Scientific Approaches to Goalkeeping in Football:

A practical perspective on the most unique position in sport

by Andy Elleray

Foreword

Congratulations to Andy Elleray for pulling together such an innovative book which uses the Teaching Games for Understanding (TGfU) approach that can enhance the performance of football goalkeepers. Andy has reflected well on the nature of TGfU, which is based on the notion that players learn best by being put into authentic situations that might be presented to them in actual competitions.

These goalkeeper games are examples of outstanding decision making opportunities that enable players to learn and develop their skills in the context of game-like situations. Such relevant and contextual practice produce better readers of the game who are more able to respond to pressure situations created during competition. When players use TGfU, they learn how to think/react, be intuitive and solve problems.

Players will enjoy enhancing their goalkeeping skills through these relevant games. They are fun, enjoyable and enhance intensity during training. Coaches will be pleasantly surprised how well the goalkeepers learn their skills and are able to apply them in game situations. In Andy's book, the goalkeeper games are a great learning tool.

The most useful benefit of Andy's games is the ability to enhance players' performance. Well done Andy!!

Yours in coaching,

Lynn Kidman

Lynn Kidman

Co - Editor of *Athlete-Centred Coaching*
Auckland University of Technology

About The Author

Andy Elleray has been working in the goalkeeping world since the age of 16 and playing since the age of seven. Over the years his goalkeeping passion took him to study at the University of Worcester where the main focus was on goalkeeper development from a coaching and analysis point of view.

During this time he played for the University side and at the age of 20 made his debut for the England and Great Britain Blind Football team playing as the sighted goalkeeper.

Coaching-wise he started work at the Worcestershire Football Association's Player Development Centre where he rose from assistant goalkeeper coach to lead coach during the four years there. This role included taking various development sessions in the local area.

After finishing his undergraduate BSc (hons) degree in Sports Coaching Science and a Diploma in Sports Management, Andy then took the role of Head of Performance Analysis at Cheltenham Town Football Club along with Centre of Excellence Goalkeeper Coach. This started the main analysis work - combining and devising methods to evaluate goalkeeping performance.

After a year of combining these roles and also running the Sports side of the Students' Union at Worcester, Andy went back to education enrolling on a Masters degree in Sports Coaching. This would open up all kinds of links and opportunities that included working at Liverpool Football Club in the Academy under the tutelage of world class goalkeeper coaches. This was where the concept of the Goalkeeping Analyst was born.

Andy's Master's dissertation focused on youth goalkeeping development in England, identifying trends and neglected areas; one being a lack of video analysis knowledge and support in many youth setups.

After finishing his studies, and the season at Cheltenham, Andy moved back to London to start a Performance Analysis role at Chelsea Football Club working in the Academy as goalkeeping analyst. He has since taken his ideas to the next level and is progressively looking into goalkeeping performance in greater detail – coaching at various levels including Aldershot Academy where he is currently lead goalkeeping coach. From a research perspective he has presented at various conferences including the World Analysis Congress, amongst others.

Andy is keen to pass on his knowledge and expertise to the next generation of budding goalkeepers.

About The Book

Goalkeeping has been a passion of mine ever since I started playing in the school playground. This book has been put together thanks to years of experiences and with the valuable input of numerous professional experts.

My Master's Degree dissertation highlighted the need for specific performance analysis support and the need for a greater understanding of the modern goalkeeper; in body, mind and practice.

Within this book I've tried to offer a good balance of practical and theoretical support into goalkeeping. Throughout each chapter you, the reader, will hopefully be able to relate to the issues I've had - and see the ways in which I've tried to solve them. From my own practical experiences right through to my current research, I firmly believe that there is still a great deal of investigation to be done and knowledge to be gained into the goalkeeping world, but hopefully what you see here is a start.

A lot of my work is confidential (between me and my goalkeeper clients) and for that reason some of the data has been anonymised or fictionalized. However, the data is realistic and accurate to the system used. The same goes with any images and some of the methods that have been used.

Admittedly, there will be academic parts to the book which may not be everyone's cup of tea - but they are relevant and at all turns they link back to relevant practical raw coaching and skills training. Hopefully by seeing the theory behind the practical application your understanding of each goalkeeping area will be strengthened.

Goalkeeping in any sport, not just football, is grossly under-researched. There is a crossover of skills from sport to sport and with the position being isolated and needing special understanding - to me that presents a great opportunity to dissect the role and focus on the attributes needed to succeed, and fundamentally how to improve them.

The real target group here is goalkeepers aged up to 18 which are where the vast majority of my experiences and research have taken place. I've found that the earlier goalkeepers are introduced to the methods I've implemented the more beneficial it is for their long term development. Repetitive learning is often advocated as the most effective way of introducing new skills and goalkeeping should be no different. Building in specific analysis, and psychological and physical training into a goalkeeper's regular development will enhance their game understanding, but more importantly help them to understand their own bodies and minds and how they function best.

My main aim here is to offer current coaches and players another way of looking at the position. To allow them to open their minds and to see that more can be done on the training pitch and in the classroom to develop the next generation of goalkeepers.

Coaching practice is, at times, based upon traditions and theories rather than actual evidential requirements. Sometimes (within the foundation phases of goalkeeping) I see goalkeepers being brought up in the same mould, the same drills, the same techniques… the same problems. Goalkeeping has and is evolving, but from a sports science point of view we have to play catch up to assist coaches and goalkeepers alike to provide them with the best possible information on how to train and prepare. Coaches also have an obligation to explore new ways to work. The speed of the play, the player's quality, the movement of the ball to name a handful of areas are forever changing and we in the keeper's Union must be equipped to handle everything thrown our way.

I've had a lot of influences in my years working in goalkeeping. They vary from coaches, to colleagues, to lecturers and teachers but most importantly the players themselves due to their passion for improving skills and performances. I've been able to look at everything with an open and creative mind.

The common rule of thumb is that to become an expert performer at any sport you need 10,000 hours or 10 years of committed and deliberate practice. Now does this have to be 10 years of physical technical training, tactical match play, or possession games? These hours could encompass a variety of actions including video analysis work, watching an ideal model in match and training situations, talking to your coach or fellow goalkeepers, training the physical and psychological attributes required (more on these later) and just absorbing yourself with everything that is goalkeeping.

Enough with the introduction. I want you to get stuck into the book to get you to look at goalkeeping in a new light. You may agree or disagree with sections of the book, but there are still theories, trends and traditions that exist which aren't maximising the potential of our young goalkeepers.

Like Einstein once said, "We cannot solve our problems with the same thinking we used when we created them."

Andy

*Views and opinions are my own and not necessarily any of the clubs or personnel that I've worked with – unless where stated.

Acknowledgements

Family: Thank you to all my family for their support over the years. Also to Danni for putting up with me working most weekends for 4 years!

Friends: Thank you for putting up with me talking about goalkeeping 24/7 and leaving coaching equipment around various houses… also for spending vast amounts of money on electricity charging laptops and cameras!

Contributors: A massive thank you to all the contributors within the book – your input has been fantastic. Also to the people who have given me advice, tips and helped me along the way. Namely the sports staff at the University of Worcester.

People and Clubs: Thank you for allowing me to express my ideas and work within some top quality football environments.

Finally, to Bennion Kearny for believing in me and supporting my project. And to Karen Wiltshire for helping me overcome the barriers.

Table of Contents

Preface
Origins and Experiences

"Don't measure yourself by what you have accomplished, but by what you should accomplish with your ability."

(John Wooden)

Goalkeeping has always been a passion of mine. Starting from when I was seven years old in the playground right up to the time of writing. 18 years on and I've not lost this desire to explore the role the goalkeeper plays within the team dynamic, and how to go about helping this position evolve.

I remember my first ever Premiership match, Chelsea vs Aston Villa in 1996, on my ninth birthday. I still recall studying the goalkeepers and how they moved, played the ball, and commanded their back lines. From this match on I was going to put all my energy into being the best goalkeeper in the world and playing for England!

A bold statement but, as fate would have it, not as bold as you might think.

Having gone through numerous playing, coaching and performance analysis environments this preface will talk about how my practical and educational experiences have helped shape the way I operate in the field of goalkeeping. This position in football has always been under-researched and not fully understood by those outside the 'Keeper's Union'.

In this chapter we will cover:

- How the role of the goalkeeper has evolved
- Why their position in the team dynamic is so important
- What the main themes of the book will be
- How each level of football has contributed to my research and coaching
- An in-depth look into goalkeeping in blind football
- The impact each football experience has had

The History of Goalkeeping

The role of goalkeeping in the sport of Association Football came to life in 1870 when law changes allowed for one member of a team to touch the ball with their hands anywhere on the pitch. The following year saw things evolve further and this player was now only allowed to handle the ball in their own half and goal area. The position of 'goalkeeper' was thus created.

In the early days, the goalkeeper was solely there to stop the ball going into the goal with most goalkeepers being big and clumsy. Further law changes in 1890 meant that the goalkeeper was only allowed to handle in their defensive penalty area, and the physical requirements changed dramatically to move the emphasis to quickness and mobility. This was the first significant change in philosophy as the goalkeeper now had to integrate with the team along with saving shots around their goal from different angles and distances.

Other law updates have directly affected the way in which goalkeepers are developed, including the 1967 change which prohibited the goalkeeper to be in possession of the ball for more than four seconds, or move with four steps. This meant that the role changed – a goalkeeper could now affect the tactical attacking area of the team due to this emphasis on recycling play quickly.

The final change was when the overall governing body of football, FIFA, implemented the 'back pass' rule in 1992 which prohibited the goalkeeper from handling the ball when played back to them directly from their own team's feet. This rule change now puts a greater emphasis on the player being able to cope with the ball at his feet. It is therefore very important that goalkeepers work on this aspect of their game on a regular basis.

Preface

Most goalkeepers have only had a dedicated coach within the past 15-20 years at 1st team level. Now virtually every professional club and many semi-professional clubs do as well. Combined with Academies, Centres of Excellence, and specific goalkeeping schools like *GK Icon* there is a whole host of goalkeeper coaching going on - not only in England but all over the world. The Football Association and UEFA run specific goalkeeper coaching courses (which I've taken) to enhance people's knowledge and application of the necessary skills.

Now we've talked about goalkeeping in general I'm going to tell a story about my football experiences and how they've helped shape my research and coaching exploits.

Experiences

The first main impact upon my coaching and performance analysis work stemmed from my playing experiences as a goalkeeper at various different levels of football. Each experience has had a bearing on the way I see and implement things within goalkeeping and a lot of this book is built around the issues I experienced for myself. So it is worth taking a short moment to run through my background briefly.

Playing Experiences

There's always been the debate in football as to whether having played the game or not should affect you being a successful coach or manager. There are a numerous examples of high profile managers who have not played the game at an elite level: Jose Mourinho, Andre Villas Boas and Arsene Wenger spring straight to mind.

Their understanding of the game and how to interact with players puts them on a different level. Within goalkeeping, however, I believe you need to have at least played in the position to truly understand the position; these experiences can only help when coaching.

My situation is very varied and complex to say the least! From a young age I always played in goal. I think I was attracted to diving around and saving the ball in the mud to be honest! Or potentially it might be the fact that I was an overweight child who didn't like running around so much! The latter is actually quite a defining characteristic of mine because, had I not held the body composition I did, I may well have ended up as a winger playing for England.

I joined my first team at 12 after playing schools football at primary school. The team was Hamsey Rangers FC based near my home in Whyteleafe. Part of the reason I signed up was not just for the desire to play but it was a new school and my Mum was keen for me to meet new people. Like any team sport the social aspect is critical.

Luckily despite a heavy beating in my 'trial' match the coach saw something in me and signed me to play. The coach's name was Cliff Baxter, a giant of a man who thankfully had a keen interest in goalkeeping, and throughout the four seasons I was with him gave up his free time to teach me the skills and techniques needed to be a goalkeeper.

In my time with Hamsey I won many awards for my performances and built up a reputation as a good goalkeeper in the local area. Representing my secondary school only aided this.

Now one thing that I always work on with young goalkeepers is being able to use both feet effectively over short and long ranges, along with being under pressure. When I was growing up playing football the goalkeeper's role was purely to stop the ball going in the net and then kicking it up-field as far as possible. To a certain extent the statement is true - the goalkeeper's main role will always be to keep the ball out of the goal but their role (as will be discussed later) is so much more than that.

I wish I had been taught to actually kick a ball! It sounds stupid but having been a goalkeeper all my life I was never actually taught how to kick a ball nor given the necessary contact time to develop my 'footballing' abilities. Although you might see this as a negative, my inability to play with my feet indirectly shaped my future football career, and actually enabled me to achieve one of my life goals.

When I turned 16 I started playing adult football and my inability to use my feet began to get noticed. My shot stopping and decision making skills within the game were extremely good but under new circumstances, and as the game evolved, I couldn't cope with these new found demands. After a couple of nasty injuries (including a broken collarbone) I stopped playing for a year or so. During my Sixth Form College years I returned to play on a Sunday with Bluacre FC and enjoyed my time there.

It was around this time I wanted to go to university to study coaching and to pass on my goalkeeping knowledge obtained over the years. I wanted to try and change goalkeeping. It may sound farfetched but my playing experiences pre-19 taught me that goalkeeping was not what it should be and that there were flaws in the way I saw the position being coached. Often I watched coaching sessions with 4/5 goalkeepers in a line making a pre-determined save with the coach stopping each time to correct mistakes. During one session I watched a 20 minute diving drill and each goalkeeper made about 10 saves. Now, for me, that's not productive in the slightest. There was no addressing using the feet. I do appreciate that time/space/facilities have a bearing but for a creative coach no obstacle is too big to overcome. Upcoming chapters will explore this in more detail.

I used to get incredibly nervous before matches, any match, even in training. I would dwell on mistakes and have constant self-doubts. I even remember a match when I was 13 where I made two absolute howlers and took my gloves off refusing to play! I wish back then that I understood (and more importantly my coach understood) how to deal with my nervous and negative thoughts. Due to my experiences of lacking confidence, and becoming increasingly concerned about what I wasn't good at, I have focused some of my research on helping goalkeepers overcome these same issues. Chapter 1 will highlight this and give specific ways to help goalkeepers young and old build confidence and make them feel invincible.

University & Blind Football

Upon moving to University I played football for 4 years merely to keep myself ticking over and to meet new people. I played with some very good players, some of whom play professional football now. A highlight was playing in front of 500 or so people in our annual Varsity match against our bitter rivals Gloucestershire, which we won 2-1.

Although the relevance to the book from the above is not as strong as other experiences it led me to making a life changing decision.

In my second semester (2006) at University I was offered the chance to join the Worcester Blind Football team. Blind football you say? Back in 2006 the sport was not as high profile as it is now, although it is still not recognised enough.

Whilst playing for the University one of the sports lecturers asked if I was interested in playing as the sighted goalkeeper for the team. As someone who likes new challenges I jumped at the chance knowing little about what I was about to face!

I remember my first session like it was yesterday. After meeting the players we did some ball skills and some communication exercises ending with a shooting drill where the coach, Dave Mycock, acted as a player to play a '1-2' before the blind player took a shot at goal.

As the goalkeeper in training you have to call the player in so they can recognise where the goal is, whereas in a match there would be someone behind the goal calling them in. The commands were pretty basic - just how many yards from goal they were. Because of their skill level they could pretty much paint a picture in their head of where and when to shoot - which is incredible.

So the drill started and I found multi-tasking very hard - calling the players in then worrying about my own position in the goal, alongside saving the ball. I guess men can't multi-task!

Blind football is 5-a-side played on a futsal pitch, with boards along the side, so the goals aren't massive (2 meters high, 3 meters wide).

I arrogantly thought to myself, 'how can they score? I can see. I have all the aces!' I quickly learned that the typical stereotype of what blind people can accomplish was nowhere near the mark to these guys. Shot after shot hit the back of the net and I was rapidly questioning what I had let myself in for.

The speed of thought and ball skill of these elite footballers was breathtaking and from a goalkeeping point of view I held the advantage. What was going on? I could see, I was a very able goalkeeper, and I didn't have to change position because of the size of the goal. The final act of the drill changed my view forever.

Keryn Seal who, in my opinion, is one of the best blind players in the world, not to mention the hardest working, picked up the ball about 20 yards from my goal. He played the standard '1-2' with Dave, controlled the ball, preceded to flick the ball over his head, listened for the ball to control, and on the first bounce half volleyed the ball past me into the top corner of the goal.

As a goalkeeper I stood there and gasped. I had just been beaten by an incredible piece of skill, not to mention a perfectly executed half volley by a person who had no sight whatsoever! Without meaning to sound crude I actually enjoyed being scored against, what goalkeeper can say that!

After the session I talked to the coaches and analysed my own performance. We came to the conclusion that because of the nature of the game I wasn't 'set' in time for any of the shots. I never knew how important the 'set position' was in goalkeeping until then. It allows you, from a movement perspective to go up and down, left and right, 360 degrees with balance and speed. I was always moving and being caught out by the shooting. This was because in sighted football you get a pretty good idea when someone is about to shoot. Their head goes down and the ball is at their feet, unless you get a Lionel Messi or a Cristiano Ronaldo type player.

In blind football players shoot when the ball is under their control because if the ball is away from them they lose focus and awareness of the ball. Combine that with toe-poked movement shots and balls can come like machine gun bullets.

This made me think about the biomechanics involved in this type of goalkeeping. This wasn't 11-a-side Sunday morning down-the-park goalkeeping - this was a new game entirely. I decided to sit down and think about my performance and self-coach. I decided to try lowering my set position and not to try catching every ball. Due to the speed and direction of the ball I was being caught too slow and too upright in my stance. The coach filmed a few sessions so I could see how I was faring, fuelling my interest in video analysis which at that point was an un-trodden path.

I found my approach effective and I was starting to make saves and block shots. For those who are unfamiliar with the sport, the ball is very heavy and is a size 3. Wearing protective padding is a must. In my first match I looked like skateboarder with knee and elbow pads! Not to mention wearing a cricket box, no explanation necessary. All this added mass does affect your movement so training 'as you mean to play' never had a better rationale.

Goalkeeping in Blind Football

In blind football saving the ball is actually not the most important part of the game you could argue. Like sighted football, effective communication and organisation within your team stops you having to make saves in the first place. More so within the blind environment because, excuse the cliché, you're the eyes on the pitch for the whole team.

I'm going to talk a bit about the requirements to play the position broken down into major areas of performance as many of the things I have learnt in blind football have informed my research and are applicable to conventional goalkeeping. Chapters throughout the book will go into greater depth, but let's take a moment to get a flavour.

Psychology

As the goalkeeper, you are the focal point of the team so total focus and concentration are essential at all times during play, not only for the performance itself, but for safety reasons. The position of the goalkeeper in blind football is one of great responsibility. Not only are you responsible for your own performance technically but the positioning of the players in the defensive third, the organisation of the team, and effective communication between yourself and the defence.

Maintaining focus and being switched on at all times is paramount as the game can change quickly. If your team loses the ball then it's your priority to get the team's shape back and to display understanding of the game and the team's tactics. The opposing goalkeeper could have the ball and it only takes one long throw for it to be down near your goal. So quick thinking and clear instructions are very important.

Sociology

Everyone who I have met in blind football has a different story to tell and comes from a unique background. A lot of the players have played together for a while so know each other pretty well. Because of the focal point of Hereford many of the players have been to the RNC (Royal National College for the Blind) or been connected with it in some way.

When first entering the sport I hadn't had much interaction with blind athletes or visually impaired people come to think of it, so I had to adjust to their needs; for example being on hand to get the water, guiding them around the playing area, and describing certain situations to them.

In both the Worcester and England squads I found that socialising with the players generally, as well as training with them, was equally beneficial. This was because I got to understand how visually impaired people went about their daily routines and how they acted. I forged very good relationships with the players which enabled us to trust each other in life and on the football pitch.

During the summer training for the Paralympics we trained twice daily and spent time at each other's houses and went for the occasional drink or sporting event.

The Worcester squad all went to Will Norman's wedding (Will was one of our newest players); we had a great time talking about football and enjoying the day. In my opinion situations such as these shape the team because I feel getting to know my team on a social basis is very important and an often neglected area of the team cohesion cycle.

I recently told someone that to represent my country at football was my dream but to achieve this in a disability sport as an able-bodied athlete I find so much more rewarding. I feel I am offering a lot more and helping others to reach their potential.

Physiology

Much like sighted football the goalkeeper in blind football doesn't need an overly efficient aerobic system although you do need a certain amount of aerobic capacity. I find this helps in decision making and being able to talk to the players for the whole game and not get out of breath. This is overlooked I feel because if you become tired your game suffers and so will your ability to concentrate and communicate.

As a goalkeeper you might have a few shots to save in a row so power from the legs and upper body will help with recovery saves and moving the body efficiently. Quick feet and good hand-eye coordination are essential to be in the correct position and stop the ball. Muscular endurance in the upper body is important because the position entails a lot of throwing so being able to hit the players' feet consistently is beneficial for the team from an attacking point of view.

Movements and Techniques

Coaches have formed a desirable starting or 'set' position for goalkeepers which require:

1. Knees bent
2. Weight forward
3. Head advanced of the body
4. Hands out in front, with your elbows bent and tucked in

Within blind football this is predominantly the case but the ball is mainly shot on the ground or around the waist area due to the ball and the shooting technique of the players. I have tried lowering my set position so I can deal with these balls but still spring up for the high shots when they come.

The basic diving and catching principles apply but sometimes due to the distance away from the goal and the power the elite players can generate - technique must give way to bravery and you just fling yourself in front of the ball and player. It can be enough to keep the ball out of the net.

Throwing technique is important because (due to the nature of the sport) you must aim to hit the players' feet. In sighted football you are told to direct the ball out in front of the player so they can run onto it. In blind football this can rarely be done because by the time the player tracks the ball, and moves into line, the ball will already be past them and the team could lose possession.

Communication

The importance of communication cannot be stressed enough. The goalkeeper's voice and position is the focal point for players on the field of play and is instrumental in organising the team to defend but also to start an attack.

The goalkeeper is in charge of the defensive third and must give clear, specific instructions about where the ball is, where opposing players are, and how far they are from goal.

I have developed my skills and commands over the months of playing the game. I like to use commands such as 'left board' or 'right board' for the position of the ball and basic numbers to confirm how far the ball is away from goal. Also phrases such as 'drop left' or 'push right' can be used for moving defenders to mark players or to pressure the ball.

Having lost the ball from a goal throw or in the final third you must call the players back into position so the team can regroup and assemble its shape once again to deal with the oncoming attack. This takes quick instructions and great trust is put on the goalkeeper by the players so that they can read the game well and anticipate where the ball is going, and what runs opponents are likely to make.

Coaching

When coaching a goalkeeper - doing all the technical work is important such as how to catch a ball and how to make a diving save, but goalkeepers also need to experience a blind player hitting a ball at them as it is usually 'toe-poked' - meaning the ball can move in irregular directions and angles because of its contact with the foot. One of the England players shoots only with the outside of his right boot which makes him incredibly hard to read so it's important the goalkeeper stands big and doesn't commit himself too early otherwise he will be beaten.

Blind footballers strike the ball very differently to sighted players with little or no back lift so it's hard to know when to set yourself. With this in mind the goalkeeper should be coached to make small short steps and movements so they can get back into their set position quicker and become more balanced to receive a shot.

When coaching 'throwing' - I use 3 types of throw, the underarm roll of quick and accurate release, the javelin for short (and usually the wider) throws, and the overarm bowl for long range throws.

The players must be able to trust you and respond to your instructions so familiarity is vital. Work with the players as much as possible to forge a relationship, know their strengths and weaknesses and learn what commands work best for individual players.

England and Great Britain

After a few rounds of league matches and two training sessions a week I was invited to become part of the England training setup. This was a massive honour and was a great reward for my hard work.

This is a good point to talk about why my lack of 'feet skills' might have been a positive. In blind football the goalkeeper doesn't use their feet at all, every distribution is thrown and because you have to stay in the 5 x 2 metre area there's no requirement to play out from the back.

So breaking it down - the key requirements for the goalkeeper would be:

- Shot stopping
- Effective communication
- Team organisation
- Throwing accuracy and appropriateness
- Concentration/Alertness
- Game understanding

All of which are my strengths as a goalkeeper. So the sport played right into my hands so to speak, enabling me to identify my own strengths and weaknesses. Something which I fully advocate and utilise when coaching or working with young goalkeepers. This will be fully explored in the psychological chapter looking at performance profiles to assess current attributes and performance.

I was able to play with the freedom of not having to worry about back-passes, through balls, crosses and goal kicks. All of which had previously increased my anxiety in matches and hindered my progress in sighted football.

International Matches

After various training camps, demonstration days to increase awareness of the sport, and fundamental training sessions - two games against Spain were coming up in May 2008. I was hopeful of achieving my dream of representing England at football, well Great Britain also as the team took up the alias at the Beijing Paralympics which were in August that year. I made my debut in the two matches against Spain, and although we lost it was an amazing experience. I made some crucial saves although I was disappointed with the goal we conceded.

Being 2nd choice in the team I knew being taken to Beijing was a long shot. I worked hard in the summer although ultimately I didn't go to the games. The team performed well and at one point there were four Worcester outfield players playing at the same time which made me proud to be part of the setup.

I recently saw that my photo (back of my head and dodgy barnet) was on the front of the FA Level 1 Goalkeeping Certificate which I guess is a good claim to fame!

The whole experience of being a sighted goalkeeper in this sport has given me the insight to investigate goalkeeping a whole lot more. From being able to look at the qualities and attributes a goalkeeper needs to succeed I'm in a good place to work with young goalkeepers to overcome the personal barriers I came across.

Coaching Experiences

I started coaching goalkeepers around the age of 16 thanks to one of my Physical Education teachers. He was coach of a local junior team and I started coaching the club's goalkeepers, mainly aged from 10-13. I began to devise new drills and exercises for my sessions based on what I thought the keepers could work on. Obviously my technical and tactical knowledge didn't have the depth it has now but from what I was taught from previous coaches and picked up from watching numerous matches - I was in a good position to start my coaching career.

I have always looked into ways in which to coach goalkeepers best, and ways to keep the practice games realistic. I have seen so many sessions where the coaches have four plus goalkeepers and each receives a shot and the coach will spend time talking through various coaching points whilst the other goalkeepers wait their turn. This can't be conducive to developing players if there's a large number of people standing around. People become disengaged, especially at a young age when goalkeepers need to be developing their all-round motor skills such as running, jumping and basic movements.

At an older age and a higher level perhaps there's a place for this but generally the higher up you go in football the coach might only have 2-3 goalkeepers per session where they can target specific technical issues. My games based coaching concept will demonstrate ways to eradicate this for younger goalkeepers and bring in an all-round development environment.

I have had the pleasure of coaching for the Worcestershire Football Association for four years taking a lead goalkeeper coach position for two of them. This enabled me to work with some of the best goalkeepers in the area who were not on the books of professional clubs and to trial my games-based theory along with some specific technical work.

This fuelled my ambition to develop the concept further and around the same time I started coaching for Cheltenham Town at their Centre of Excellence and Development Centres where I could carry on this process. In the development centre I was faced with a group of 10 goalkeepers of varying ability in half a sports hall, with whatever equipment I could bring along… and a bag of balls. A challenging environment! Not player wise but it would be impossible and unproductive to work in technical isolation. So developing my concept was rather forced upon me, but in a good way!

The last few years have seen performance analysis and coaching come together. At a variety of different levels, such as Worcester City and more recently responsibilty for the Academy keepers at Aldershot Town, all areas of this book have been based around the daily exploits spent with goalkeepers of all shapes and sizes. Fundamentally all the chapters of this book will assist coaches in structuring some practices, dealing with different issues, and adding variety to goalkeeping curriculums.

Performance Analysis Experiences

My current speciality is performance analysis, and I feel it's important to give a brief insight into what I've come across here. In my opinion performance analysis is a fundamental part of the coaching process and if utilised in a correct structured way can have a massive influence on athletes.

My introduction to this field came by way of a 3rd year degree work placement at Cheltenham Town for the Youth Team (where I was coaching at the time). Here I got a taste for filming, coding and developing statistics (my distribution system for goalkeepers). After this I got the role of overseeing the analysis for the 1st team whilst still working with the Youth Team where possible.

Being able to work under high profile and experienced coaches gave me a first-hand view of professional football and how the industry operates. A high pressure environment where results are the most important part, totally different to youth development where the focus is on the player's progress and giving them the tools and guidance to succeed.

At the time I was working in both fields: filming matches and training sessions within the Centre of Excellence and working on different feedback methods for goalkeepers - viewing their performances along with the 1st team. In the Centre of Excellence we would chat about different performance areas: what we did well and what we could improve, along with group discussions looking at professional goalkeepers and how they worked.

The book will highlight many of the methods used, not only at Cheltenham but in other clubs and football environments. Worcester City being one where I was 1st Team goalkeeper coach.

In this period I touched upon psychology - looking into performance profiles and ways to deal with anxiety and build confidence in goalkeepers. Something which, as stated before, I struggled with in my own performance.

My time working in professional Youth Academies have had a massive impact on what I'm doing at the moment but without spoiling upcoming chapters I will leave you to read about these experiences later.

Having the opportunities to work solely in goalkeeping performance analysis has enabled me to break the position down into key performance indicators, of which the chapters are named. The aim is for the grassroots coach or goalkeeper coach to be able to take some of my methods straight into practice. Although some systems do require cameras and computers, there are systems that can be replicated quite easily if the coach has the willingness and desire to implement them.

Playing Other Sports

The influence of other sports on my goalkeeping concepts cannot be underestimated. At university where my concepts were taking shape I played a variety of different sports that conjured up ideas of new drills and exercises. Handball, Basketball and Gaelic Football were three key ones. With goalkeeping being predominantly a motor skills position (running, jumping, kicking, catching, throwing) these sports encompass all the moves a goalkeeper will make. With short explosive actions these benefitted me first as a player and later in my coaching sessions.

Being able to play these sports gave me a real feel for the movements involved. At each turn I tried to relate what was going on back into the goalkeeping world – taking bits from each sport.

Reading and searching for goalkeeping literature was a big part of my studies at University: I read that Tim Howard played Basketball, Peter Schmeichel Handball, and Pat Jennings Gaelic Football. So if these exceptional goalkeepers had backgrounds in other sports why couldn't I try and develop goalkeeping attributes away from the technical practices? Using other sports as training environments could only be of benefit. It obviously did the above three examples no harm. What were they doing before being a goalkeeper? No doubt honing their skills in a different environment but they had obviously developed the necessary attributes to be a goalkeeper; all they needed was game and tactical understanding.

More on this area and the benefit of taking elements from other sports into goalkeeper training will be discussed in upcoming chapters.

Summary

I really hope that this goalkeeping book complements what's currently out there for coaches, players and anyone generally looking into the goalkeeping world.

My playing experiences and getting to understand the goalkeeping role in the thick of grassroots, adult, university and elite football have had a big impact on my philosophies.

I feel physically experiencing these feelings, thoughts, and situations, teaches you how to apply them in real life. You can learn a lot on coaching courses but actually playing the game and being involved in the environments I have been involved in - allowed me to figure out where goalkeeping has the potential to go and, in some areas, *needs to go*.

Within the book I'm not going to go into detail in every area of sports performance as there are plenty of books out there focusing exclusively on injury prevention, plyometric training, technical coaching points and general biomechanics and psychology. What I've tried to do is relate everything to goalkeeping: giving suggestions and reasoning behind doing particular types of training and performance enhancing methods rather than giving hundreds of examples, plus a mass of scientific information. It's at the coach's discretion to investigate some chapter areas for themselves and use the information effectively how they want. The book will offer tips and suggestions on how to include performance analysis and the games based theory in a useable development plan.

Science and research means that the field of goalkeeping is always changing... this book looks to do the same... Let's get cracking!

1

Goalkeeping Psychology

"We are all creatures of habit. We can do most things without even thinking about them; our bodies take charge and do them for us."

(Earl Nightingale)

To start off the book, let's take a closer look into the mind of the goalkeeper. Psychology in any sport is fundamental to performance, whether it relates to boosting confidence or coping with anxiety. Being able to channel your focus and deal with the tasks at hand, or being able to block out all pressures and distractions, is crucial.

There are myths and preconceptions about sports psychology, starting from 'mind control' right through to expectations of lying down on a sofa talking about your problems! But maybe the biggest one is the misperception that psychological skills training is only for 'problem' athletes. Goalkeeping has been very much under-researched from an academic perspective although coaches and goalkeepers themselves have come up with various ways to achieve more generic optimum peak performance. I had my own troubles with my mind (self-doubt and not coping with nerves which disrupted my progression as a goalkeeper) - I only wish I had the understanding (and my coaches did) that I do now.

With the assistance of professional goalkeepers, coaches, and specialists in sports psychology, this chapter will go into the goalkeeper's mind and look at what can impact on performance. But bear in mind that this is no quick fix. Like physical and technical skills - psychological skills must be trained regularly.

As a goalkeeper you need to be mentally strong. Dealing with mistakes, being a scapegoat for goals and having your performance scrutinised at every turn is part and parcel of what you can expect playing between the sticks. The goalkeeper must be the calmest player on the pitch and be ready to deal with setbacks, frustrations and difficulties which – when it comes to the crunch – are the difference between winning and losing.

People say goalkeeping is 100% psychological, some say 90%, some say 80% but it doesn't matter what percentage you put on this area - it's a crucial part of the position and one that can make or break a goalkeeper. You must be as brave as a lion, as cunning as a fox, as fearless as a grizzly bear and as confident as a shark. No this isn't animal farm - but such attributes must exist in a goalkeeper if they want to deal with the trials and tribulations that come with the different coloured shirt and special gloves.

Have belief and passion to achieve what you want in the game. Take heart in the fact that young goalkeepers can make it to the top level of the professional game. Examples include Iker Casillas and Gianluigi Buffon who broke through in their teens. In the modern era the young goalkeeper boom has happened with Hugo Lloris, Joe Hart, Manuel Neuer and David de Gea. If they can do it… so can you! But whatever level you want to play at psychology is an important area. Frans Hoek discussed how goalkeepers can be placed into two types: reaction and anticipation. Both have different strengths and attributes and knowing which goalkeeper you're dealing with as a player, or coach, will impact on the type of training required.

'Want' to save the ball. That's the biggest thing I can say. If you want to keep that ball out the goal, if you want to be the leader of the team, if you want to be unbeatable and positive at all times… you can. It's all about self-confidence and belief in your own ability. Showing commitment to the position will breed a winning goalkeeper.

In this chapter we will cover:

- How psychology plays an important part in the goalkeeper's world
- What attributes goalkeepers must posses
- Ways in which to enhance psychological attributes
- Experiences from the 'Keeper's Union'

This chapter has been co-authored with Gavin Wilson, so it's worth taking a moment to offer a brief biography.

Gavin Wilson is one of the UK's premier Sports Performance coaches and has achieved outstanding results in enhancing the sporting performances of athletes, coaches and teams by assessing, evaluating and developing strategies using the latest psychological techniques available worldwide to enhance confidence, motivation, mental toughness and focus. Gavin has also produced a hugely popular CD and MP3, entitled "Eye On The Ball", specifically for goalkeepers. More information on Gavin and MINDSi can be found at the front of the book.

A Goalkeeper's Life

It's a tough life being a goalkeeper. By far the toughest position on the pitch, and yet the most important. In addition to technical skills, and physical and tactical competencies, the key to becoming a top goalkeeper is his mental strength. For that reason, mental training should be a vital part of all goalkeeper training programmes.

Many coaches focus on physical techniques to become a successful goalkeeper but constantly neglect the mental side. Is this down to a lack of knowledge and understanding of the benefits psychology can have? I very much think so!

Being a goalkeeper says something about your psychological and your mental toughness. One thing that goalkeepers quickly have to get used to, when starting out, is "taking the blame", more often than not unfairly. And most frustratingly of all, most of the criticism comes from outfield players or indeed the coach, none of whom have probably ever been brave enough to don the keeper's gloves. It often

3

seems that everyone is a critic and an expert in the art and science of goalkeeping.

From a psychological perspective, the goalkeeper engages in arguably some of the most demanding and difficult situations within modern-day football. Due to the specialist nature of the position, it is essential for both goalkeeper, and goalkeeper coach to understand the psychological requirements of the position.

Without sounding like a broken record, if I had known about the ways in which my mind can affect performance when I was younger and strategies to enhance them, maybe I would have progressed further in the game... you never know! But I'm now making it my mission for young goalkeepers everywhere to see the benefits sports psychology can bring and to enable goalkeeping coaches to utilise its considerable power and influence.

The Nuts and Bolts

Bearing in mind my own experiences (playing and otherwise) and dialogue with people in the game, we're now going to explore different psychological attributes and relate them directly to goalkeeping. We shall look at what the attribute is, then look at how to go about becoming a master of it. We shall end each section with a few experiences from professional goalkeepers to help you relate to the realism of goalkeeping psychology.

Each section will have scientific content but I urge you, as a coach, player or parent, to investigate each attribute more to get extra details on them. Each attribute could have a chapter, or indeed a book on its own. This chapter is designed to give an understanding to a good level of each attribute and enough for you to directly affect said attribute positively. There are academic tests, questionnaires and scales referenced that allow a goalkeeping coach to investigate matters further in a structured manner.

It goes without saying that you will know your goalkeepers better than me or Gavin. Psychology can be a delicate subject but the methods shown are designed to be relatively unobtrusive and structured in a way that can be used across ages and abilities.

Here's what's going to be studied...

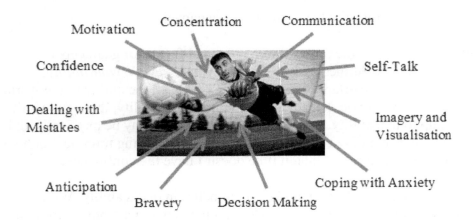

Motivation — Concentration — Communication — Self-Talk — Confidence — Dealing with Mistakes — Imagery and Visualisation — Anticipation — Bravery — Decision Making — Coping with Anxiety

Confidence

Confidence is a fragile and delicate thing. At its peak it is the best feeling in the world – I feel 10ft tall and amazing; I have no doubts and believe I am the best. But at its lowest it can be a lonely, cold feeling of doubt and frustration. Self-confidence has been proven to be a major factor in sporting success. Not only for goalkeeping in football but for athletes in any situation.

Confidence is typically understood as an attribute possessed by subjects who trust their own abilities and judgement and are self-reliant and assured. Confident athletes enter competitions in the knowledge that they will achieve their goal with a resolute and secure approach and a belief or degree of certainty. I will keep a clean sheet! I will distribute the ball effectively! I will be a leader and inspire my team!

However this passage does not convey the unstable features of confidence that can be built, damaged and destroyed by events and personalities. This relates to Albert Bandura's theory on self-efficacy which describes a belief as the capacity to produce desired results under specific conditions. "As conditions change, so might someone's belief in their competence to reach a certain level of performance, as might the strength of their certainty as well as the generality of their self-efficacy."

A confident athlete can move from conscious control to automaticity which is a key ingredient in order to produce peak performance. In other words, the confident performer *does not think* about the job at hand they just perform the action or skill. Thus persuading athletes to surrender conscious effort to motor

5

control involves trust and belief in their own capacities.

Confidence is one of the most important mental factor for goalkeepers. Confidence can be defined as *how strongly you believe in your ability*. Confidence is so important because you may have all the ability in the world to perform well, but if you don't believe you have that ability, then you won't perform up to that ability. For example, a goalkeeper may be physically and technically capable of executing unbelievable saves during training, but he won't attempt the same save in a match if he doesn't have the confidence.

Confidence is a deep, lasting, and resilient belief in one's ability. With confidence, you are able to stay positive even when you are not performing well. Confidence keeps you motivated, intense, focused, and emotionally in control when you need to be. You aren't negative and uncertain in difficult matches and you're not overconfident in easy matches. Confidence also encourages you to seek out pressure situations and to view difficult conditions and tough opponents as challenges to pursue. Confidence enables you to perform at your highest level consistently.

Confidence is the belief that if you do the right things, you will be successful. Confidence demonstrates faith in your ability and your preparation. It should not, however, cause you to expect *success*; this belief can lead to arrogance and overconfidence. It can also cause you to become *too focused on winning* rather than on *performing your best*. This perception can lead to self-imposed pressure and a fear of failure.

A misconception that many goalkeepers have, specifically young keepers, is that confidence is something that you are born with, or that if you don't have it at an early age - you will never have confidence. In reality, confidence is a mental skill, much like technical skills, *that can be learned*. As for any type of skill, confidence is developed through focus, effort, and repetition.

Courage

I think it a good idea to address bravery and courage in this section. Physical courage has been said to be an innate part to your personality and can't be taught – although it can be worked on by putting the goalkeeper in the same physical situations as they would be exposed to in a match. The physical side can be described in goalkeeping as diving head first at an attacker's feet or ploughing your way through bodies to punch a cross – 'fearless' these goalkeepers are called. As a coach you need to translate to your young goalkeepers that being physically courageous is part of the role. Some young goalkeepers have this no fear attitude and thrive on the collisions and stand offs; others shy away and retreat to the safety of their goal line. Recreating situations and building a goalkeeper's confidence in training, putting them in real game 1 v 1s, crosses and other 'fear' situations will help build courage.

When I was 16 I broke my collarbone in a collision with an opposition striker. It was a break that put me out of action for a good eight months but the damage it did psychologically was irreparable. Bones and muscles can heal but losing my 'fearless approach' stifled my game. When I made my comeback I was hesitant with 50/50 challenges (half-hearted challenges will lead to more injuries), stayed on my line for crosses, and was late on 1 v 1s – all of which brought me criticism for not commanding my area. My technically ability hadn't changed but my mindset had.

Here is something that might be considered trivial. Several times now, I've seen that when young goalkeepers get braces on their teeth it can impact on their bravery. I've coached goalkeepers who one week were flying around at attackers' feet and the next were not so keen to get involved – I assumed they were having a bad day but after further investigation (talking to one 12 year old keeper in particular) I discovered he had just had braces fitted and was feeling a bit uncomfortable. After 3-4 weeks he got used to them and was back to his old self. This conversation clicked in my mind, and I recalled that I had experienced the same discomfort when I was the same age. Why am I recalling this story? It's really important that goalkeeping coaches understand issues as seemingly trivial as keepers getting braces – and realise how what-appear-to-be small issues can impact hugely on performance.

Now courage doesn't necessarily have to be physical - involving collisions and confrontations. One example I've seen was a goalkeeper who received a back pass, then played a 1-2 with the centre back, then misplaced the next pass straight to the opposition attacker. This attacker broke through on goal and was brought down for a penalty by the centre back – and the resulting penalty was scored. The very next play the goalkeeper received the ball in virtually the same position, played a 1-2 with the right back, then played a penetrative ball into his midfielder to turn and travel forward – taking two opposition players out of the game in the process. Courageous and brave – yes! Self-confident – yes! Considering what had occurred a few minutes earlier, it was terrific to see this keeper push his previous mistake out his mind and believe in his own ability to play this pass; after all he'd done it hundreds of times in matches without giving the ball away. Even Xavi or

Chapter 1

Iniesta gives the ball away occasionally. Accept that mistakes and bad outcomes will occur but if a goalkeeper has confidence in their own ability, giving the ball away won't faze them. Like we all say, if the goalkeeper makes a mistake it's usually a goal.

The given example didn't happen overnight, of course. It took years of practice for the keeper to be comfortable in his skill and the belief that 'no matter what' he could execute this skill whatever the situation.

How

Now let's look at how to build this vital attribute of confidence into goalkeeping success. For me one of the biggest ways of building and maintaining confidence is to watch videos of your own successful performances and think back... asking yourself... how did that feel? What did I do there? Where were my hands and head when I saved that shot? You get the idea.

By re-creating and reviewing your best games and training sessions - positive reinforcement will stand you in good stead for success. Let's examine other contributing factors and start by looking through a relevant theory from Albert Bandura and talk through some key points related to goalkeeping.

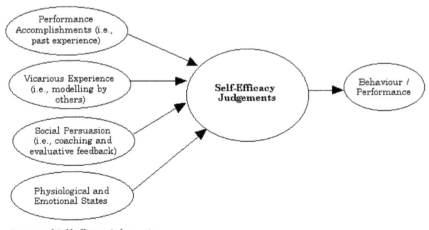

Sources of Self-efficacy Information

Performance Accomplishments are the strongest contributor to sport confidence. When you perform any goalkeeping skill successfully, you will generate confidence and be willing to attempt something slightly more difficult. Improving goalkeeping skills and techniques needs to be organized in such a way that they progress gradually and allow you to master each step before progressing onto the next. A good goalkeeping coach will understand this and help a young keeper progress step by step. They will also understand that personal success breeds confidence, while repeated personal failure diminishes it.

On the subject of Performance Accomplishments, I would also advise any goalkeeper to list their Top 10 goalkeeping successes and to look at this list daily until a time when they can readily recall it – in order! *Always remember the good times.*

Vicarious Experiences – or more simply put "Being Involved with the Success of Others" - can also significantly bolster your confidence. For young goalkeepers this can often be done by having an idol and modelling your style, technique and goalkeeping performance on your hero. In effect, it evokes the reaction: "If they can do it, I can do it". Another commonly used word for this, in the field of psychology and NLP, is "modelling" - i.e. you model someone else's behaviour and performance.

For a goalkeeper who currently doesn't have an idol I would strongly suggest they get one and then watch them, in detail, as often as possible – either on TV, live during matches, or in training. A final tip is to encourage a goalkeeper to focus their attention on a top keeper who has a similar style or similar characteristics to themselves (or even looks or physique) as this will improve the vicarious experience and boost confidence.

Verbal Persuasion is a way of changing attitudes and behaviour by using positive words and phrases, either from a coach or from the goalkeeper themselves. The latter is known a *self-talk*. In football, coaches often try to boost confidence by convincing goalkeepers that the challenge ahead is within their capabilities: "I know you're a great keeper, so go out there and show everyone what you can do!" A goalkeeper may then want to reinforce this by repeating the message over and over to himself as a form of self-persuasion. A tip here is to avoid stating what you want in the negative; so, rather than "I really don't want to let a silly goal in today," try "I really want to be awesome today." Accordingly, your mind will not need to consider what is not required in order to arrive at what is required.

Another useful tip is for a goalkeeper to write down some key words or phrases such as "unbeatable", "awesome", "clean sheet", "confident", etc. These words can be written on cards or even on the strap of goalkeeper gloves to act as a constant and positive reminder before and during matches.

Imagery Experiences are to do with goalkeepers recreating images of successful goalkeeping performances in their mind. Through creating such mental representations, mastery of a particular goalkeeping technique or type of save is far more likely. This is also referred to as *visualisation* and it is a very powerful technique to boost confidence but it does need to be constantly practiced. Keepers - use the power of your imagination to remember your previous and future goalkeeping sporting successes. More on this later.

Physiological States can reduce feelings of confidence through phenomena such as muscular tension, palpitations and butterflies in the stomach. The bodily sensations associated with competition need to be perceived as being 'facilitative to performance' and this can be achieved through the application of appropriate stress management interventions such as breathing and relaxation techniques.

When looking at Physiological States, I would recommend that goalkeepers try to identify how they feel before and after matches and devise a strategy of how these feelings can be used to have a positive effect on performance. For example, try and recall a match where you felt physically tense, maybe even nauseous, before kick-off but where you performed superbly during the game. And then remind yourself how that superb performance would not have been possible without having those feelings.

Emotional States refer to the final source of self-confidence and relate to how you control the emotions associated with matches - such as excitement and anxiety. Very often, the importance of the occasion creates self-doubt, which is why it is essential to control your thoughts and emotions. Again 'visualising' your successful goalkeeping performance will help here. Learning relaxation techniques that you can use if feeling tense, angry or nervous will pay dividends. Learning the art of relaxation is of great importance to any sportsman striving for peak performance. As well as helping keepers reduce mental and physical anxiety, it boosts concentration levels and thereon improves the goalkeeper experience.

Relaxation techniques can be used prior to games or, if practiced enough, during games. And it has been scientifically proven that relaxation responses are accompanied by feelings of mental wellbeing and emotional calmness. A win/win for any goalkeeper.

A good way in which to gain a physical measure of your self-confidence is by performing two tests:

Sport-Confidence Inventory

The Sport-Confidence Inventory measures different levels of confidence relating to an individual's belief in their ability to execute the skills needed to succeed in their sport. I've used this test in the past with good success as the results open up how goalkeepers think they deal with mistakes, problems faced, and how well they focus. From a coach's perspective - results from the inventory enable you to create plans and speak to goalkeepers to build their self-belief – and importantly your belief in them.

The following book has this inventory in it: Vealey, R.S. (2005). *Coaching for the Inner Edge*. Champaign IL: Human Kinetics.

Example

Matt Murray – Former England Under-21 Goalkeeper

"Throughout my whole career I always battled with my self-confidence. I had to work hard with my sports psychologist to learn the technique of 'thought stopping'. I would always get very nervous before games and found it hard to stop images of making mistakes getting into my head. I learnt how to replace them with positive thoughts. On the morning of games I would write a list of all the things I was going to do in the game - for example:

- Brave
- Dominant
- Good communicator
- Great distribution

"These are known as 'affirmations'. I would always follow the same routine from when I woke up to kick off. I always trained hard to make sure I was as fit and as sharp as I could possibly be. I would analyse games with my coach - watching videos and talking them through. We would then work on things - working on my

11

weaknesses rather than my strengths. For example, if it was raining I would worry about the ball being slippery but my coach would say: "Only worry about what you can affect so make sure your technique is a good as possible and that will equip you for whatever you have to deal with." You must not concentrate on making mistakes, you must concentrate on what you have done well. As I got older I was able to deal with pressure more effectively. I decided to focus on it being my chance to shine rather than on failing."

Coping with Anxiety

Anxiety is a feeling we all experience at some time or other. This feeling can take the shape of nervousness, fear, or unease. Anxiety has been associated with negative performance but when at a certain 'optimum level' it can actually enhance performance.

Within goalkeeping anxious feelings can obviously impact on performance, and when negative thoughts enter the mind they can inhibit a goalkeeper's ability to do their job effectively. To identify anxiety, and put it at ease, must be at the top of a coach's priorities. Some goalkeepers, of course, thrive on these 'butterflies', whereas others struggle to control them and let worries control their body language.

Anxiety can be broken down into three different levels: cognitive (thought processing), somatic (physical responses), and behavioural (patterns of behaviour).

Cognitive – Indecision, confusion, negative thoughts, fear and poor concentration

Somatic – Sweating, muscle tension, clamminess and increased heart rate

Behavioural – Lethargic movements, playing safe, introversion and avoidance of eye contact

Anxiety can also be broken down into two main types: trait and state. Trait anxiety exists in someone's personality and can affect their daily life. State anxiety, on the other hand, is seen as a temporary change in someone's demeanour due to an outside factor; so in our language if your goalkeeper is usually a calm and jovial character, but come match days becomes a nervous wreck, this would show state anxiety.

(IAMS) Immediate Anxiety Measures Scale

Overcoming and dealing with anxiety is touched upon in the previous section under "Physiological States" and "Emotional States". Ways in which one can measure and understand a goalkeeper's anxiety can be done using (IAMS) the Immediate Anxiety Measures Scale.

This scale looks at anxieties at particular points in time, so it is very useful just before performance. It measures:

Cognitive anxiety which is the mental component of anxiety and may be characterised by thoughts, such as concerns or worries, about your upcoming competition; for example, about the way you perform or the importance of the event.

Somatic anxiety is the perception of your physical state and may be characterised by symptoms such as physical nervousness, butterflies in the stomach, tense muscles and increased heart rate.

Self-confidence is how confident you are of performing well in your upcoming competition and may be characterised by factors such as achieving your competition goals and performing well under pressure.

Intensity refers to the *amount* or *level* of cognitive anxiety, somatic anxiety or self-confidence that you are experiencing.

Directional interpretation refers to the extent to which you regard the intensity of these anxiety and confidence symptoms as positive or negative towards your upcoming performance.

Frequency of cognitive intrusions refers to how frequently you are experiencing these anxiety and confidence symptoms.

The test can be found using the following journal article via an appropriate academic textbook or internet search. Thomas, O., Hanton, S. & Jones, G. (2002) An alternative approach to short-form self-report assessment of competitive anxiety: A research note, *International Journal of Sport Psychology*, 33, p325-336

If you want to go the empirical route of measuring anxiety in order to better understand an individual's thinking, two additional tests can be considered:

Chapter 1

The (SCAT) Sport Competition Anxiety Test

This is a simple test that measures overall anxiety in sport performance. You can check your goalkeeper's scores and look for the relevant signs during performance if they score highly. Again you can find this test through an internet search or use the following academic reference. Maartens, R. (1990). *Competitive Anxiety in Sport*. Leeds: Human Kinetics

The CSAI – 2 (Competitive State Anxiety Inventory-2)

The CSAI-2 is an instrument used to measure cognitive state anxiety, somatic state anxiety and state self-confidence in competitive situations. This questionnaire again will help you understand how goalkeepers react and see the effects anxiety can have.

Now let's take the time to look at the real world nerves experienced by Richard Lee – Professional Goalkeeper, and author of the acclaimed book *'Graduation'*.

"Nerves stem from thought processes. It is therefore essential that your thought processes are positive otherwise the mind can run havoc. Many believe 'strength of mind' is something you're born with. It isn't. Many will adopt a character that will see them succeed in 'pressure' situations but this can be learned, worked on, and improved, like any other skill.

"Combine positive images with powerful self-talk, eliminate all negativity and see how great you can feel. The reality isn't always what your mind thinks it to be, you have the ability to create your own reality. Make it a good place to be."

Decision Making

A goalkeeper's decision making in football is crucial due to the ever changing nature of the environment in front of them. Decisions include where to kick the ball, whether to come and deal with a crossed ball, or what technique to use to catch the ball.

Decision making can be defined as the process of making a choice between alternatives when the outcome cannot be known in advance. Taking the above example of whether to come and deal with a crossed ball - the alternatives would be to catch the ball, punch the ball, or leave the ball to be dealt with by the defenders.

Decision making involves often complex deliberations, such as predicting probable consequences, balancing moral and technical considerations, and attending to the likely impact of the decision on others. No athlete makes the appropriate decision at all times. This comes down to factors including experience and muscle memory.

The process of decision making is pretty complex! So without regurgitating a textbook I will just touch upon the 'phase' system involved.

The Perceiving Phase – in this phase the goalkeeper is looking to address the situation and is working out what information is important. So, for example, when considering a cross - decision making would incorporate the flight of the ball, left footer or right footer delivery, defensive and attacking positions and the environmental conditions. With experience this phase becomes shorter and more autonomous.

The Deciding Phase – the goalkeeper is now deciding what action to take. Using the above example - shall I come, or stay and catch or punch?

The Acting Phase – where the goalkeeper physically carries out the action.

Obviously all of the above takes place in a fraction of a second. So it's important you don't overload your mind with lots of questions about the situation you're faced with. As experience increases you will know how to respond to a whole host of scenarios. In football, no two attacks, saves or crosses are the same; the decision making process however stays the same. Within practice sessions, incorporate decision making elements into the exercises (as the ability level increases a keeper should be able to handle a lot more). The goalkeeper should be allowed to solve problems at every turn.

A clear mind free from distractions which enables the athlete to focus solely on the task at hand is the winning approach. In goalkeeping you survive due to your decision making skills. As a coach ask your goalkeeper, "What is your thought process when you make this move?", or "What went through your mind when you made this decision?" Questions like these will invoke an interaction between athlete and coach – potentially to help unclutter the mind when faced with a split second decision.

Chapter 1

Small hesitations can prove costly so being positive and sticking to your decisions is crucial. This is why goalkeepers can carry on playing into their late 30s. Their decision making processes are grooved and they can place themselves in appropriate positions, despite their inevitable decreasing agility and reaction times, as they have been faced with real-life game experiences before and can process situations quickly. There's no substitute for experience.

Anticipation in goalkeeping is being able to read the game situation and your opponents. Being in the correct position allows for tough saves to become easier and for you to be one step ahead of the opposition. Anticipation in goalkeeping has been researched in the last few years. Results found that total gaze fixation time and average gaze fixation time were longer when a kick was anticipated successfully. Also information obtained through the peripheral vision system (while fixing one's gaze on an optic clue) was deemed the most important element to successful anticipation.

A study by Savelsbergh *et al* found that with penalty kicks - expert goalkeepers were generally more accurate in predicting the direction of the penalty kick and, waited longer before initiating a response. They also found that expert goalkeepers used a more efficient search strategy involving fewer fixations of longer duration to less disparate areas of the display. The novices spent longer fixating on the trunk, arms and hips, whereas the experts found the kicking leg, non-kicking leg and ball areas to be more informative, particularly as the moment of foot-to-ball contact approached.

In essence, expert goalkeepers reduce the amount of information to be processed by using their peripheral vision to a greater effect. Expert goalkeepers can anticipate where the ball is going and what their next actions must be; for example, telling their defence to shift left or right, or positioning themselves in an appropriate position in the goal area to save a shot.

I read an article on Petr Cech and how he uses different techniques to improve his peripheral vision. One being a screen that contains 500 lights and he has to hit the light as soon as it lights up. Another is a machine that fires out different coloured balls at varying angles and speeds. As Christophe Lollichon quotes in this article, "You mustn't move your head but only your eyes, as that's how to improve your peripheral vision, which is essential as a goalkeeper who has to spot dangers coming from all sides." And although this type of equipment is only available to those at the top level it's certainly interesting to see how goalkeepers are looking to prepare and train in the modern era of football. Further into the book, the vision and awareness section will look further into this.

If you are a coach your training environment must replicate the situations your goalkeepers are faced with on a match day. Without harping on about the benefits of varied decision-making based practices it is worth stating that these environments breed a goalkeeper that can respond to whatever they face in a match. Specific match based practices, team tactical play, or tailored game practices are the way forward here.

We must arm our goalkeepers with the tools needed to fight the opposition. To respond to every type of shot, from every type of distance. From giving them numerous ways in which to distribute effectively to the defensive, midfield and attacking thirds, to show them different set plays they will be exposed to and how to handle subtle changes of movement from the opposition.

Is playing out to my left back the right pass? How can I distribute early down the field? What is the best option now to build an attack? The game changes so fast that the movement of one player can change the picture the goalkeeper sees.

Let's return to Richard Lee, professional goalkeeper for Brentford, and formerly Watford, and learn what he has to say about decision making.

"Decision making is arguably the most important element for a goalkeeper; the good news is that this is something that can be taught via realistic training drills. Exercises as simple as playing a variety of different through balls with someone bearing down on goal and leaving the keeper with the decision to come and collect or hold their ground is a very beneficial one. Similar drills for crossing can also be useful. Neither have to be too complicated provided they are realistic and test the goalkeeper in this specific area. Linked to this is the mental aspect, often bad decisions will come from a cluttered mind."

Motivation

Not just in football, or more specifically goalkeeping, motivation in any sport has been found to be of fundamental importance in stimulating success in performance and training. Goalkeepers need to be motivated. It's an essential ingredient for a successful performance between the sticks. Keepers must be motivated to take to the field on a cold wet morning on a churned up pitch, behind a dodgy defense, or when they are about to face the league leaders.

Motivation is a combination of the drive within us to achieve our aims and the outside factors which affect it. Motivation in sport can be defined, in a simple way, as the direction and intensity of individual effort, and it's key for determining *why* athletes do anything within sport.

Motivation has the following two forms: intrinsic motivation and extrinsic motivation.

Intrinsic motivation is an inbuilt desire to become competent enough to master specific tasks. It is all about learning, developing, having fun, playing for pride and being the best goalkeeper that you can possibly be. It is about the joy and satisfaction of participating and competing. It's about improving on your past goalkeeping performances. It's about you and not about the opposition.

Extrinsic motivation on the other hand is all about the glory, the plaudits, the medals, the trophies and maybe even the fame and fortune. The motivation comes from other people. It's all about the winning; sometimes at all costs. It's about the result. It's about your opponents and not about you.

For a goalkeeper to improve the mental side of his game, it is important that he or she understands both intrinsic and extrinsic motivation. Intrinsic motivation is what is required for sustained long term success; as a goalkeeper you need to love what you do. Extrinsic motivation also has its benefits, but usually just for the short term, and as long as it is not overused.

Reliance on extrinsic motivation will not sustain goalkeeping success as external rewards will not maintain motivation over the long haul. You need to supplement one with the other. Intrinsic motivation must be the major factor for long term sporting success. Learn to love goalkeeping.

Unfortunately in football, as in most sports, the tendency is to focus a larger amount of the time on motivating athletes extrinsically – by trophies, medals, certificates, prize money and so on. As a goalkeeper do not put too much focus on these status symbols. And if you are a coach, play down these external rewards and do not use them as a carrot for your goalkeeper. Instead, create a fun learning environment that encourages and praises improvements in personal goalkeeper performance and development – not just the results.

Being able to see how, why, and to what level, goalkeepers are motivated is vital for coaches because it allows them to offer assistance for players to reach their goals. For example, laying on extra challenging training or offering external rewards as discussed. If you want to explore and gauge motivation, the (SMS) Sports Motivation Scale is to be recommended.

Pelletier, L. G., Fortier, M. S., Vallerand, R. J., Tuson, K. M., Brière, N. M., & Blais, M. R. (1995). Toward a new measure of intrinsic motivation, extrinsic motivation, and a motivation in sports: The Sport Motivation Scale (SMS). *Journal of Sport & Exercise Psychology*, 17, p35-53

Now, let's taking a working example of motivation. Please say hello to Scott Brown – Professional Goalkeeper.

"I love football. I love playing. When I am not playing I want to lay down and often think and remind myself what I have done, what I have sacrificed to get to that point in my career, and how much it makes my family proud when they come and watch me play."

Concentration and Attention

Concentration and attention for goalkeepers is fundamental to success. This is because of the nature of the position; goalkeepers will often have large parts of the match where they will not be directly involved in play yet will be called into action in a split instant. Maintaining focus throughout a match is a difficult task, particularly for some younger players with limited attention spans.

Concentration and attention are needed for skill execution but although they are linked – they are different. Attention is when an organism focuses on certain features of the environment. Selective attention is the process where an individual is confronted with multiple stimuli in a situation and must select one aspect of them and attend to it. Concentration, on the other hand, involves focusing only on performance-relevant cues in your attentional field. In other words, only focusing on cues that help you to perform to your best. These cues can include tactics, relevant technical information, and your opponent.

The best keepers in the world are masters of concentration (or focus) – they can tune out everything that doesn't matter, and focus only on what does.

There are numerous external factors that can potentially cause disturbance or disruption to the goalkeeper during game situations. They include: the crowd, the weather, a mistake by a teammate, and lengthy periods of time without seeing the ball. It is essential for the goalkeeper not to allow external factors to have detrimental implications on their performance, especially when these factors are outside the goalkeeper's control.

Chapter 1

Let's look at Cricket briefly. When batting it's been said that in between balls it's important to think about something un-related to the task you're performing in order to 'take a break', but then to refocus back to the task at hand once in your stance again. A batsman could be there for six or seven hours a day, or three long sessions, so being able to break this time down can help keep the batsman remain mentally fresh and alert.

For goalkeeping it has been shown that within a match the goalkeeper can't focus solely on the ball; they must orchestrate the defence through communication and direction, and be in an appropriate position in relation to the ball. There is a lot of 'multi-tasking' to be done so focusing on relevant information is paramount.

The goalkeeper's 'Funnel of Attention', devised by Bill Beswick and Eric Steele, shows the attentional demands on a goalkeeper when the ball is in different areas of the pitch.

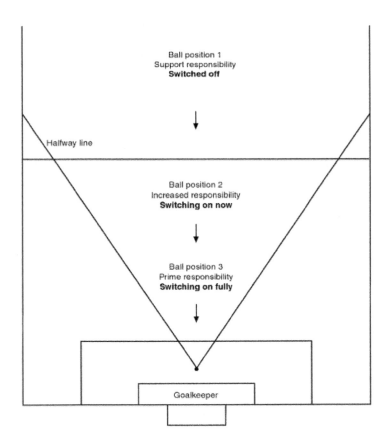

Parts of this model have been questioned a professional manager, notably a top Premiership manager who England's first choice goalkeeper plays for. After a few mistakes leading to goals, he said: "I think for a young goalkeeper it is important to always have full concentration. But I think that [he] sometimes loses his concentration. He is always very assured except sometimes. It is important to always have concentration, always." I guess this manager isn't saying that a keeper needs to have optimum concentration 'always', rather that - with the speed of counter attacks and corners for your team - the ball can be down your end in a matter of seconds so being prepared to respond is crucial. Being able to switch the amount of attention required is difficult. Being ready and alert at that crucial moment can be the difference between winning and losing for a team.

I was watching a League of Their Own (Sky TV programme) recently and the same goalkeeper as above was on the panel. James Corden (the host) asked him what you do when not involved in the play. He responded that one match "I planned my route home." I wonder what his manager thought!

If you are in a title challenging team you could argue that you're less likely to be involved 'directly' in the play because your team will have the lion's share of possession. The key is to be ready once called upon. How many times have you seen world class keepers make a crucial last minute save to hold on to a 1-0 win? That separates the good from the great goalkeepers.

The flip side would be playing for a team that's struggling at the wrong end of the league. As the goalkeeper you would swamped with wave upon wave of attacks (although you could say a top team like Chelsea had to endure three games like this in the Champions League winning year of 2011/2012, so there are exceptions in certain games and competitions).

It can be said – *true focus lies between serenity and rage!*

From a practical viewpoint a good way of building concentration is *after* a session, particularly after a challenging one, where the goalkeeper can be taken to one side and asked to do some reaction work. An example might be to give the goalkeeper a series of throws with a tennis ball:

- 10 to the centre (two hand catch)
- 10 to their dominant side (one hand catch)
- 10 to their weaker side (one hand catch)

Simple exercises such as this will test a keeper's ability to concentrate when their mind and body is fatigued after a session. There are various other exercises you can do involving smaller balls, and getting your goalkeepers to work differently than they have done in the training session.

A goalkeeper can do a number of things to remain focused, particularly during periods of inactivity and when the mind starts to wander. For example, you can immediately take a deep breath, tell yourself a word like 'FOCUS' combined with a physical reminder, for instance, a single clap, or a tap of your boot. Another useful tip is to separate the game into different periods, for example in the professional game some keepers have been known to mentally separate a 90-minute match into three 30-minute periods, with the aim of achieving a clean sheet within each individual period.

There is a questionnaire (called the **TAIS Attentional Style questionnaire**) that can be given to goalkeepers to assess their attention style. This questionnaire will show how goalkeepers respond to external stimuli. This could be distractions to their performance, their engagement when performing goalkeeping skills, and how they think whilst performing these skills.

Nideffer, R.M. (1976). Test of attentional and interpersonal style. *Journal of Personality and Social Psychology*, 34, p394-404.

More from Scott Brown: "Concentration is another major part of keeping, that's why the likes of Iker Casillas are such good goalkeepers because they have very little to do and then are called upon to make saves at vital times in the game. For me I just set myself little targets during the game, firstly I say get to 15 minutes, then 35, then half time and the same in the second half so it just breaks the game up a bit."

Goal Setting

Not the big white things with nets hanging off them! Here we are talking about an aim or an objective to improve your goalkeeping performance and development.

Sport psychology assumes that goal-setting is the key to motivation. In order to motivate yourself, you need to create clear, sharp goals.

Put simply, when you set goals correctly, your goals will allow you to achieve results that you never thought possible. Also, if you don't have goals then you won't be motivated to improve and your goalkeeping performance will hit a plateau – or even decline!

Goal setting is a very powerful way of thinking about your ideal goalkeeping future, and for motivating yourself to turn your vision of this future into reality.

The process of setting goals helps you choose where you want to go, and what you want to achieve. By knowing precisely what you want to achieve, you know where you have to concentrate your efforts. You'll also quickly spot the distractions that can, so easily, lead you astray.

Goal setting is used by many of the top sports professionals. Setting goals gives them a long-term vision and short-term motivation. It focuses their acquisition of knowledge, and helps them to organize their time and resources so that they can fulfil, and sometimes exceed, their potential.

By setting sharp, clearly defined goals, you can measure and take pride in the achievement of those goals, and you'll see forward progress in what might previously have seemed a long pointless grind. You will also raise your self-confidence, as you recognize your own ability and competence in achieving the goals that you've set.

Setting challenging goals gives goalkeepers the incentive to get out of the bed in the morning and go improve.

Here are the key factors that should be used when setting all types of goals:

- Make them SMART (Specific, Measurable, Achievable, Realistic and Time constrained)
- Be positive - express goals positively – "Focus on my excellent technique which I have developed in training," is a much better goal than "Don't make a stupid mistake." The mind cannot process a negative thought. Want me to prove it? Ok, **don't** think of a purple elephant; whatever you do, **don't** think of a purple elephant. See?
- Be precise - set precise goals, putting in dates, times and desired statistics so that you can somehow measure achievement.
- Prioritize - when you have several goals, give each a priority. This helps you to avoid feeling overwhelmed by having too many goals, and helps to direct your attention to the most important ones.
- Write goals down - this crystallizes them and gives them more force. Keep them visible!

- Keep goals small - keep the low-level goals that you're working towards small and achievable. If a goal is too large, then it can seem that you are not making progress towards it. Keeping goals small and incremental gives more opportunities for reward.
- Set performance goals, not outcome goals - you should take care to set goals over which you have as much control as possible. It can be quite dispiriting to fail to achieve a personal goal for reasons beyond your control! For example, saying "My team will win every match this season," is unreasonable and completely out of your control.
- Set realistic goals - it's important to set goals that you can achieve - but DO make them challenging!
- Use imagery (visualization) – imagine achieving your goals. Really imagine it! Your mind cannot distinguish between your imagination and reality. Visualizing your future makes it more likely to turn your vision into reality.
- Rewards – make sure that you give yourself an appropriate reward for completing each goal.
- Evaluate - regularly review your goals and adjust accordingly.
- Support – enlist the help of your friends, family and coach to help you achieve your goals. You can't do this on your own!

An Example of Setting Goals for Young Keepers

This is how would I help motivate a young keeper and help him set some goals. Let's set the scene.

There is a young goalkeeper. He is only 11 but has a tremendous technique, attitude and physique. He is not yet linked with a local professional football club but he plays for a good club side, and also his school team. However there is a fear that he just takes one game at a time and has not really thought through a timeline that could help him achieve his burning ambition, and obvious potential, to be a top professional goalkeeper. His name is Harry.

The first step is to help Harry set some goals and aide his development, and this would involve explaining to Harry how sport psychology could help him achieve his dreams. So, I would provide him with a basic overview of sport psychology, find out what motivates him, and discuss his ambitions.

Then, once I have gathered information, I would explain the benefits of goal setting, such as:

- Persistence - goals will help Harry persist with goalkeeping over a period of time and help him keep sight of what he wants to achieve.
- Attention – will help Harry focus on the important aspects of improving his goalkeeping performance.
- Effort – will provide Harry with the incentive to mobilise and direct the intensity of his efforts towards his goals.
- Strategies –will provide Harry with new strategies to achieve his desired outcomes.

I would then follow this up with an explanation of the principles of goal setting and explain the acronym SMART (Specific, Measurable, Achievable, Realistic and Time Constrained).

I would then explain what we mean by Short Term (each day, within a week or a month), Medium Term (within three months) and Long Term (within a year or beyond). Also I would explain the pros and cons of outcome, performance and process goals.

Writing things down in a footballing notebook, an example of each type of goal, could be something like the following:

Short term: "Each week I will attend specific goalkeeper training with a qualified goalkeeper coach and record details of each session, so that I can regularly evaluate my development."

Medium term: "Within three months, I will have successfully played a match in the next age group with my club or at school."

Long term: "Within two years, I will have successfully completed a trial for my local professional club and been accepted into their Academy."

These goals, and Harry's achievement towards them, will need to be regularly reviewed, to make sure he is on track. I will also reward Harry for achieving any of these goals - maybe I will offer him a free pair of goalkeeper gloves.

Once any of these goals have been achieved – set new ones. The learning and the development never stops.

A very useful way of using video for small performance targets is to film a practice, then look back through the video to evaluate what the player has just done. Now, as a coach, you can get targets, for example:

You've just done a 1v1 practice that you filmed with three goalkeepers. After looking back through a small section of footage you've noticed that Johnny, your 10 year old keeper, goes to ground far too early and lets in a number of goals. Here you can say, '"Johnny can we stay on our feet longer for the next 1v1 practice?" By seeing this target on video, he can understand the target, and also why it's being set – if he doesn't commit too early he can increase his chances of saving the ball. The video aspect to the above will be explained in greater depth in future chapters.

Performance Profiling

Performance profiling is a tried and tested way of athlete assessment that gets them to identify their perceived strengths and weaknesses. I've used these at grassroots and professional level with great benefit. Psychological, physical, technical and tactical attributes can be listed on these profiles with specific attributes analysed - based upon match requirements.

The benefit of performance profiling is that it helps monitor changes; athletes take ownership of their development and help the coach draw up an appropriate development plan (although this final point shouldn't be reason alone to create a programme).

Profiles are created by listing certain attributes relevant to the athlete's sport and specific requirements, in the examples shown, to goalkeeping. These can differ depending on what you want to find out. The example is a general goalkeeping one – I've done profiles based purely on technical attributes such as goal kick distribution, diving left, dealing with corners; you can go right into detail with these.

The two images below illustrate two ways to fill in a profile (a blank copy is available upon request).

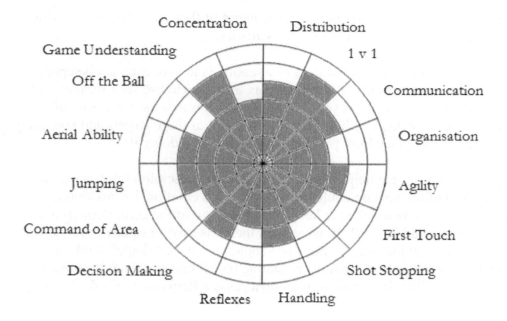

To score each profile, get each athlete to rate their perceived current level of performance. The further away from the centre mark - the higher the score (on the example above they are rated out of 7).

Using the example shown, which is fictitious, but meant to be completed by a goalkeeper, the profile would show what areas the athlete perceives to be weaker, namely command of area, and concentration (amongst others). Strengths are game understanding and decision making.

A coach would then analyse the profile by noticing strengths and weaknesses – and through discussion with the goalkeeper talk about ways to best improve on certain attributes. It's also common for the coach to benchmark scores that they would expect from a goalkeeper of a certain age or ability – and by doing this goals can be set – although it's a subjective process where views can differ.

An all-round goalkeeper who is strong across the board must be the ultimate goal for a coach and these profiles can help show this. Profiles should be redrawn regularly (after a pre-determined time) to highlight what areas are improving, and what (potentially) new areas need development.

The key to this process is *honesty* in establishing what your strengths as a goalkeeper are, and as the coach being able to devise training programmes (although as stated previously not solely because of these profiles). Using video is a great way of backing up the profiles statistics.

A simple way to invoke ownership to any session is to give each goalkeeper a small target for the session. This might be as simple as to use your weaker foot when distributing, or work on your explosiveness towards the ball. And, of course, the use of video will help provide evidence of these targets and positively reinforce a keeper, "Hey look you can do it, here's you doing it!"

Using 'buzz' words also helps trigger a reaction. If the session topic is reactions then the word of the session could be "desire". This emotional word would appeal to the goalkeeper when linked to keeping the ball out of the goal. Perhaps a more technical term could be used; if the session theme is staying square onto the ball and maintaining saving shape – the word could simply be "shape". Link this to the key technical points like not over-rotating the shoulder and having hands forwards. I find dropping these words into a session helps maintain focus and session aims.

Imagery and Visualisation

We have already talked a lot about *imagery* (or *visualisation* as it is more commonly referred to) but what is it and can it really help goalkeepers?

Visualisation is one of the most powerful tools we possess to improve goalkeeping performance. By using our minds to imagine performing at our best, we condition our bodies to excel.

Imagery refers to the process of rehearsing actions in the mind using all five of our senses. Imagine what you would see, what you would hear, and what you would feel to make an action as real as possible.

If you were a runner competing in the marathon, you can imagine yourself running the 26.2 miles along the lake front. If you're a triathlete, you can use imagery to mentally practice the swim, bike, and run leg of the race.

When goalkeepers practice visualization they establish a link between feeling, visualizing, and performing, and it is for this reason that the keeper's ability to relax is crucial. When goalkeepers relax and visualize themselves performing their sport, they link that relaxed state to images of an ideal performance.

Benefits of Imagery:

- Improves concentration
- Enhances motivation
- Builds confidence (because you see yourself doing what you want to do)
- Helps control emotional responses
- Helps in building or acquiring skills or strategy
- Prepares you for matches
- Helps you cope with mistakes and setbacks
- Enhances problem-solving

Here is an example of a visualisation script that Gavin has written to help goalkeepers. It is beneficial if you, or someone you know, records this and you listen to it whenever you need a boost or want to enhance your mental training. Alternatively why not write and record your own version?

I would like you to sit comfortably in a chair, in an upright position, with your spine straight. Now close your eyes, breathe slowly and deeply . . . and begin to count down slowly from ten to one . . . relaxing more and more deeply with each count. 10 . . . 9 . . . 8 . . . Feel yourself going deeper and deeper . . . into a quieter, more relaxed state of mind . . . 7 . . . 6 . . . 5 . . . deeper and more relaxed . . . 4 . . . 3 . . . 2 . . . 1 . . . You are now in a very deep, very calm state of mind.

Now see yourself in that special spot where you are completely at peace with yourself... where you are totally happy... it may be under an oak tree in the forest, or next to a stream in the woods, or floating in a boat on a lake... it's a place you love to be because it's so peaceful. And once you're situated in that spot, then you see before you what appears to be a television screen...and as you watch that screen, you suddenly see yourself... you are on the screen... performing on the pitch... in goal... between the sticks.

And see with you that one person who has always been your goalkeeping idol... look at what they are wearing... their kit... their gloves... you watch them play... you copy their body language... you copy their style. Their every move is your move... you and they are one... excellent timing... excellent positioning............safe hands........excellent communication......superb distribution.........swagger.....confidence....... you are in sync with your goalkeeping idol...

Chapter 1

And also see that individual you want to excel for... the one person who, throughout your life has been an inspiration for you... the one person who has stood by you through good times and tough times. You know there are many people who love you...who care about you... they are with you... they are for you... (PAUSE).

You are relaxed... you are calm. The referee blows the whistle... the game is on. You are saving everything...you are distributing the ball accurately... you feel the wind in your face... you are doing what you do best... you are looking and feeling unbeatable. You are relaxed and calm. You see the ball... yet you see the whole field. You know what you will do with the ball before it comes to you. You know how you are going to deal with every type of shot and cross... you are totally prepared for this game. You are performing at your best... (PAUSE).

And finally, the game is over... see yourself... tired, but happy.... you are sweating... there is a towel around your neck... everyone is patting you on the back... giving you high fives... hugging you... congratulating you. See yourself enjoying the reward you promised yourself . . . you did it . . . you made it happen . . . you . . . are awesome (PAUSE)

and now, take approximately 30-seconds to slowly open your eyes. Thirty Seconds.

And now some more from Richard Lee:

"As mentioned previously, it is vital that come game time you have tuned into your Optimum Performance State. This is different for everyone but gaining this understanding of yourself will give you a fantastic base to build from. Imagery/visualisation are great ways of doing this.

"An exercise as simple as putting on some music and mentally running through what you may need to do in an upcoming match is a very powerful tool. You'll often feel the adrenaline start to flow as you think through potential scenarios. This is because your brain will treat the situation as being real and in doing so, the same synapses in your brain will fire therefore helping prepare you as you think through a variety of positive images in your head. David James was well-known for his pre match mental prep, often mimicking actions in his goal-mouth prior to a game being played, all very useful when it comes to playing the game."

Self-talk

Human beings, whether they realize it or not, are in constant conversation with themselves. Sometimes these conversations are spoken out loud, but more often than not these conversations are in your head. Both of these are methods of *self-talk*.

Often the messages are positive, for example "I am unbeatable", "I am fast" or "I can do this". But sometimes the messages can be negative, for example "I am rubbish", "I am going to lose," or "I am never going to save this penalty."

The key with self-talk is that whatever you are telling yourself is very, very powerful. Therefore it is important to remember that you have control over the messages that you tell yourself which means that you can harness the power of your thoughts to improve your sporting performance.

As a result of utilizing positive self-talk goalkeepers are able to:

- Enhance self-confidence
- Enhance motivation
- Maintain the appropriate focus
- Help control anxiety at key moments

Research has shown that the mind cannot process a negative, therefore all self-talk must be stated in the positive; so for example:

Instead of a keeper saying something like: "I am going to play terribly today," they need to say, "I am going to save everything today."

To boost self-talk, it is recommended to record these key, positive statements onto your iPod or onto notes that you can keep on your person and refer to at key moments. Some sportsmen and women often write these key, positive statements onto their sports equipment – and I know a number of professional goalkeepers that write key, positive words on the straps of their goalkeeper gloves and then refer to these in key moments. Words like "Great Save", "Focus", "Unbeatable."

It has been shown that actually saying positive key words and statements out loud is more beneficial than saying them internally. So, before and during a match, don't be shy in saying any of these key, positive words and phrases out loud. It will give you a great lift.

Self-talk is a key component of sport psychology and its powerfulness cannot be underestimated.

Richard Lee: "How you think will affect the way you feel. The beauty of this is that you are able to guide your thoughts in a positive way and this applies with self-talk too. By feeding positive messages to yourself you'll feel heightened confidence, the reason being that the unconscious mind reacts to what it is fed. Continually feed it positive messages and you'll feel good. Doubt yourself or beat yourself up about mistakes and you won't feel so good! In truth much of goalkeeping is based on opinion, therefore it's essential that your opinion of yourself is a great one."

Dealing with Mistakes

We've all been there! Young goalkeepers will make mistakes, whether it is a technical error or a decision making one, it's all part of the learning process. The key is to limit mistakes and not let them affect your performance – whether this is in matches or training.

I've seen and been involved with many young goalkeepers over the years that beat themselves up over errors in training. Concentration is a big part of this because, in training, goalkeepers have a tendency to switch off from the task if they see the exercise as easy, or they expect what the exercise has to offer (such as prescribed drills) and become lazy. Couple this with training environments that seem to mirror a social interaction (rather than a focus on performance and improving skills) then mistake-ridden sessions will occur; not through lack of skill and understanding but purely because concentration lapses.

An appropriate training environment for goalkeeping should embrace mistakes. By this I mean that if the goalkeeper sees a mistake as disrupting the session, or is scared to try new techniques, is this conducive to learning and expressing themselves? Training is there to try new things and work on the goalkeeper's all round game – so as a coach you need to reassure players that should they make an error, they need to either figure the solution out for themselves, or be told and then shown; depending on your teaching method.

I know coaches who, when scouting goalkeepers, make a special point of noticing how they deal with a mistake. Do they dwell on it for the next 10 minutes or re-focus and face the next action with a determined mindset? You can tell a lot from a goalkeeper by how they handle a setback. Although with experience these situations will become easier.

It is inevitable that every goalkeeper will make a mistake during a season; however, it is essential for a goalkeeper to have a positive mindset, enabling them to believe that they can save everything thrown their way. In reality, this is unrealistic, as it is the unavoidable outcome of being a goalkeeper to concede the occasional goal! It is essential that the goalkeeper must not be defined by their mistakes; they must react positively to them. Dwelling on a mistake WILL be detrimental to the performance of a goalkeeper.

How

It is important for a goalkeeper to attempt to mentally erase any mistake which has just occurred (at least for the duration of the game), and re-establish their focus on the task at hand. The mistake has occurred, it cannot be rectified, and the goalkeeper can still have a positive influence on the remainder of the game. Positive self-talk, reminders, and reinforcements will allow you to rediscover your focus, and allow you to react positively to the experience. Learn from that mistake and move on. Never make the same mistake twice!

Something I used to do (and still do when playing) after conceding a goal, is just to think about it briefly for a couple of seconds before play restarts, then wipe my forehead with my hand or finger, then flick it away. This might sound strange but effectively I'm wiping that moment out of my head and carrying on with the task at hand.

Scott Brown: "I think that psychology is a massive part of goalkeeping, you can have all the ability in the world but if you're not right between the ears then you have no chance. It can be a very lonely place out there and you need to be mentally very tough.

"I remember one game a few years back I was playing for Cheltenham and there was a game coming up that was on exactly the same Tuesday night as there had been one year previously. In the previous year's match I had made a mistake that had cost us at least a point and I went into this game thinking that it was going to happen again. Then, the opposition team changed ends, just like the previous year, we took the lead just like the previous year, and I made a mistake just like the previous year. I know that dealing with mistakes is something that I need to, and want to, work on further and believe it will help me no end."

Chapter 1

All goalkeepers will have their own way of dealing with mistakes or setbacks. For young goalkeepers it is important to help them overcome setbacks and remain confident and positive until the end.

Communication

The final attribute that needs addressing is communication. Communication is an interpersonal skill that can have a massive impact on any given situation in football – impacting on the feeling and thoughts of the team.

Verbal (oral feedback, instructions, or praise) and visual (a positive or negative gesture for example) communication dominates the goalkeeper's role. Combine this with actions that show some demeanour – such as a player walking away when being spoken to, or not showing some kind of acknowledgement to acknowledge they've heard or seen a command can have an impact as well.

I frequently get asked at youth level: "How can I get my goalkeeper to talk more?" Well there's no easy answer, although I would say that two things are apparent:

1. Most young keepers don't know what to say
2. And they don't have the confidence to address their team

The first point can relate to tactical understanding. When you're a young goalkeeper there's so much information to take in, mainly on the technical side such as focusing on how to physically save the ball and the situation being faced. It goes without saying that the goalkeeper can see the whole picture from their position – working on communication can keep your team in solid shape and players in correct positions – this means less work you have to do in a match.

Controlling the defence takes game understanding and experience. Giving the goalkeeper appropriate scripted commands, or trigger words are a good start! Some examples might be:

- 'man on' or 'time'
- 'step up' (followed by distance)
- 'mark' (followed by name)
- 'slide left' or 'slide right' (when the ball moves vertically)
- Arranging walls and defensive set plays

All commands should be clear, short and sharp, using the appropriate tone of voice. Don't commentate, you're not John Motson! If you're monotone, and constantly talking, your team will switch off and not respond quickly when you actually require them to. Of course you should focus on the players you can directly affect – like organising your defensive shape when the ball is in the attacking third.

As the coach it's important to show examples of when to use these terms, either in training, through video recall, or by watching live games a player is not involved in. This is why specific game based exercises and sessions are so important – along with integration into the team.

The second point (they don't have the confidence to address their team) is relevant to the confidence section. Again, it is important for the goalkeeper to integrate with the team to form a relationship and create cohesion with them. I think if you get the first point right then the second will take care of itself – the thought of saying the wrong thing or 'not knowing your team' can make you very placid. I speak from experience here!

Of course when wanting to receive the ball, a goalkeeper's commands should be verbal and visual; for example, when wanting to receive the ball on their right foot from a defender: "Right foot John," (showing their right hand at the same time). Making eye contact with that player is important also, especially when leaving the goal mouth to receive a ball. The defender can see you change position and not play the ball where they saw you last, but where you actually are,

Whether verbal or visual, it's crucial in practice sessions that a keeper practices both, and that the goalkeeper understands where and when to use them. The key is to be loud and specific. Every goalkeeper is different and personalities will dictate your goalkeeper's type of communication – but once again, giving them the necessary tools and feedback to perform will help a great deal.

Summary

As you can see there are a number of key ingredients that allow a goalkeeper to be mentally prepared for the roller coaster existence of a life in front of the sticks. These ingredients include focus, self-confidence, use of imagery/visualisation, an ability to deal with pressure or setbacks, motivation, and the ability to manage nerves. Creating a presence and being committed to your own learning as a goalkeeper is vital. Don't let anyone or anything get in your head and distract you from the tasks at hand. Trying your best as a coach to put your goalkeepers in a confident and committed frame of mind, before a training session or match, will increase productivity. Some of the methods here will hopefully breed this.

The key should be to develop an optimum, balanced and personalised approach to goalkeeping. Getting to know 'what makes a keeper tick' is crucial as everyone is different. That's the beauty of sport. And life!

Match warm up routines are a good example of psychology in its entirety – creating a routine that makes a keeper feel comfortable, confident, prepared, positive and ready to face whatever is thrown at them.

When looking at mental strength there are three resources I can point you in the direction of. I'll point out that, coincidentally, both books are published by this book's publisher – Bennion Kearny.

1. Richard Lee's book *Graduation: Life Lessons of a Professional Footballer*. In this book Richard talks about his experiences in football and particularly a season playing for Brentford. He writes about how important the mind is and how powerful it can be… he writes about his experiences with hypnotherapy and yoga amongst other things… a must read for budding or current goalkeepers - believe me!

2. *Soccer Tough: Simple Football Psychology Techniques to Improve Your Game* by Dan Abrahams. *Soccer Tough* offers practical techniques from sports psychology that will enable footballers (not specifically goalkeepers) of all abilities to actively develop focus, energy, and confidence.

3. My chapter co-author Gavin Wilson has produced a hugely popular CD and MP3, entitled *Eye On The Ball*, specifically for goalkeepers.

Generally speaking, a goalkeeper's negative mindset is associated with their personal attitude or approach to goalkeeping. Negative thoughts, disbelief in ability, poor preparation, and poor mindset, are all detrimental to performance. The key method in conquering these negative associations is for a keeper to take ownership of their own development. If you want to be the best goalkeeper that you can possibly be then you must do everything in your control to train relentlessly, think positively, and evaluate your performance in training and game situations.

Despite the clear individualistic and position specific requirements, the goalkeeper still needs to be part of the team and contribute to the team's ethics and culture. There may be slight bias when this is said, but *they are* the most important player in the team. A great goalkeeper can win a team points and keep them in the game - examples of Peter Shilton for Nottingham Forest in the Brian Clough era, and more recently Ali Al-Habsi at Wigan spring to mind. The goalkeeper should be part of the team, not apart from the team.

When all is said and done, it is essential for you to discover your own winning formula and optimum performance state.

2

Goalkeeping Physiology and Athletic Development

"Be quick, but never hurry."

(John Wooden)

This chapter will be co-authored with Michael Main. Michael is currently head of strength and conditioning for Hampshire County Cricket Club. He has a strong background in football having worked previously at Coventry City Football Club and played at a high level. Michael is a highly experienced strength and conditioning practitioner having worked with elite athletes for a number of years. He holds a Master's degree in strength and conditioning as well as a number of other qualifications.

Looking at the chapter ahead, Michael will provide an excellent point of view from both a general physical and, more importantly, a goalkeeping specific viewpoint. Together we look to provide an outline into some of a goalkeeper's main physical attributes, giving tried and tested examples along the way. There are references to other sources that are very specific to goalkeeper conditioning too. What this chapter looks to do is introduce the basics and perhaps give alternative exercises to improve certain attributes (rather than traditional methods you might have seen or used before). A great number of the exercises will be field-based because a gym, or gym equipment, may not always be available for training, and for young goalkeepers 'overdoing' physical development can be dangerous in the long run.

In this chapter we will cover

- Why physical development is important for goalkeepers
- What the goalkeeper does in a game
- The physical demands of goalkeeping
- The physical attributes goalkeepers need to be proficient at, and how to develop them
- When to work on these attributes
- Injury prevention

Physical Importance

In this day and age physical training in football is becoming much more than a 'tick box' approach as part of an elite program. It is very much a specific area, bespoke to individual players and specific positions (goalkeeping being one).

There is a plethora of different approaches to physical training in sport. Every sport has different physical demands and responses – indeed every position within a sport has physiological differences. Football is no different in that respect, and taking the goalkeeper as our example – we can note how he or she has a very different physical makeup compared to other positions on the pitch due to the tasks keepers are asked to perform.

Often commentators' compliment players using words such as *powerful* or *strong* and it is becoming more and more obvious that, at the highest level, players are finely tuned physically. This plays a large part in preventing injuries, maximising performance, and lengthening a player's career.

A multidimensional approach to physical goalkeeper coaching and training will be a key objective within this chapter. We are not going to go through every muscle, bone or joint for different actions because we'd be here all day! In any case thinking about movement patterns rather than individual muscles is more beneficial. The chapter isn't designed as a detailed strength and conditioning (academically based) physiology manual – there are many generic publications that do that well. This is about taking a goalkeeping specific outlook onto a player's physical attributes and how to go about developing them in a safe, practical and realistic environment.

The physical demands of the goalkeeper's position have changed considerably over the years and thus so have the specific training and athletic development regimes. Goalkeeping can take guidance from many different sports which provide transferable skills (discussed in upcoming chapters) so that goalkeeping coaches can take the goalkeeper out of technical goalmouth training to develop skills in isolation.

Imagine your goalkeeper has the ability to… jump as high as an elite basketball player… the ability to be as fast out of the blocks as an international sprinter … the ability to be as powerful as an american footballer… the ability to be as flexible, balanced and agile as an Olympic gymnast… All of these will be a massive advantage. So taking pieces of other sports' training and applying them, in the right environment, to a goalkeeper's physical development can't be a bad thing!

Goalkeeping exercises will naturally improve a goalkeeper's overall match fitness, as long as training meets match requirements. Laying on exercises and sessions that isolate key physical attributes are extremely beneficial. This is why the emphasis to work on possession and distribution during training sessions is so great – because if this is what a keeper is faced with in a match they should be physically ready to deal with 40+ actions.

Long gone are the days when a keeper's physical conditioning was the same as the outfield players – going for long runs or doing continuous exercise (which will hinder developing their explosive nature). The current repetitious nature of goalkeeping drills must be managed in a way where you substitute quantity for quality; highly repetitious goalkeeping practice can be detrimental.

Think about every time a goalkeeper dives… a huge amount of force and impact goes through their bodies - so finding the optimum amount of time to train certain techniques should be high on a coach's list of priorities – doing short, sharp exercises with good rest periods in-between will address this. All in all, a safe and appropriate environment is key; an environment that is age specific, meets the demands of the position, and of course the individuality of the goalkeeper themselves is a high priority.

Before we start, if you want an extremely practical and simple goalkeeping workout, there is a highly recommended DVD compiled by Richard Lee of GK Icon which covers a whole host of ways to improve different areas of goalkeeping. This DVD can be found at www.GKWorkout.com; along with this, and the exercises suggested here, you should be more than covered.

Of course all exercises used in training must be performed in a safe environment, and with the correct form to *enhance* safety and effectiveness. Make sure you, or the goalkeeper you're training, is physically able and capable enough to perform exercises in the gym; exercises such as box jumping or plyometric exercises for example. Young people's bodies are still growing, developing and changing at a fast pace – so be aware of the dangers of the wrong type or load of training.

Some of the exercises will overlap the emphasis on a particular attribute, as many are interconnected. Use this chapter as a base for where to start your goalkeeping physical development programme.

What Do Goalkeepers Do?

From an overall perspective it's important to get a better idea of what actions the goalkeeper will face in a match. This can then impact on the most appropriate training and exercises that will mirror what a keeper is faced with in a match. As we shall see, in the biomechanics chapter, the position is one of generic sport and body movement patterns, but placed in a unique environment causing these movements to be challenged.

A study in 2008 investigated the activity profiles of elite goalkeepers in the English Premier League over 109 matches involving 62 different goalkeepers.

The results were as follows: (incidentally, these are mean averages of the distances.)

- Walking – 4.025km
- Jogging – 1.223km
- Running – 0.221km
- High speed run – 0.056km
- Sprinting – 0.011km

Overall the goalkeeper covered an average of 5.6km. 73% of the time they were walking and there were brief occasions of short-sharp bursts of high intensity. The length of time spent doing each action was headed by walking, with standing still being the second most time consuming action.

As goalkeeping enthusiasts, we all know that goalkeepers will have periods of inactivity but studies of this nature prove this, giving us a better insight into energy systems and what types of training the goalkeeper should be exposed to.

We must focus on high intensity, explosive actions with good rest periods. Within a match the goalkeeper will have sufficient time to rest before each high intensity action (saves, crosses, through balls), although previous studies have shown that in the latter stages of matches, the chances of a goal being scored increase due to the fatigue of the outfield players. However, the situation of the match and the opposition's attacking prowess will have a considerable bearing on match involvement.

The game based coaching theory (at the end of the book) will expose the keeper in the developing phase to more actions will breed familiarity and build some of the physical attributes we shall soon discuss. Of course these games will involve high intensity activity but require good rest periods – along with periods where keepers won't be diving or throwing themselves around at maximum velocity.

From a physical viewpoint goalkeepers must be trained to use both feet. Not just so they can play effectively but for developing co-ordination and muscles on both sides of the body – in turn this will aid the goalkeeper in diving, jumping and generally moving in all directions

Give Me Energy...

The overall energy system the goalkeeper uses is called the anaerobic system. This basically means – 'without oxygen'. Although predominantly anaerobic in nature, physical exercise requires a certain amount of general aerobic fitness for general bodily function.

Goalkeeping emphasizes anaerobic efforts of brief duration when the goalkeeper is involved directly in play. Therefore anaerobic power is important in accelerating the muscles during short movements. This relates largely to what they are faced with in a match – this can be opposition driven and externally paced, for example shots, set pieces or through balls; or team driven which would include back passes and supporting positions. Aerobic exercises emphasise long durations of exertion such as continuous running or cycling. In small doses they are fine for goalkeepers but asking them to work for long periods of time doesn't reflect match requirements and wouldn't be considered sensible training. As well as this, spending hours in the gym building muscle mass or getting an aesthetically pleasing body doesn't correlate to good performances, in a lot of cases too much muscle mass hinders speed, agility and flexibility.

The Physical Demands of Goalkeeping

Firstly, it is important to understand what is meant by physical demands. Areas such as exercise physiology, components of fitness, and any physical factors likely to affect a performance outcome all contribute towards the physical demands of goalkeeping.

Physiology is a complex and scientific area in sport and football. In its rawest form it can be defined as: 'the way in which a living organism or bodily part functions'; in football terms: 'the way in which a player performs physically.' Without being able to understand the basic physiological demands associated with a sport and specific positions within - it can be extremely difficult to train effectively. As already touched upon, the demands of football differ and vary depending on the individual player in any given position.

Football in general is a multi-directional intermittent team sport played at a range of intensities and speeds. If we look specifically at goalkeeping as a position, the general physical attributes needed would include power, speed and reactive agility with a high amount of decision making. From a physiological viewpoint it is very much an anaerobic position. Having analysed goalkeeper involvement across a number of matches, the game play they are typically involved in is usually for a split second or for short periods of time (e.g. shot stopping, collecting balls into the box, or goal kicks). It is rare to see a goalkeeper leave the eighteen yard box during a game unless taking a free kick or collecting the ball. This speaks volumes in regards to the way keepers should be trained physically.

We should take a moment to expand on a few of the statements made in the previous paragraph. The statement of goalkeeping being predominantly anaerobic in nature is widely accepted within elite football. Anaerobic exercise or energy production can simply be defined as 'intense exercise which metabolises energy without the need of oxygen'. During games the goalkeeper will spend the majority of time uninvolved from a physical perspective (e.g. standing or walking sub maximally). At the highest level goalkeepers can take anywhere up to and beyond 40 distribution actions, make numerous saves and repeat sprints over short distances. It is important to note that the majority of actions a keeper completes in a game are dynamic, explosive and quickly followed by long periods of recovery or low level activity. This would suggest the majority of energy production is anaerobic in nature (Creatine Phosphate – ATP Production).

We will talk more about this later in the chapter in regards to the integration of anaerobic functioning into training.

With the above in mind, pitch based training should be based around short sharp drills incorporating speed, agility and jumping with long rest periods to maintain quality. When it comes to speed and agility, preplaced and positioned ladder drills are maybe not the way forward - multi-directional movement drills or acceleration speed drills are more appropriate. Constant reinforcement of good basic technique coupled with repetition should transfer theory into a better performance outcome. When looking at jumping and bounding drills, the key effectiveness indicator is the quality of the movement involved. As a coach, gaining a basic understanding of the basic biomechanical and physical aspects associated with *running mechanics*, *change of direction* and *jumping* and *landing* will only improve the quality of fitness and technical drills.

It is also important as a coach to appreciate the load associated with kicking, and monitoring this load where possible. The mechanical forces exerted during a long distance kicking action have a huge load on the muscularity, tendons and joints of the hip knee and ankle of both legs as well as the lower back region. It is an important aspect of goalkeeper coaching and the physical conditioning of goalkeepers which passes 'under the radar' so to speak. Aspects of a goalkeeper's strength, range of movement and flexibility are crucial to prevent injury in repetitive kicking actions. On-going strategies such as heightened mobility and flexibility should help reduce the risk of injury and under-performance when kicking.

Starting the Journey

Physical work completed at younger ages can potentially shape that athlete's or goalkeeper's career. Often people talk about models of Long Term Athletic Development (LTAD) and relate this to physical, social, technical and psychological progressions. With this in mind, adaptable specificity is key to developing young keepers physically. The LTAD should be about quality education, appropriate content, and justifiable progression. It is certainly not a set-in-stone process as each athlete/goalkeeper is different and will therefore progress differently. Often coaches, sport scientists and other people who have contact with young sportspeople get them to do drills, exercises or work which is detrimental to that individual's development. This may be due to them being too physically or technically weak to complete the task. In many cases a lack of coach awareness relates to why someone should or should not be doing a certain drill/exercise. An example might be gym based weight training, or high intensity speed drills. This highlights the importance and duty we have as coaches to understand our area of expertise thoroughly and show a willingness to be educated and develop - so our practices can too.

Goalkeeping at the highest level involves big multi-joint powerful movements from jumps to sprints, catching to throwing, all of which are multi-directional and done at high speed in an explosive nature. The big question that needs answering is that of 'how' a young athlete can work towards the highest levels of physical performance commensurate with modern day goalkeepers e.g. Ben Foster (West Bromwich Albion FC) or Joe Hart (Manchester City FC). Undoubtedly a huge amount of technical competency is required to succeed in professional football but one would argue modern goalkeepers have many 'must have' attributes and physicality is one in its own right.

Working with any young athlete of 9-14 years of age is a crucial time to develop basic athletic competency. This will put them in a good position when more specific demands are placed upon them. Squatting, lunging, jumping/landing, running and basic body weight strength exercises are crucial at this age (See the following table). All these basic movement patterns give a solid foundation to develop performance from. In addition they set the athlete up in regards to trainability when the right time presents itself for strength training. Without reinforcing these fundamental areas you may find yourself playing catch up which is always difficult with the demands of a high level schedule. Another pertinent area which must be included across all ages is flexibility and mobility. Young athletes will be growing at different rates and this growth can be massively detrimental to performance. Two areas associated with this are: a reduction in mobility, and a reduction in flexibility. At every contact, whether it is a technical or physical session, both dynamic flexibility/mobility pre-session and developmental flexibility post-session should be completed.

Athletic Competency Exercises Age 9-14yr

Squat Exercises	Lunge Exercises	Jump/Land	Body Weight Strength
Double Leg Squat	Split Squat (Static)	Double Leg Hop + Stick	Press Ups
Single Leg Squat	Forward Lunge	Single Leg Hop + Stick	Pull Ups
Single Leg Step Ups	Backwards Lunge	Lateral Hop + Stick	Inverted Rows
Lateral Step Ups	Overhead Lunge	Squat Jump + Land	Plank (Front and Side)
Overhead Squat	Lateral Lunge	Drop and Stick	
	Bulgarian Split Squat		

Later on…

When approaching 14-18 years of age all of the above should be on-going. Continuing 'good movement' coaching will only help progress things further. If good fundamental movement competency is present then a fantastic opportunity to start some effective strength training presents itself. At these ages, young athletes will be in a good position to see some good strength adaptations due to maturation in which testosterone levels are high and adaptive change to skeletal bone, muscles and joints is accelerated.

Michael: "From previous experience I have not worked with many 14-18 year olds who haven't got issues with fundamental movement. Usually this is associated with missing the window of opportunity at age 9-14 where quality athletic development exercises should be coached and progressed appropriately. Issues are also commonly related to growth changes and detrimental change to an individual's movement patterns, flexibility and mobility. When faced with these issues, along with limited contact time, it can be a long process to get back to a positive position in which the athlete is moving with good competency and ready for effective strength training."

Physical Goalkeeping Attributes

Now let's investigate some main goalkeeping attributes. A lot of the attributes are interrelated, this means you need effective muscle strength and activation for speed; power for agility and dynamic saves; overall body co-ordination and proprioception to move effectively.

Many of the attributes can be combined together into an umbrella term; for example SAQ (Speed, Agility, Quickness) or ABC (Agility, Balance, Co-ordination) – all these work hand-in-hand for the goalkeeper so training them all will give a keeper a rounded and competent physical makeup.

Below, an attribute or physical component will be introduced and a selection of example practices provided. The games based theory will show a number of exercises that can help improve some of these attributes. The usage of other sporting activities in a goalkeeping tailored environment will supplement a keeper's physical development.

Each physical component in its entirety is rather large. What we've done is give necessary depth and practical application rather than purely listing the components, or indeed packing each section with lots of information.

Strength

Strength in the lower limbs is of obvious importance in football: the quadriceps and hamstring groups must generate high forces for jumping, kicking, tackling, turning and changing pace. Strength and mobility in these physical areas will aid the goalkeeper in performing said actions, especially when performing motor skills. The ability to sustain forceful contractions is also important in maintaining balance and control especially when being challenged for possession. Isometric strength is also an important contributory factor in maintaining a player's balance on a slippery pitch and for ball control.

Combined with this - the goalkeeper must carry and control their body through non-linear motions, as discussed in the biomechanics chapter, so strength training must not be one-dimensional and should be performed by putting the body through many different directions.

For a goalkeeper almost all the body's muscle groups are important for executing positional skills. The vertical jump and short sprints are actions that require leg (gluteals, quadriceps, hamstrings) and core strength (abdominals and trunk muscles) training.

The term 'functional strength' (training the body for movements that they would perform in their sport, rather than simply isolating target muscle groups) highlights the fact that typical weight training exercises (for example how many bench presses you can do) do not replicate sports specific movements. The use of core stability methods such as medicine balls and dumbbells are very prominent. One research article found a 58% increase in strength over fixed form programmes of weight training machines when using core stability techniques. They also found that these exercises can help work on power, flexibility and balance. This type of training is recommended for explosive sports that require speed of movement. Research suggests that the most important strength factor in goalkeeping is not that of the maximal kind but *functional* from different starting positions. Using free weights would therefore increase the range of motion and promote muscle balance. Moreover, elastic strength, being the ability to overcome resistance with a fast contraction, will help the goalkeeper in moving their hands and feet fast to react to the ball.

In any case the key point must be to use 'functional strength' during goalkeeping actions and to "make maximal use of the strength available." (Hans Leitert)

Having good and effective core strength for a goalkeeper is vital. When these muscles contract they stabilize areas of the body such as the pelvis, spine and shoulder girdle to create a solid base of support. When this occurs a goalkeeper becomes able to generate powerful movements of the extremities. Basically the core muscles stabilize and assist powerful movements because they all initiate from the centre of the body. Muscles here would include the abdominals, obliques, hip flexors, hip adductors and the gluteals. And of course training the core muscles will assist with injury prevention and aid with postural imbalances.

Exercises

Squat exercises are a crucial area for developing good movement competency in many sporting actions. For a keeper, jumping and making saves originate from a squat position. Repetitions of body weight exercises with constant technical reinforcement will mean that, as a young athlete changes physically, movement patterns will not be as affected. In addition having these fundamental movement patterns and competencies will provide a better platform for training at a later age (loaded strength and power variations). Without good basic unloaded movement patterns - it is difficult, as a fitness or strength coach, to maximise strength training. Bad movement patterns are associated with injury risk. It is also worth considering that making someone stronger and more powerful using strength training - when they have poor movement - dramatically increases the risk of injury.

Similar to squatting movement patterns - lunging is also utilised when keepers are running into jumps, making saves either side of their goal, and kicking. From a training perspective a similar emphasis on good biomechanics, competency and control is needed in order to maximise training when the athlete is older. Both lunge and squat patterns, when completed correctly, require a large amount of mobility and flexibility. At the 9-14 age range, when growth can cause deterioration to both mobility and flexibility, squat and lunge patterns can aid in positively identifying changes and providing feedback. I am a big advocate of videoing movements and using movement screening to monitor progressions and regressions in movement patterns. A good coaching resource with more detail for athletic development and physical competency is *Movement Dynamics* (Kelvin Giles).

Here are a few examples of some exercises that work the core. The exercises in the table above are relevant here.

- Planks
- Squats
- Push up and sit ups
- Lunges with a twist
- Supermans
- Back bridges

Some other examples of equipment and programmes that can develop core strength are:

- Swedish gym balls
- Medicine balls
- Wobble-boards
- Yoga
- Pilates

Another area to consider is that of bodyweight strength exercises using the upper body and trunk. As the game is developing, the stature and shape of players is changing dramatically (*especially* goalkeepers). Using some basic pushing and pulling exercises to develop basic strength and upper body control will put a young athlete in a good position for upper body strength training exercises at an older age. In addition general trunk stability through the use of planks and side plank variations will again provide a platform to move on to more demanding trunk strength exercises, and will help develop the athlete's ability to stabilise the spine. This is essential when moving into higher level strength training and loaded strength exercises.

Gym Based Exercises

Some gym based exercises that can be used on older, and more physically developed, goalkeepers include the following:

For each exercise, five repetitions are recommended – calculate this from your one rep max.

Jerk Balance

- Stand with feet together, with the barbell positioned on the front shoulder
- Dip the knees and hips, drive up quickly extending the arms overhead and the legs into a split stance landing
- Return to the starting foot position and lower the bar to the front of the shoulders

Chapter 2

Wide Grip Assisted Pull Ups

- Lie face up beneath the barbell
- Grip the bar with an overhead wide grip
- Keeping the feet together, push the hips up so the back is flat
- Pull until the chest touches the bar, slowly lower to the starting position then repeat

Barbell Split Squat – each side

- Standing in front of the barbell rack, walk forwards and position the barbell on the rear of the shoulders
- Carefully walk backwards a couple of steps
- Start with feet in a split stance, bend the front and rear knee to 90 degrees; keeping the chest up and both feet pointing forwards, extend the knees to return to the starting position

Push Up Pull – each side

- Start in the push up position, holding a dumbbell in each hand
- Brace the core and pull one dumbbell towards the chest – drawing the elbow back as high as possible
- Slowly lower the dumbbell back to the floor and repeat on the opposite side
- Ensure that the hips don't move from side to side during the exercise

Dumbbell Shoulder Press – each side

- Standing with feet together, hold the dumbbells in both hands and extend the arms overhead
- Keeping one dumbbell overhead, slowly lower the other dumbbell to shoulder height, and press back to the starting position; then repeat

Dumbbell Upright Row – each side

- Stand with feet together and hold a dumbbell in each hand
- Alternately pull each dumbbell up towards the shoulders, raising the elbow as high as possible – slowly lower and repeat

Power

Power, in short, is the combination of speed and strength. Muscle power is a function of the interaction between force of contraction and the speed of contraction, and is associated with the explosiveness of the muscle. The relationship between force and speed of contraction and the subsequent point at which peak power occurs varies between athletes with peak power occurring at 50–70% of the maximum weight that can be lifted for one repetition. A fundamental way of increasing muscle power is to increase maximal strength, particularly in untrained athletes. However as stated above this may not be the best method of training goalkeepers.

For most athletes, increasing muscular power is a primary goal. Despite a relationship between power and strength training, power is a separate component and any training programme must be adjusted when working on power. Strength training forms the basis of muscle power and also forms the basis of most sporting abilities to a large extent.

Power has been identified as a vital component in jumping based on the fact that a superior ability to execute the movement explosively typically results in a more desirable performance. Speaking to a Norwegian Athletics coach last summer he told me that the highest scorer on the vertical jump test was a sprinter!

Chapter 2

Exercises

Exercise 1 (The Travelator)

This exercise emphasizes the goalkeeper walking/jogging then having to react quickly. As discussed previously the goalkeeper spends the vast majority of their time walking and moving slowly (compared to their high intensity bursts) so this exercise is designed accordingly. You could use hurdles and speed ladders for example as well – although keep the distance of the travelator to a maximum of 10 yards.

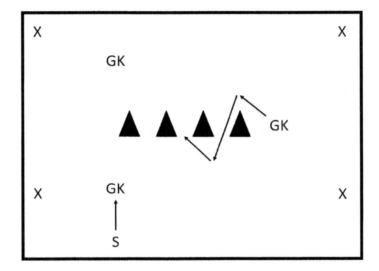

The goalkeepers will be moving around the grid with a ball, either bouncing or dribbling or passing between each other; but working at a slow pace. When they decide to move to the top of the travelator (shown by the cones) they will move fast through the cone layout, then revert back to the speed they were working at before.

The travelator can take a couple of different forms depending on what you want to work on.

Speed: the same as above but the travelator is a sprint to get to the ball (b) located at the end of the distance shown by the two parallel lines – the distance would be between two and eighteen yards relating to the common sprint distances.

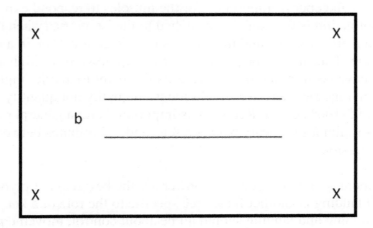

Footwork: cones (x) can be different colours, and the keeper needs to touch specific cones as he goes through the cone setup. Or just simple quick feet through them, changing direction quickly. Once again the same as the original travelator diagram… just with a different travelator setup in the middle.

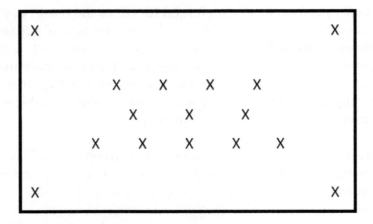

Chapter 2

Plyometrics

Plyometrics seeks to enhance explosive reactions through powerful muscular contractions through rapid eccentric contractions; allowing muscles to exert maximum force in the shortest amount of time possible – which for the reactive and intuitive goalkeeper is important. For the muscles to respond explosively, the eccentric contraction is then quickly switched to the isometric (when the downward movement stops) and then the concentric contraction, in a minimum amount of time. This allows the goalkeeper to jump upwards as high as possible. Plyometrics have been found to have benefits for lower extremity injury prevention. Plyometric exercises should focus on quality not quantity and performed at 95-100% effort. Recovery is important here; a general rule of thumb is to allow 1-3 minutes recovery between sets, and 3-5 minutes between exercises in a training session.

Ultimately, increasing both speed and power are the key goals of plyometrics. Jumping and landing is another huge area specific to the role of a keeper. At a young age jumping and landing should all be about control, movement quality and stability. Developing the ability to jump dynamically, but with good execution, is essential before moving on to maximal jumping exercises.

Plyometric training can be an important tool for developing explosive power in goalkeepers but you put the player at serious risk when engaging them in such training if basic jumping and landing control is poor. This control ties in with squatting and single leg squat variations massively. If you watch the take-off and landing phases at top level - the impact forces and loading that goes through the lower extremities when a keeper dives and jumps is huge; therefore the movement *quality* needs to be of a high level to reduce the risk of potential injury. In Michael's experience, working with many young athletes (and in some cases older athletes), the ability to sub maximally jump (and land) is really quite poor and those with poor squat, single leg squat, and lunging movement patterns are usually the ones with poor jumping and landing competency. It again reinforces the importance of these fundamental movement and athletic competency exercises for long term development.

Ultimately the goalkeeper needs to have sufficient strength, flexibility and proprioception before starting serious plyometric training. There are many lower intensity versions of plyometric type training that can be done too.

Some example exercises will be given from a practical viewpoint. They wouldn't be classified as 'explosive plyometrics' but more like jump routines. A good tip is to think of yourself as a ball and bounce as a ball would – use the stretch reflex and/or elastic energy. There are websites and books dedicated to plyometrics – if you are looking for a detailed plan or programme then visit these resources.

Two such resources that can be recommended are the book: *Jumping into Plyometrics* by Donald Chu; and a very informative website: *www.ericwongmma.com*

Exercises

Exercise 1

There are a number of exercises and movements that can be done with just a flat cone (or higher one) and a ball.

Have the goalkeeper stand either in front of a cone, or by the side of it.

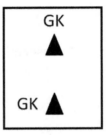

Some simple exercises would include:

- Hopping over the cone with a ball – focus on landing in a controlled manner whilst trying to maximize height and lateral distance.
- Bouncing a ball in one hand whilst hopping around the cone – keeping the head level, with upright posture, engaging the core muscles.
- Two footed jump over the cone (lateral) – landing in a set position – looking for maximum height and distance.
- Two footed jump over the cone (horizontal) – same as above but change the direction.
- One footed jump over the cone (lateral and horizontal) – step with the nearest leg for the lateral jumps.
- Incorporate the ball into the above by adding a catch, or save at the end of the jump.

Exercise 2

Box Jumps. Stand on a box (or stable elevated platform), jump to the ground, and jump up again. Usually no more than 20-30 inches high. The physical process the body goes through here can be seen in the above paragraphs.

Exercise 3

Hurdles work. Place hurdles close together so the goalkeeper has to bounce over them with a variety of different take off positions. These can include:

- Bunny hops
- Single leg hops
- Lateral and horizontal hops.

Main Coaching Points:

- Landings need to be stable – if consecutive jumps are being done then land on the front part of the foot ready to load again.
- Warm up before the exercises
- Take offs need to be explosive
- Focus on the take offs and landings – head up will increase control and stability in the posture
- Conduct when muscles are fresh
- Quality not quantity, with rest
- Limit to two sessions per week

Physical Speed & Reaction Time

Physical speed and reaction time have been paired together because of the nature of quickness. 'Speed of body, speed of mind'. Reaction time would normally be considered a psychological attribute but with its physical implications to goalkeeping performance – it goes hand in hand with physical speed.

Speed can, in simple terms, be described as how quickly something gets from A to B. In goalkeeping terms: speed to come out for through balls, speed to re-position, to support the play and of course to save the ball. Lateral speed across the goal area and vertical speed towards the ball would be commonly used measures (along with backwards speed to re-position). If a goalkeeper is physically quick in all directions – it will give them a significant advantage.

The key in speed training for goalkeepers is to improve acceleration – this is the first five yards. The goalkeeper will never really reach maximal speed because this occurs anywhere between 30-50 yards, a distance which they rarely, if ever reach.

Keeping body movements short and concise will retain balance as well as enabling the keeper to be in a position to 'set' at any point. If movements are too big, it will take longer to regain a set position and time to readjust if the ball changes direction. Physiology-wise the key muscles used here would be the upper and lower leg muscles – along with our core and gluteals.

A simple and relevant definition of *reaction time* would be the time that elapses between a stimulus and the response to it. I think it goes without saying that decreasing your goalkeeper's reaction time is of real benefit, which segments from previous chapters would support, including decision making scenarios (game based theory) and the usage of short, sharp goalmouth practice.

Exercises

There are many exercises that can help a goalkeeper improve their speed, away from strengthening the leg muscles in isolation, and gym based work. The following are field based activities that only require basic equipment. Some key points are that the initial steps could be short and sharp whilst using the arms for maximum drive.

I'm a huge believer in using reaction balls (ResponseBalls – see Chapter 11) and also different sized balls – this will make the keeper focus on a smaller object to save which is harder.

Chapter 2

Exercise 1

The emphasis on speed here is very plain to see. The coach (or other GK) will call out a coloured cone, the GK will have to reach this cone as quickly as they can; there are quite a few progressions for this exercise.

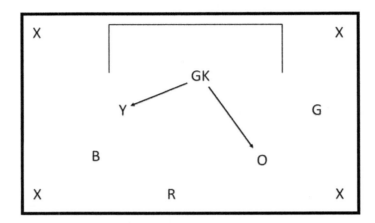

- Simply get the GK to touch the cone.
- Have the GK slide through the cone as if they were faced with a contest.
- Start with a server hitting some balls at the GK before the colour is called to create a multi stimulus setting.
- Replace the cones with balls, and name them 1, 2, 3 etc.
- Add in a GK as an attacker (or an actual attacker if you have access) to put pressure on the GK when they are coming out.

Exercise 2

The grid acts as a den as the goalkeeper can't go outside the coned (x) area. The coach or server stays outside the grid putting balls in that the goalkeeper must play back to them before the ball goes outside the grid. To bring another dimension to this exercise the goalkeeper will have to touch a coloured cone (shown by the black circles) before they play the ball. Speed of body, speed of mind.

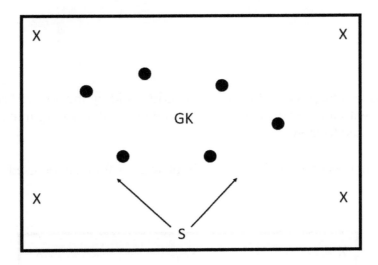

Exercise 3

A very simple speed exercise that can be used during warm up (training and match) to assist the decision making process whilst working quickly into a save. Place the cones no further than 10 yards away from the server. The goalkeeper will be moving around the grid, performing dynamic stretches or mobility exercises. When a coloured cone is called the goalkeeper will touch this then move into the small goal to make a save. Repeat this 10 times.

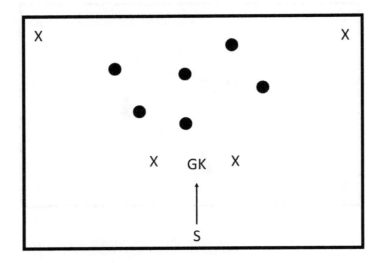

Chapter 2

Exercise 4

Goalkeepers will be passing the ball in the grid avoiding the cones. The goalkeepers without the ball will be working then need to spring into action when the ball is passed to them.

Conditions such as two-touch, one-touch, or weaker foot can be used.

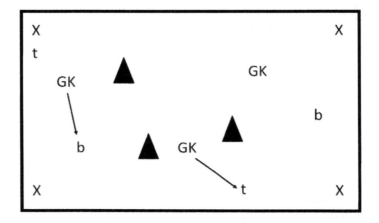

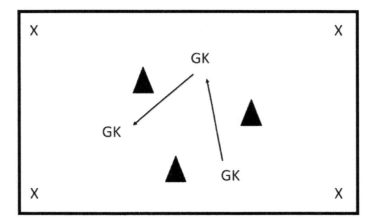

Exercise 5

To work on reaction time, during shooting practice, have players or obstacles stand in the way to obstruct the goalkeeper's view. They can then react off subtle changes in the direction of the ball, and from the player's movement – which can affect their positioning for a shot. In a match there will always be players in the way in some shape or form so this practice setting will benefit reactions.

Exercise 6

Crazy catch, rebound boards, and rebound nets are fantastic tools for working on general reactions. Balls can come at different speeds and from different directions – they add a varied dimension to training environments.

Exercise 7

Relating to the use of other sports in goalkeeper training, along with the vision and awareness section, using smaller balls will enhance reaction training. A great practice is to mix a reaction based saving practice with small coloured balls (size 1 or 2 footballs). Ask the goalkeeper to, for example, catch a certain coloured ball and then punch/parry another coloured ball – here they'll have to react to the visual cue of the colour and then act upon it.

Exercise 8

Further to the above exercise, the coach/server will strike size 1 balls (between three and five) into one half of the goal for the keeper to react to – using fast and strong hands. Once these balls have all been served a size 5 ball will be struck into the other half of the goal for the keeper to respond to. Distances can vary but for the small balls six yards is a good starting place – size 5 can be any distance or angle (balls on the diagram not to scale).

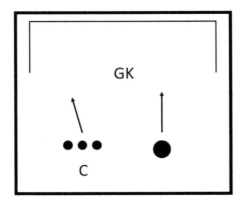

Overall many goalkeeping practices will naturally breed reaction training. The above are a selection of suggested exercises that will work well as part of any warm up to get the mind alert.

Agility

The consensus is that *agility* is defined as the ability to rapidly change direction and react to different stimuli, without the loss of balance or control of body. This is a requisite of many sports, particularly team and racquet sports. From an injury prevention view, agility helps with muscle activation and helps prevent niggling injuries.

The traditional definition of the ability to change direction rapidly has been redefined as *change of direction speed* and within goalkeeping has been pointed out as being crucial. This is because of the need to change direction quickly and frequently, mainly over short distances, and mostly through two different types of agility: planned (or programmed) agility, and reactive (or random) agility. After looking through specific football and goalkeeping research it has been seen that reactive agility is commonly used because of the change stimuli keepers are faced with in a match.

I'm going to include *balance* and *co-ordination* in the agility section as they are very much an element of agility. Balance is a fundamental for a goalkeeper and involves the maintenance of the body's equilibrium while stationary or moving. In turn, the ability to stop and change direction cannot be underestimated and builds into many goalkeeping actions. Of course strength and speed play a big part in balance and co-ordination, as well as the timing of actions and rhythm. When a top keeper moves they look aesthetically pleasing, and very smooth.

Co-ordination is linked very much to the biomechanical aspect of goalkeeping. Focusing on footwork and jumping should be attempted, as well as breaking down key elements of an action. Of course goalkeeping is a position that contains physical contact – by maintaining balance during aerial challenges and if they are nudged, for example, a keeper can remain in a stable position to withstand this physicality and still move.

Training can be slow at times when working with younger goalkeepers, but bringing all these components together after movement training is beneficial. Should goalkeepers be gymnasts?! Combining the above you could say so!

Examples of how to train all these components will be shown in a moment. There are many general exercises that can be done but many often fail to address the specific conditional requirements for a goalkeeper.

Before they're shown I want to mention the term *athleticism*…

Throughout goalkeeping the term 'athleticism' can be heard a lot of the time. This term, in its original sport-related form, was established in the 19th century in English public schools when referring to physical prowess and athletic sporting game ability. The qualities of athleticism are seen as flexibility, strength endurance, balance, agility and explosive coordination.

The National Basketball Association (NBA) in America uses an 'Athleticism Draft Fitness Test' for their incoming crop of potential players. This consists of a series of tests that look at different fitness components such as power, speed, agility and strength. These tests could be transferable to goalkeeping because of the type of actions they advocate: the initial speed to collect the ball over a short space of time, the ability to jump and beat opponents to the ball, and the ability to change direction quickly in relation to the ball and changes in play.

Chapter 2

Exercises

These exercises will look to build up the above attributes. Various bits of SAQ equipment can be used such as hurdles (from 12 inches to full Olympic sprinting height), resistance belts, and fast feet ladders can also be incorporated. Again look at what actions and movements goalkeepers make in a match and find ways to train them.

Exercise 1

A great balance exercise is getting the keeper to stand on one leg as you hit balls in and around their body to catch. Do this off both legs, also.

Exercise 2

Wobble boards are fantastic for improving balance. Use wobble boards regularly and ask the goalkeeper to look firmly at a ball to retain shape. Move the ball around so the keeper gets used to keeping their body still – whilst using their peripheral vision. If the player has the ability, get them to stand on the board and hit balls straight at them (gently!) – this will be a test of balance but also core strength for retaining body shape and set position.

Exercise 3

The 'working cone' exercise builds co-ordination and balance. It's a simple exercise where the goalkeeper works either side of a cone doing the following actions and playing the ball back to the server.

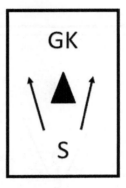

- Left/right foot volley
- Half volley
- Thigh to volley
- Tennis ball one hand
- Reverse hand tennis ball
- One palm back to server (sizes 3-5 balls)

Exercise 4

Using a small goal or two poles – simply hit a selection of tennis balls towards the GK using a tennis racquet; this could also perhaps go into the reactions section as well.

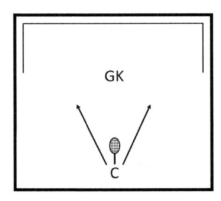

To provide more of a 'co-ordination element' try to obtain different coloured balls, or colour the originals somehow. Ask the GK to catch all green balls with their right hand, and then the others with their left hand.

Exercise 5

For eye-hand co-ordination racquet sports are great. Ping-Pong, tennis, badminton and squash are advocated examples. For general body co-ordination for young goalkeepers, these sports, used at different points in training, can provide a necessary and effective variation.

Flexibility

Flexibility has been identified as a frequently ignored component to an athlete. It is important because of its injury prevention capabilities and its relationship with agility and dynamic movements - which relate to goalkeeping attributes.

Some factors effecting flexibility would be:

- The elasticity of tendons and ligaments, and muscle tissue along with the skin
- Bony structures which can limit movement
- Age and gender
- If the goalkeeper is recovering from injury (or in the process of recovering)
- Temperature of the joint and the environment

Flexibility represents the range of motion specific to a joint, and can be dynamic or static. Dynamic flexibility involves the range of motion during movement of muscles around a joint. Static flexibility defines the degree to which a joint can be passively moved through its full range of motion. Developing muscle around joints improves stability and flexibility, although bulk strength training isn't advised. Hence, the functional strength requirements of goalkeeping should develop enough muscle to sustain stability and flexibility due to factors stated in the strength section.

Dynamic Flexibility - the ability to perform dynamic (or kinetic) movements of the muscles to bring a limb through its full range of motion in the joints.

Static-Active Flexibility - the capacity to assume and maintain extended positions using only the tension of the agonists and synergists while the antagonists are being stretched. For example, lifting the leg and keeping it high without any external support (other than from your own leg muscles).

Static-Passive Flexibility - is the ability to assume extended positions and then maintain them using only your weight, the support of your limbs, or other equipment. An example here would be the splits.

Some authors state that active flexibility is harder to develop than passive flexibility. Not only does active flexibility need passive flexibility in order to assume an initial extended position, it requires muscle strength to be able to hold and maintain that position.

Changes in flexibility occur after stretching exercises and practicing sports specific movements. Since goalkeepers need to produce quick, dynamic movements and increasing flexibility will prove beneficial. There is great discussion regarding stretches and which are the most effective. Stretches are either dynamic (involving motion) or static (no motion). Each can be broken down into many sub-sections and all, you could argue, have a part to play in maintaining flexibility, preparing the body for exercise, cooling down and preventing injuries.

Cooling down and stretching also reduces the chance of DOMS – Delayed Onset of Muscles Soreness, where lactic acid builds up. A failure to get rid of lactic acid during exercise causes this soreness.

One of the best flexibility resources around is the DVD called *Flexibility Express: Flexibility and Functional Strength in No Time* by Thomas Kurz.

Test Me!

As far as I'm aware (although I may be wrong!) there are no standardised goalkeeping-specific physical tests in operation. A lot of testing that I've seen (and in the past have taken part in, or conducted) is very general. Some of them I would imagine you've heard of, and used, and they can all be readily found on the internet.

- The bleep test
- The aero test
- The 12 minute copper run test
- The Illinois agility test
- Standing vertical jump test
- One rep max
- Sit and reach test
- Various sprinting tests with measuring gates

The list could go on no doubt. What would a coach gain from the knowledge that a goalkeeper can get to level 12 on the bleep test? Or run for 12 minutes at a good pace? Sure they could gauge aerobic capacity, which is useful as a foundation for fitness, but for transferability to match requirements would this data prove useful?

However, some of the above are very useful. Any standing jump test gives a good measure of the goalkeeper's power and leg strength. Add force plates into the equation and you can generate a reading of their power output, velocity, and force generation.

Sprinting tests over a certain distance are again a transferable measure. As said previously, the ability to accelerate up to 10 yards is crucial. You could even use existing penalty box markings as a measure – so goal line to 6 yards, goal line to penalty spot, 6 yards to penalty spot, or 6 yard box to the end of the penalty area.

The Illinois agility test measures changes in direction and explosive speed – this is a good test if you're planning pre-season testing with goalkeepers.

Injury Prevention

You should be cautious to avoid highly repetitive exercises where there is a great deal of strain on the body, such as jumping, sprinting and recovery saves. Remember that, in a match, the goalkeeper normally gets a good rest period in between high intensity physical exertions. This is why younger goalkeepers should train in shorter periods and whilst repetition does breed habit make sure the environment is set up correctly.

Matters such as growth spurts should be handled carefully because the bones will grow faster than muscles during this time. A coach should try and obtain all the necessary information to recognise this where possible.

It seems simple but maintaining flexibility, stretching before and after sessions and matches, and looking after health naturally will make for a physically capable goalkeeper.

There are numerous ways to help avoid injury – no doubt as a coach you'll have your own tried and tested ways but the following are some commonly used measures:

- Perform thorough warm ups and cool downs
- Prepare sufficiently in terms of food, fluid and hydration
- Get sufficient rest and sleep
- Avoid training if you're fatigued
- Introduce new training programmes gradually
- Utilise sports massages
- Follow the information in the flexibility section

Chapter 2

Summary

Within this chapter we have covered a broad spectrum of physical requirements – and given some background into each with exercises that can help enhance certain physical attributes. At the end of the day the goalkeeper needs to be prepared for what they're going to be faced with in a match.

A lot of the methods and practices in this chapter will aid the promotion of general co-ordination, both eye-hand and body. From reactive exercises to increasing mobility and agility all attributes will work together; hopefully in sync and perfect harmony. Footwork patterns will develop and the goalkeeper's movement will be smooth and adaptable.

Looking at the exercises above, it is clear that there is no need for an abundance of equipment or huge amounts of time. All that is really needed is adequate space and good coaching. The vast majority of exercises can be incorporated in warm ups before skills sessions. This is ideal as they will not only act as an appropriate warm up but also aid physical development. If 15 minutes of the warm up can include a number of the exercises relating to a certain attribute, before you know it young players are doing this work three times a week or more. This could significantly impact on their individual development.

The biomechanics chapter and this one are closely related. The way the goalkeeper moves and goes about their business on the field of play will be a massively determining factor upon their performance – if they're not physically capable of conducting their role, how can they be successful? Saying that, do not expect everything of the younger goalkeeper. Their training should build the foundations and framework for when they *can* reach maximum strength and power. Building the right mechanical movements, bodily control and proprioception at an early age will stand their development in good stead. Don't expect an 11 year old goalkeeper to play a 50 yard pass, or a 10 year old goalkeeper to jump and touch the bar of a full size goal! Their time will come when they fully develop and reach their top physical prowess.

Of course a thorough and appropriate warm up and cool down should be conducted – the practice chapter gives some advice, but in the warm up make sure all the physical needs of the goalkeeper are met.

The overall aim must be to produce a powerful, strong, fast and reactive goalkeeper – they are not called cats for no reason you know…

3

Goalkeeping Biomechanics

"A successful man is one who can lay a firm foundation with the bricks others have thrown at him."

(David Brinkley)

The modern day goalkeeper needs to be dynamic. An athlete - powerful and explosive. They need to be able to move fast but at the same time able to control their bodies. They need to sometimes be unorthodox and keep the ball out of the net by any means necessary. They need to be adaptable. The human body is never robotic or static, it should be adaptive. The basic technical and physical foundations in goalkeeping are crucial so knowing what they are, and how to work on them, is so important to the coach. Modern day footballs move so quickly – the flight and trajectory are not keeper friendly. Couple this with the pace of the sport and decisive movements can make a big difference for the goalkeeper.

The key is to create good habits by practicing appropriate, safe and adaptable techniques that can be etched into the goalkeeper's memory through suitable skills and techniques training. If you find yourself in a position where you're looking to correct techniques, try teaching new ones instead of spending time changing current behaviours.

I think the modern day goalkeeper cannot be confined to the football pitch. For game understanding and positioning the 'pitch' is clearly crucial but I propose that utilising elements of movements from other sports, specific strength and conditioning techniques, and being in different training environments will add much needed dimensions and variation to goalkeeper practice. If the goalkeeper doesn't have the physical capacity to perform their required tasks biomechanically then they are at a massive disadvantage – this is why at a young age this should be worked on (perhaps more than positioning around the penalty area which can be taught as the goalkeeper gains more experience and is exposed to more complex settings). If a goalkeeper is physically and biomechanically competent then a large part of their development battle has been won. In turn, tactical/positional elements will become easier because the keeper can physically do 'what they need to do' in order to be in the right place, at the right time.

Playing as an outfield player (goalkeeping specialisation will be discussed in the practice chapter) gives a young player better overall co-ordination, balance and agility. In my experience some of the best goalkeepers I've coached played as outfielders for a numbers of years before turning to the goalkeeping position, or even continued to play whilst in goal. This gave their body more variation biomechanically and perhaps more 'general athleticism'. Of course this is my experience but confining the goalkeeper to the position from the age of 6/7 could be considered detrimental.

The emergence of goalkeepers reaching the top level at an early age may perhaps be attributed to the new generation having bodies and minds that are well suited to the demands of modern day football. By this I mean they understand the new technical and tactical advances and evolutions in the game such as the emphasis on distribution and the need for quick and flexible movements.

This chapter is not designed to show how to catch or parry or punch every ball right down to the finest technical points; we would be here for hours. Instead it is meant to show some frequent movements and actions a keeper would be expected to perform in the position along with how using elements from other sports will develop an athletic and dynamic goalkeeper. Biomechanics is a detailed, and at times complex, discipline within sport. This chapter looks at the basics and tries to appeal to the general goalkeeping coach. Within each action there can be variations of angles of take offs,

Throughout this chapter I have harnessed expert opinions and methods alongside, as usual, my own first-hand experiences. I frequently see limitations in some current goalkeeper training environments so hopefully some of the suggestions and areas looked at will give your training a new dimension. At times there is a discrepancy between match and training ground techniques – by this I mean (as coaches) are we training/teaching players how to perform certain exercises, or are we training/teaching *real life goalkeeping*? A poignant question and one that we shall endeavour to answer in this chapter and beyond.

Note: The physiology and athletic development chapter will go into more detail about how to develop different movements and physical attributes necessary for goalkeeping. In turn, and where possible, images from actual training and matches are used (where allowed) to gain a more applied perspective.

In this chapter we will cover

- A brief look into some biomechanics
- Goalkeeping movement and action analysis
- How (and why) to work on different movements
- How playing other sports benefits goalkeeping in football

What is Biomechanics?

In simple terms biomechanics can be defined as the study of *the mechanics of human movement*. Within this chapter the primary focus will be on the qualitative nature or cinematographic analysis (basic and intermediate) focusing on goalkeeping movements and techniques that are used in real life situations.

From an injury prevention point of view biomechanics can help identify issues related to poor technique, insufficient strength, bad preparation and insufficient range of movement throughout key joints and muscles. Screening is very common throughout football. It is used regularly for individual programmes and to help build appropriate training loads.

Detailed biomechanical tests and analyses encompassing statistics, EMG for muscle activation, force plates and high speed cameras are used within different sports institutes and universities to dissect small technical details and produce useable data for a variety of different actions. Some proposed and upcoming tests for goalkeeping will be touched upon later in this chapter.

I'm not going to crowd this chapter with a large number of scientific terms – I'm looking to keep the information as real life as possible and coach/player friendly. There are some very good sports biomechanics books available and one which I would highly recommend is: *Introduction to Sports Biomechanics* (2nd Edition) by Roger Bartlett. This book covers everything needed to understand biomechanics from a general athlete's point of view.

Within goalkeeping, there are various movement skills that the player needs to master, but few of the actual training and match based actions have been subjected to biomechanical analysis. The most obvious are fundamental motor skills, such as jumping, kicking, throwing and catching which make up the majority of the goalkeeper's movements when faced with common situations in a match, such as shots on goal, distribution, and crosses.

The movements goalkeepers make can be classified as 'non-linear' and 'irregular' which means a keeper must be able to control their body in every possible direction. In developing functional strength the body will work in its natural freedom rather than a single plane of motion which will aid the goalkeeper's movements through a more flexible state.

The ultimate aim is to get the goalkeeper moving from A to B as quickly as possible – along with developing how they co-ordinate and balance their body to be able to make diving saves, jump through players, and change direction quickly. For example, moving across the goal area and re-positioning are frequent movements and creating overload environments will get the goalkeeper used to moving quickly. Moving across the goal can take many forms – some coaches use side steps, some use lateral running and some advocate crossing over, but again it's up to the goalkeeper to use whatever method is comfortable and appropriate for them. Rhythm and timing are crucial in this respect. Along with being physically ready on the balls of your feet to move quickly. Biomechanical investigation can help these areas.

Let's get Technical…

When looking for the key elements of 'what makes a goalkeeper' it's important to analyse the observed techniques of movement and the relevant 'critical features'. These features should be fundamental to improving the performance of a certain skill or reducing the injury risk by performing that skill – sometimes both.

It has been said that the fundamentals of goalkeeping tasks require a solid foundation involving an effective 'set' or 'ready' position. The below has been identified within existing goalkeeping literature. This will be a good place to start with the basics – with more explanation and examples further on.

'Set' or 'Ready' Position

- Head - Forward, with eyes firmly fixed on the ball.

- Hands - In front of feet, shoulder-width apart, elbows in front of the line of the body and fingers pointing towards the ball.

- Feet - Weight on the front studs (not on heels as this will inhibit the ability to move quickly and respond to directional change)

'Catching' Position

Start with hands forward as it enables the keeper to lead with his or her hands as the ball approaches. There are three advantages to this.

- A keeper is able to watch the ball into their hands

- They can follow any movements, or change of ball direction

- They can use their arms as 'shock absorbers'

From a movement perspective if the hands come round the ball then it will take longer for contact to be made. This delay will result in potential spilling. Balls above the eye-line for young keepers can be especially difficult – this could well be down to the fact of needing to move more than one body part in co-ordination for the age.

Chapter 3

'Diving' Position

- Head - Behind the ball

- Hands - will lead, take the ball as early as possible and keep the elbows in front of the line of body

- Feet – Step off the nearest foot to the ball, off the front studs at a 45 degree angle

The 'diving' position references the 45 degree angle of diving, or at least diving forward to try and reach the ball. One question to ask is what degree or angle the power step should be at to provide optimum velocity and drive (more on this is in the summary). If you observe a goalkeeper making diving saves the angles they dive at is never exactly 45 degrees forward; in fact it rarely is. The way goalkeepers have to move is very irregular and nonlinear so the focus would be to train the goalkeeper to save balls in the various different ways needed. When a keeper moves with his hands towards the ball it is important to avoid 'chopping down' (when the hands move vertically down towards the ball) because the ball (more often than not) is neither caught nor parried cleanly, hence the need to take the ball early. Diving will be explored a bit later on.

It is suggested that this 'ideal model' is most commonly exemplified by an elite performer, but it can be argued that this 'template' approach involves little need for creativity and is lazy. But one might question whether there is an 'ideal' model of technique at all? There are certain fundamentals to adhere by but if you look at the top goalkeepers in the world – can their movements be considered orthodox? Not really!

Because of the high level nature of these 'ideal models' there is the assumption that the ideal or elite performance is applicable to all athletes performing the skill. There is agreement among movement analysts that there is no universal 'optimal performance model' for any sport's movement pattern. Within goalkeeping, for example, each individual has a different technique when performing movements like catching, diving and jumping and generally in football orientated tasks such as kicking – no two actions are ever the same.

Overall what works best for athletes under task constraints is deemed effective despite actions sometimes not being 'technically proficient'; for example, as long as the goalkeeper catches the ball safely and consistently, despite not following the exact features discussed previously, should the coach make changes to the player's technique? Some coaches' argue that so called 'unorthodox' styles must not be coached out of players but that the goalkeeping coach must offer alternative techniques to the goalkeeper, so they don't become reliant on just one isolated technique.

A recent (2008) study in Denmark looked into the biomechanical profiles of elite and sub-elite goalkeepers. In short the study consisted of measuring actions such as short sprints, vertical jumps and leg strength measures. The researchers concluded that biomechanical parameters are of 'minor importance' for the assessment of a goalkeeper's skill level. They suggest that tactical understanding and qualities such as positioning and anticipation are more important. Although this can be seen as true, to a point, and based upon my years of experience watching training sessions and matches, I believe the way the goalkeeper moves and controls their body to be of the utmost importance the higher you go in the sport. Elite goalkeepers certainly move more efficiently and at times make challenging situations look easy. For example, something which video analysis has demonstrated to me is that goalkeepers spend a lot of time moving backwards at various different speeds – or 'dropping off' as it is commonly known. This highlights the need for balance and the need to adapt and change direction regularly keeping the head and hands forwards.

What to Look For?

I'm now going to examine some actual examples of goalkeeping performance. As suggested in the video analysis chapter, analysis can be seen as reactive. A tip when looking at things from a qualitative perspective is to use the following four stage model. I've put a shortened summary by each.

1. *Preparation* – gathering knowledge, establishing critical features of the movement or technique and developing an observation strategy.
2. *Observation* – gathering information from videos and determining where to observe from (vantage points/angles).

3. *Evaluation and Diagnostics* – strengths/weaknesses, errors and critical features versus the ideal.
4. *Intervention* – appropriate/structured feedback, related to the needs of the overall technique and training plan of the goalkeeper. Focus on one correction at a time.

When conducting your own video analysis or general observations, remember the key points on camera angle and where to place yourself when working upon a particular goalkeeping topic. Having iPads with apps, or computer software (such as Kinovea) can assist in slowing down movements and comparing goalkeepers, by looking at different angles of the body and highlighting key performance indicators by zooming in on the video.

The performance and video analysis chapters cover a lot of the above since looking at different movement patterns requires analysis.

Set Position

The set position is the optimum position that allows the goalkeeper to move in any direction. It is usually performed at the point when the ball is about to be struck in the keeper's direction. Every goalkeeper has a different set position. Some have their arms spread wide, some like to be lower, and some like their feet closer together. It's crucial for a well-balanced goalkeeper not to set their feet too wide because the increase in length will inhibit quick movement and it takes longer to move into line for balls in and around the body. One thing that is fundamental not just in the set position, and which sounds obvious, is that the goalkeeper's feet are on the ground when they are about to be faced with any situation. The reasons for this are:

- If a keeper's feet are on the ground they can move. It sounds simple but if a player's feet are in the air when a striker shoots the ball how can the player dive?
- In the time it takes for a keeper to plant his feet the ball will already be on its way – decreasing the time he can react considerably.
- Keeping feet planted on the front of the foot allows for quick movements in any direction.

It is not always possible to be 'set' in and around the goal area because of the speed of play and the quickness with which the ball is played. To combat this, the goalkeeper must be flexible and agile, and able to control their body's directional changes at different speeds. For momentum purposes if the keeper sees the ball going in the direction they're going already, there's no need to set as such because setting will slow them down and can result in not getting close enough to the ball. These situations usually happen when the keeper is out of position and trying to re-adjust or trying to make up ground back across the goal line – a low cross or cutback for example.

The rule of thumb is that the closer the ball is to the goalkeeper the lower the set position needs to be. A lot of coaches I've worked alongside support the notion of being set regardless of where the goalkeeper is in position to save a shot – this maximises their options because they give themselves a chance of going in any direction responding to the ball rather than the direction they might be moving.

The following image shows two goalkeepers being compared on a split screen – with a focus on body positions. In this case the body position at the point of impact from a shot in a technical exercise.

Your first question might well be... how do you know when the ball is struck? You cannot see the server! Good question – with the close up view you can see the goalkeeper on the screen in order to focus on their body. So, to gauge when the ball is struck, you listen to when the ball is struck from the audio to pinpoint the exact frame.

The two images above show two goalkeepers - one with higher hands on the left, the other with lower hands on the right. Every keeper will have a natural stance but if their hands are somewhere near the centre of the body they can go up or down, left or right efficiently. Both goalkeepers have their feet on the ground at the point the ball is struck. The goalkeeper on the left is more on his toes – which will allow him to move quickly and sharply if he has to adjust to a struck ball.

I once coached a goalkeeper who would move his feet very wide once a ball was struck. Whether this was coached or simply a general habit I don't know. Whatever the case, this movement inhibited his ability to respond to a ball outside the line of his body, or to change position as his weight was distributed too wide to be able transfer his body towards the ball. He could still dive but with this base he didn't get the maximum distance possible – resulting in potentially reachable balls going in the goal.

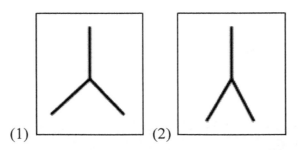

(1)   (2)

The two images above represent a very simplistic way of looking at this – if the body weight is spread wide (2) rather than closer to the body (1) it's harder to move and propel one's bodyweight either side.

Another issue within the set position is that if the position is too low - the goalkeeper's ability to create the relevant force to dive will be considerably reduced. When faced with 1 v 1s though, the goalkeeper's position should be lower to counteract the quick nature of the situation, but for shot stopping a well-balanced and comfortable set position is so effective.

Key Points:

- Every keeper will have a different and more comfortable set position
- Being balanced with head and hands forward is key
- If the set position is to low then the force-generation for higher balls can be compromised
- Weight should be on the front part of the foot to allow for increased range of movement

I'm now going to take you through four goalkeeping actions – catching, jumping, diving and kicking.

Catching

Being able to catch the ball is a goalkeeper's bread and butter. There are a whole host of catching positions but this section aims to cover the fundamentals which translate across most situations.

The following photo shows a real life situation where video analysis focuses on where the goalkeeper is catching the ball.

From a coaching perspective, we are looking for the goalkeeper to take the ball early with their hands forward, and not too close to the body, for a more solid catching position. In turn, we want the keeper to avoid pushing his hands towards to the ball as overly extended arms and hands reduce the ability for them to act as shock absorbers - diminishing a keeper's catching ability. Analysis can also be carried out when facing the player to examine whether they are moving into line with the ball, and whether the keeper's head and hands are also behind the ball.

When coaching goalkeepers – whatever your philosophy or country – I would always advise that you teach keepers the skills of catching, parrying and deflecting. This will give the goalkeeper *options* when faced with a type of shot. No two shots are quite the same; speed, height, trajectory, wind direction, ground conditions they are all factors that will be different at any one time. If a keeper goes into a match with a predetermined plan and thinks: "right, I'm going to either catch everything or deflect everything," he limits his options a great deal.

One common theme I see when goalkeepers drop the ball is that their arms swing back in an almost skiing-type motion. This does two things:

- Makes the hands late to meet the ball
- Causes the arms to meet the ball from the bottom – which causes upwards contact

The figures below show an example set position, and then what this motion can look like.

This ski action is a common reason, especially with younger goalkeepers, for dropping the ball and being late in making initial contact with the ball.

When it comes to catching shapes or positions – if the goalkeeper catches the ball cleanly and safely there's an argument to leave the technique alone if, of course, it doesn't follow pre-determined coaching points. The key comes in giving the goalkeeper different options to deal with different balls – so until trends of dropping or spilling occur (possibly because of technique, or maybe just concentration) then to coach this original technique out of a player might be the wrong approach.

Key Points:

- Every keeper will have a different catching style
- Watch out for palms coming over the ball, or going under the ball – this will result in spillage and the ball potentially breaking through the hands
- Using the traditional scoop, cup, or W catching shapes will translate to most situations when catching

Jumping

I think every goalkeeping coach would agree that getting their goalkeepers to rise above their opponents to take a cross is a crucial skill. Being aerially dominant gives a goalkeeper a great advantage. Exact ways to work on this will be shown in the physiology chapter.

It's widely considered that the aerial ball for a goalkeeper is one of the hardest actions to master. They need to judge the situation from their own technical and movement perspective, decide how to deal with the ball, and think about the players in their immediate vicinity.

Jumping is what is considered a 'ballistic' movement. These movements can be divided up into different sub-sections but the three of jumping preparation, action and recovery are commonly used.

- Preparation – lowers the body enabling stored elastic energy to be utilised
- Action – a synchronised movement with all leg joints extending and plantar flexing together
- Recovery – Time in the air (making contact with the ball) and a controlled landing (to re-adjust position or looking to distribute the ball)

Like a lot of areas in this book – the mechanics of jumping could be a whole chapter in itself. When you're looking at counter movements, forces and utilising energy you can go into great detail.

Without listing all the major technical coaching points associated with jumping, much video analysis has been geared towards examining the correct timing of the jump (hours of video work done here). Mistiming comes from anticipating the high ball or cross too early. A lot of young keepers are too eager to get to the ball, and this leaves them with a lot of work to do if they misjudge the flight and have to scamper backwards. A tip is to count to one, giving yourself 'a moment' to assess, then plan your route and technique to that ball, or re-adjust into a position ready for a potential attempt on goal.

Upon jumping, the protection leg (i.e. the leg opposite to the take-off leg) should have the knee driving upwards with the toe also pointing upwards – called dorsiflexion. With the toe being in this position the protection leg's muscles are now engaged and activated – allowing for a stronger base and jumping shape. Two legged jumps from the ground will produce more force and therefore height but you'll lose the protective element of the one legged action. My suggestion is to work on both jumps then allow the keeper to make a tactical decision as he is being challenged. Sometimes they need the protection, and sometimes the two legged jump is best. It's all about using the appropriate action at the right time…. decision making!

You are also looking for the arms to be slightly bent at the elbows offering a stronger shape compared to when arms are locked. I hear the term "catch (or make contact) at the highest point" a lot. Now, this could be 15 feet in the air which is impossible to reach. Instead, you're looking to make contact at the earliest possible opportunity - taking the most appropriate route towards the ball based on the flight, speed and trajectory of the ball. The quickest route to the ball would obviously be beneficial as this would allow less time for the attacking team to react to the ball. Again quick dynamic movements.

When the goalkeeper lands there is stress on the lower extremities and the forefoot usually contacts the ground first. This will cause knee and hip flexion which reduces the amount of body mass involved in the initial collision with the ground, amongst other things. When the goalkeeper catches a ball and lands they have six seconds to release the ball – so they are made to move quickly to distribute and at times counterattack. Don't substitute speed for a safe and balanced landing.

Key Points:

- The athletic development chapter will give tips on how to improve jumping
- Jumping of some kind exists within a great deal of goalkeeper movements
- Being able to out-jump opponents will give keepers confidence in coming for set pieces and crossed balls

Diving

Diving is, hopefully, a movement that is not needed too often in a match. But when this desperate situation arises, being able to choose *when* (once you've gone you can't go back) and *how* will ultimately produce important saves for the team.

When diving for a ball, the key for the goalkeeper is to move their whole body weight towards the ball as quickly as possible. This means the velocity of the dive must be to take the shortest route to the ball, moving one's Centre Of Mass (COM) as quickly to the ball as possible. This is why smaller goalkeepers are known to be good at getting down to low shots; because their COM is lower they can reach the ground quicker – although there will always be exceptions and I know taller goalkeepers who can hit the ground like lightning!

For balls on and around the ground - dive low and fast. Keepers need to avoid 'up then down' (inverted U Dive) as this will take time and the angle of approach to save the ball will be wrong. For higher balls – avoid 'down then up' (the U Dive) as reach will be compromised – a keeper should use his body force to dive up and at the ball.

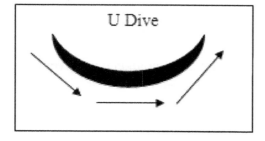
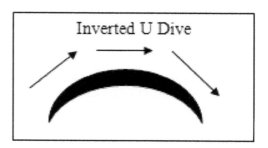

The above depicts this movement. The arrows show the body pathway.

When doing cinematography analysis I find it useful to break down diving technique into three separate areas:

- Initiation
- Take off
- Ball contact

Within the initiation stage the 'Power Step', as it is commonly known, is so crucial in getting the correct velocity towards the ball. By loading the weight through the inside leg (mainly quadriceps and hamstrings) you can generate the necessary force to spring and propel the body. The older and more physically developed a keeper gets the more you'll see increased height, power and distance from the diving mechanism.

The arms also play a part in the dive, but going either one or two handed towards the ball can impact on distance; usually if you go one handed for a ball (where the goalkeeper needs to dive full length) allows for more distance – although every goalkeeper is different. The angle of the step will dictate where the body will go and the angle of dive – for example if the step is backwards the body will follow.

So many times I see goalkeepers at every level collapse the nearest leg to the ball when looking to save a ball then needing to dive to reach. The below action shot illustrates this leg collapse.

A common issue with the diving movement is that, at times, the nearest leg leaving the ground forces the goalkeeper's body weight backwards. This movement limits the amount of distance and power a keeper can get with a dive; anything around the body span can be saved but anything slightly out of reach will go past. The more surface area a keeper can get on the ground with this step the more force that can be generated in propelling his body towards the ball.

For balls in and around the ground you want to 'lower and load' the legs but respond to each ball, high or low, with correct body propulsion. A common theme amongst younger goalkeepers is that they don't get in the necessary position to dive at their maximum. But, of course, the younger they are the less force they exert towards the ball. Again it's about creating good habits so when they develop in maturity they will be able to reach balls higher and further away from their bodies.

This image shows a dive with no drive towards the ball. Notice how the ball goes in about two thirds inside the goal.

The angle at which the body is positioned has a big impact on diving ability. If you're fighting past the front leg to save the ball then you're in the wrong position because this leg will get in the way when making the save; for low balls this is a problem.

Working round the front leg causes the body shape to go back and the ball to go in. Also over rotation of the shoulders towards the ball causes a backwards body shape.

An example of the inside leg working forwards and the body working backwards – you want the body to work in sync. Invariably where the head goes the rest of the body will follow.

The above technical issue is primarily for balls hit from further out. The closer the striker gets to a keeper, however, the more likely the need for a reaction save, which is a strike stopped by whatever means necessary. Reaction saves are easier the closer the attacker is. A goalkeeper needs to use his whole body to make the save.

The above technique is for balls 'wide of the goalkeeper' but for balls either side of the goalkeeper and within diving range some coaches teach 'the sweep' where you kick your legs under your body with head and hands behind the ball, and legs and feet away from the ball.

The sweep, however, can be problematic if not performed correctly as you can create an 'in-between' technique where you neither sweep or dive – as shown above - where the goalkeeper can be in two minds on which technique to use and therefore does not use the appropriate one for that particular shot. Therefore if teaching the sweep make sure the goalkeeper understands when and in which context to use it.

The extending of the arms is also extremely important. Top-hand (stays in the air longer), bottom hand or both hands - getting maximum distance can be the difference between helping the ball in, or helping the ball away from goal. Too many times I've seen goalkeepers not extending their arms to try and reach the ball – thinking the ball is already past them and not putting in the necessary effort. Keepers need to build good habits – effort and desire to save the ball is expected! For tall goalkeepers coaches should not allow them to rely too much on the length of their bodies to make saves, Obviously this will be an advantage in many instances but without developing the power step and quick movement they will be caught out.

Key Points:

- Drive and explode towards the ball
- Extend arm(s) towards the ball
- Angle of body during the dive is important
- 'Want' to reach the ball – effort and commitment
- Emphasise spring and agility

Some modern day goalkeepers use their feet to save low shots. This technique is sometimes used when there is a deflection or the goalkeeper loses sight of the ball and sees the ball late, perhaps through a crowd of players. It would be used, as it's quicker, to direct the ball away from goal when faced with a quick decision like a fast, low shot. Manchester United's David de Gea is a good exponent of this demonstrating how you can save shots with any part of your body, not just your hands! I would not necessarily advocate this for novices who are not in control of their bodies just yet. Top keepers practice techniques like this and are *in control* of what they are doing in this situation. Nonetheless, if you cannot use your hands then being able to co-ordinate your body to save the ball with other body parts gives you a huge advantage.

With blocking, or spreading the body, it goes without saying that the goalkeeper needs to make themselves as big as possible (think of Peter Schmeichel), keeping the body square on will enable the keeper to see the ball for as long as possible, and remain in a better position to spread. An over-rotation of the shoulders and/or a dip in the hips invariably comes from a lack of bravery or fear of getting hit by the ball.

Specific muscles and athletic development will be talked about in the physiology and athletic development chapter – this is the same for all the movements and actions.

Kicking

The ability to kick and distribute the ball effectively and over different ranges is most certainly a common theme in this book. So when it comes to the biomechanics of kicking a football we could spend a lot of time discussing the different muscles, bones and joints involved. Without sounding like a 'cop out' the depth of my own analysis towards kicking has been mainly visual using biomechanics software looking at hip, upper and lower leg angles, as well as rotation of the hips. There are better placed people than me to provide more in-depth biomechanical kicking analysis – some of whom will be referenced further on below.

Goalkeepers are faced with a variety of kicking tasks in a match – a stationary ball, playing two touches, bouncing a first time pass to a teammate, or clearing a ball as far as they can.

Kicking a stationary ball (goal kick or free kick) can be broken down into individual phases, which can each be broken down further for coaching points and analysis.

- Approach
- Planting foot forces
- Swing-limb loading
- Hip flexion and knee extension
- Contact with the ball
- Follow through

Rather than going through flexion, extension, abduction and adduction, etc at every point, if you're interested in the fine details about the biomechanics of kicking I would recommend a journal article called. *'The biomechanics of kicking in soccer: A review'* by A. Lees, T. Asai, T. B. Andersen, H. Nunome, & T. Sterzing – which can be obtained by contacting myself or doing an internet search.

Also a great website for further reading is *www.sportsinjurybulletin.com/archive/biomechanics-soccer*

The key with kicking is practice and familiarisation of match situations so that a keeper can trust himself when faced with multiple options: Shall I switch the play? Can I play first time? What does my weight of pass have to be when passing to this player, with this team shape? I was rarely exposed to kicking and general passing exercises as a child because I was just stuck in goal working on 'traditional goalkeeping skills'. This is why I struggled with goal kicks. Goalkeepers should be part of possession and team based training – not just for tactical and game understanding reasons, but to practice the type of match kicking they will be exposed to. Biomechanically their bodies will become used to the kicking mechanism. Everything pointing in one direction will allow for a comfortable and effective technique. The games based chapter has a whole host of exercises where goalkeepers are kicking within different situations.

Finding a technique that's comfortable and consistent is crucial, it's not about pure brute strength: co-ordination and balance come into play – of which the physiology chapter will go into more detail. But using both the instep and outside of the foot is important, and of course both feet!

Key Points:

- Goalkeepers must be efficient in kicking (passing) stationary balls, moving balls and using both feet
- Practicing with both feet, and playing in possession and outfield practices will assist biomechanical and technical development

Incorporating Other Sports

Goalkeeping is comprised largely of motor skills. These skills can be developed away from technical drill based exercises using specially designed games. But how can playing other sports impact upon goalkeeping? And how might other sports translate to goalkeeping?

Incorporating other sports is valuable for the development of a goalkeeper because they put players in similar situations, working on the same actions and muscle groups, the same movements, and the same trains of thought. But by being different sports they bring nuanced differences, fresh interest, and even increased motivation to training. The sport doesn't have to be played in its entirety within training – although a group game of Handball and Basketball is a fantastic way to take small drills and exercise. I have seen professional goalkeepers at the top level encompassing some of the sports listed below within their training. The following section will focus on younger goalkeepers because, in my experience, utilising other sports with this age range generates the most benefit - right up to elite youth level.

The overall aim is to make goalkeepers faster, stronger, able to jump and spring higher, and react quicker to save the ball.

Goalkeeper training can take place away from the goal area and football pitch. Although training needs to replicate match situations and requirements developing different and appropriate skills in other settings is valuable. Relating to the game based concept of goalkeeper development, I am a firm believer that combining these types of sports at any level and ability of goalkeeper will considerably enhance their overall range of movement. Especially in the developing and foundation years of goalkeeping (before 12). Exposing players to different movements, skills and situations will add much needed variability to the way they respond to football match environments. For me playing different sports in combination with football specific exercises and matches was crucial.

Take elements from different sports and work them into a development plan. The variety of training will inspire goalkeepers and add a competitive fun element – much like specifically designed games. Each of these sports offers something to a goalkeeper, and importantly to the goalkeeping coach. The key theme throughout though is that they develop crucial decision making skills and related movement patterns.

Handball

- Reaction training using smaller balls - using all the body to save
- Throwing accuracy
- Catching at various heights and speeds
- Jumping to challenge for balls
- Quick footwork and copying movements of opponents – great for timing
- Fast paced nature of the sport is ideal for 'general' conditioning

Dodgeball

- Reacting to loose balls (similar to through balls or 1v1s)
- Throwing accuracy
- Catching high paced balls – getting into good habits when trying to catch where possible

Volleyball

- Jump timing – working on when to jump and getting used to assessing multiple stimuli
- Strong wrists and quick hands – Oliver Khan a great example of a goalkeeper who had amazingly strong wrists and arms. The benefit here is that he could beat the ball away and out of danger if he couldn't hold the ball.
- Reacting to differing situations – although a different sport the goalkeeper needs to be adaptable and make appropriate decisions for themselves

- Recovery from the ground – if you've gone to ground the game continues (much like a 2nd or recovery save) so being able to re-position and take stock of the new situation is worked on

Ice Hockey

- Angles and distances – looking to be in an appropriate position with regards to the shooter and puck
- Presence – being able to develop a no fear attitude and making yourself hard to beat, a leader.

Water Polo

- Building diving and jumping actions in water will strengthen leg muscles – as it's much harder to move your body through water than air!
- Strong wrists and quick hands
- Catching and interception of balls at different heights

Racquet Sports

- Eye-hand co-ordination
- 360 degree movements
- Control and composure in play
- Responding to opponents and reacting to differing match situations
- Balanced at the point of impact (can move in any direction) – set position in goalkeeping
- Footwork – racquet sports players are associated with fast feet and playing the sport will develop 'quick feet' that goalkeepers need to possess

Basketball

- Jumping – the challenge of out-jumping the opposition, much like volleyball, working on the timing of the jump. The height basketball players can jump gives them a massive advantage.
- Catching – in lots of different situations – lots of opportunities to catch with the game and drills
- Throwing – building up strength and co-ordination within the throwing element
- Quick bursts of dynamic movement – much like goalkeeping the sport is explosive – so training the body to react in this way will have huge benefits

Gaelic Football

- Kicking – in any position in the sport you need to be able to kick accurately and long
- Physical challenges in the air – in every position aerial challenges are crucial – these build up the goalkeeper's confidence in these situations. There are some good drills that can be done that replicate this contact element.
- Speed and agility – the sport is very fast paced so drills work on small sprints and being able to change direction quickly

These are only a few sports taken from my own personal experiences and observations. After watching the 2012 Olympics I've seen many more that I believe can transfer over and some new sports I'm excited to try out. There are many books and training resources out there that for each different sport to get training exercises from.

Many of a goalkeeper's movements have not been subjected to field based scientific analysis or quantitative measuring - which leaves a big gap in being able to concretely evidence the most effective skills.

More detailed biomechanics research involving a quantitative approach in goalkeeper specific environments are planned within the next year to 18 months. This will involve measuring force plates along with EMG (Electromyography is a technique for evaluating and recording the electrical activity produced by skeletal muscles) for muscle involvement and activation to see what the most dominant muscles are, and what the most frequent movement patterns for goalkeepers are.

A selection of tests have been proposed to answer the following questions:

1. Is the 45 degree power step, that's considered optimum, actually the best angle the body needs to produce the most velocity and power?
2. Does the body react differently when the goalkeeper is being told where the ball is going to make a save? This can be examined using high speed cameras to track the smallest of movements.
3. How do we train to employ the optimum amount of force for movements such as diving and jumping?

Summary

The techniques and actions talked about in this chapter are a guideline to goalkeeping performance. Every goalkeeper will have different ways to move, save the ball, and conduct themselves in general. But to get the most out of goalkeepers, they need to be coached and trained with techniques that will actually prove effective in matches. Many of their actions are externally paced so the need to be quick in response and move accordingly is fundamental. This is why I can't stress enough (as a coach) how teaching the goalkeeper a variety of different and relevant technical movements will equip them for the demands of the game – it's up to them to choose which ones are effective for them…you just create the environment for them to be able to practice these technical movements. Being decisive in these movements is crucial; maintaining balance whilst moving quickly and loading.

Incorporating elements from different sports is definitely coming into goalkeeper training more and more. If you look at 'how high' basketball players can jump – it makes sense to utilise their training methods. It can only be positive. Handball enables keepers to react to changing environments and ball speed will improve reaction times. In turn, racquet sports develop fast agile feet and boost eye-hand co-ordination. The main takeaway point is that these skills are transferable and are very similar to football goalkeeping actions. But like a well-built house - goalkeepers need a solid foundation to work from, and that comes from how well they can co-ordinate and move their bodies.

With advances in biomechanical analysis research, and the fact that many elements of goalkeeping have not been subjected to biomechanical testing, upcoming research will help us understand much more thoroughly how goalkeepers move. Indeed if the goalkeeper makes *x number of saves* each session how does this equate to the stress they put on their bodies? Should there be a limit on the amount of repetitions before fatigue sets in and quality diminishes?

The chapter looks to open up some thinking and experiences within goalkeeping biomechanics. It also demonstrates that knowledge is incomplete and it will be a significant area for better understanding in the future. In the next chapter, we shall examine goalkeeping video and performance analysis..

4

Goalkeeping Performance & Video Analysis: Part 1

"Everything that can be counted does not necessarily count; everything that counts cannot necessarily be counted."

(Albert Einstein)

As commonly identified, the role of the goalkeeper is highly specialised, ever-changing but somewhat neglected at times. The ways in which goalkeeping performances are analysed from a statistical and biomechanical point of view are few and far between, leaving a lot up to individual views and philosophies. The position requires specialist understanding and training and thus must be analysed in the same way.

I hear the expression "paralysis by analysis" occasionally! Although the crux of the saying is true – that too much data and information can swamp and overload an athlete or coach – when analytical feedback is specific, structured, and relevant then the information can be beneficial and informative, and enhance performance. I fear people who use this saying have had a poor experience of performance analysis. Many world-class coaches state that winning or success is about fine margins – as Clive Woodward wrote in his book: "We would question everything, change anything and leave no stone unturned."

So any way of extracting extra information and understanding can't be a bad thing. A goalkeeper's role in the modern game is one of great importance both to the defensive dynamic, and attacking potency of the team. Despite the primary role being – in simple terms to 'keep the ball out the net' – a goalkeeper's impact in building attacks, organising team shape and needing to think like an astute outfield player is highly important. The position can be dissected at length from an analysis point of view because, unlike a squad of 20+ players, you can look in detail at the small number of goalkeepers you have at your disposal. A study (unpublished Master's thesis) on youth goalkeeper development structures carried out in 2010 highlighted that there was a clear lack of implementation and understanding of performance analysis within goalkeeping; since then I've tried to bridge this gap and this chapter reflects this.

The aim of the present chapter is to try to better inform coaches and goalkeepers of current performances, both in training and in matches. The systems presented in this chapter give suggestions as how best to collect data for goalkeepers to give another view on activity. Due to the distinct lack of ways in which goalkeepers are currently analysed I've tried to devise useable and appropriate systems to look into the different areas of goalkeeping. Statistical information is good to a point but if there's visual footage available to back these statistics up, then the more powerful they can be.

At each turn I've tried to give reasoning for how and why information is collected. Ultimately anything that can give the goalkeeper an extra performance insight will undoubtedly have a positive impact: coaches will have more information to back up coaching points, practice can be tweaked, and keepers will be able to work on areas that need development, whilst maintaining their strengths.

In this chapter we will cover:

- A general outline of performance analysis
- Video analysis
- Viewing matches differently
- Types of software available
- How and why to provide feedback
- Structuring the analysis

All of the systems and methodologies have been established based around my experiences within football and goalkeeping, and the below diagram shows where the GK Analyst sits within the system:

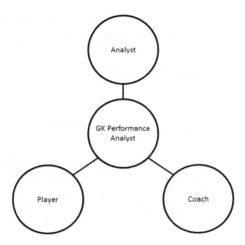

In my experience, performance analysis at each level of goalkeeping is different. The further up the age and level groups I've worked with. the more it's about fine tuning and the more results driven (e.g. at professional level) it becomes. Most of my in-depth work has taken place at both grassroots and professional youth level where the emphasis is on development; helping goalkeepers reach their full potential and helping them get to where they want to be within football.

Performance Analysis in General

With performance analysis providing one of the key building blocks of the coaching process, and the role of the analyst becoming prominent in professional sport, the ability to aid the coaching process has never been more important.

Analysis procedures today break down specific sporting actions and focus from an objective point of view, based on facts; not relying on subjective feedback (opinions). Measures such as motion analysis, biomechanical analysis, video feedback and physical monitoring are frequently utilised, so the scope to develop skills such as feedback to enhance performance, prevent injury, and to record match related actions have never been more possible.

The primary purpose of performance analysis in a coaching context is to provide

Chapter 4

information about sports performance that will assist coach and player *decision making*. Added to this is the opportunity to bring about positive behavioural change; in fact, this is one of the key aims when looking at goalkeeping analysis.

The following image shows the coaching process in its simplest format, with the circle indicating the position in which the analyst traditionally enters the process.

The Coaching Process (Cross & Lyle 2002)

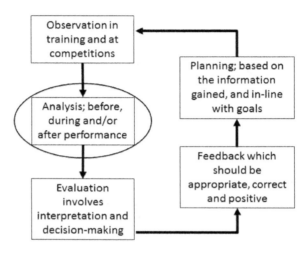

Building on this further, another diagram detailing specific analyst actions during the performance process has been developed.

Performance Process (Hughes et al 1983)

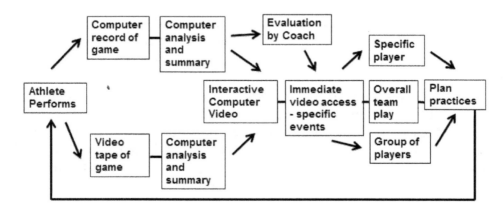

Goalkeeping in football is considered a specialist position and therefore needs specialised training, and an understanding of the role in its entirety. While there have been books written on training practices, technical advice and session content there has been little evidence of research into specific types of programmes, coaching structures and methods utilised to successfully help goalkeepers reach their full potential.

The lack of video and performance analysis systems in place specifically for goalkeepers is (at least from a historical perspective) staggering, both in terms of implication, knowledge and methods in place. The vast majority of the current literature focuses mainly upon the fundamentals of goalkeeper development such as drills and exercises, coaching points, a goalkeeper's role within the team, and the main duties they perform rather than specific academic research.

As mentioned above, goalkeeping is more complex in today's football than it has ever been and from an analysis point of view this increases the difficulty of dissecting performance due to the varied responsibilities keepers are faced with, and expected to execute. Depending on the team, the demands are different. Teams who play out from the back need to be comfortable with the ball at their feet (Victor Valdes and Barcelona), versus those who have to play more direct football (traditional lower league football), versus teams who are faced with high amounts of pressure (when playing against the 'bigger' profile teams) or faced with long periods of time without direct involvement.

Why Use Video Analysis?

The old cliché states: 'A picture paints a thousand words', well imagine how many words go into a piece of video!

Video is an extremely powerful tool and can be a key component in monitoring a goalkeeper's development and performance. It adds a new dimension to coaching and reduces the gap between subjective (views and opinions) and objective (evidence and observations) reasoning allowing for *evidence* to be provided.

Video domains whether they are iPhones, iPads, PCs, YouTube or social media are a massive part of young people's daily lives in this day and age. Even children as young as 7/8 (maybe younger!) know how to use this kind of technology. As sports coaches we should embrace this wealth of technology available and use it to our advantage.

Chapter 4

The key is to pinpoint specific video to use, and then put across the footage in a structured and effective way. The following section looks to provide suggestions and show established methods of video analysis for various levels of goalkeeping. In turn, it has been well researched in sport as a whole that the older an athlete gets, the harder it is to change behaviours and techniques because athletes become grooved and habitual. So start using video early on in a player's career.

A quick side note: one big piece of advice I can give to any new *keeper* is to watch (either live or on the TV) how goalkeepers move, how they deal with different situations, their body language, how they deal with setbacks, what they do in their warm-ups. Video is a great way to watch top quality goalkeepers go about their job and pick up tips from the greats.

A key rationale for video use to be employed is to work around the KPIs (Key Performance Indicators) that you adhere to. Now within goalkeeping there are many attributes a keeper needs to be proficient at. Video can help investigate the following:

- Handling and Catching (how and where)
- Shot stopping (reaction, parrying and recovery)
- 1 v 1 (when taking the ball, angle of approach and timing)
- General position on the pitch (support positions without the ball)
- Crossing (timing, movement, decision and positioning)
- Distribution techniques (long/short kicking, throwing, dealing with back pass and appropriateness)
- Set plays (positioning and defensive organisation)
- Communication (at times where audio and video can meet)

Using video, each of these elements can be developed, monitored and enhanced through training and match systems. In this chapter there will be visual examples – the biomechanics chapter will go into a bit more depth about what you can focus on during video and technical feedback.

Recording instruments and software are readily available now with the advancement of digital cameras, iPhones and iPads. You don't need thousands of pounds worth of hi-tech hardware and software to be effective. I still use my first hand-held video camera for my own coaching and analysis work. At times, I even use an iPhone! A couple of apps on the market currently include: *Coach's Eye* and *Coach My Video*.

There is quite a lot of video analysis software available – here are 2 pieces of *free* software which I can recommend.

1. *Kinovea* – Biomechanical Analysis Software – www.kinovea.org
2. *Longo Match* – Match Analysis Software – www.longomatch.org

As long as you have a camera and some analysis software, you are ready to roll. Again relating to the main ethos of the book, be creative... open your mind to creating different systems and ways of operating within goalkeeping. Try something new and move away from constraints and traditions... experiment and evolve your coaching.

See the Match Differently

Video analysis can also be used outside training, during actual match situations. When a match is shown on television, footage only takes the goalkeeper's role into account when they are directly involved in play (unless you have an extremely wide-angled lens). Over 80% of the time (based on a 2008 study) keepers are not involved in play so they do not get filmed. So what do they do without the ball and how can we get a better picture of the whole goalkeeping performance?

You should consider filming matches from behind the goal to get the goalkeeper's view of the game. Being in an elevated position is ideal for this type of analysis but ground level can be just as effective – you lose most of the depth but can still pick up the vast majority of what you're looking for.

The analyst should specify the optimal positions for observation for a particular movement – again so you can see the critical features to understand angles, planes of motion, and technical coaching points.

Chapter 4

Videoing, then assessing footage, will enable you to look at:

- Goalkeeper positioning without the ball
- Starting positions for counter-attacks
- Positioning from a keeper's team's set plays (final third of the pitch)
- Angles of support
- Communication
- Organisation from defensive set play

Camera Positioning

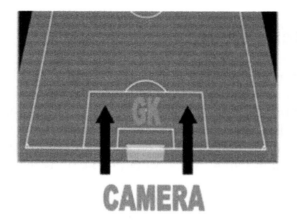

You can now see what the goalkeeper sees. This opens up a whole new dimension of video options and will help a great deal with the above review areas.

Depending on the resources available, one effective methodology I've used before is to have two separate views played together – creating a 'goalkeeper player-cam' – where you can see where the goalkeeper is, on the pitch, along with a more general match view taking into account where the ball is at all times.

This player-cam can be behind the goal (as stated previously) or level with the penalty area to just include the goalkeeper and the surrounding area. Both views are watched simultaneously so the goalkeeper can be viewed at all times. This would depend on the type and indeed amount of software and resources you have at your disposal, however. It would look something like this on a screen:

Match Review: Goalkeeper's Multi View

A 'side on' view can be achieved in two ways and can be used without the traditional match view. The two photos below are examples of different views you can use.

This first view is a close up, and directly covers the goalkeeper to see their movements.

Match View 1

The second view focuses more on the goalkeeper's positioning from shots and general game play.

Chapter 4

Match View 2

These camera views open up all kinds of analysis and feedback options. With the goalkeeper being in view all the time you can pick up their starting positions and specific movements along with their manner throughout the game. And using a zoom function on a camera will also vary the type of footage you can get. Due to the distance from the pitch, their communication can also be picked up through the camera recording which allows for organisational analysis. Of course, this form of analysis is somewhat dependent on the equipment available, however with one camera directly on the goalkeeper you can pick up a great deal of information; probably more than just using a traditional 'TV' view to film just the goalkeeper's actions.

Match viewing and reviewing of this nature can help the goalkeeper understand how there is more to the role than saving shots and kicking the ball out. How can they affect the team positively from a good starting position? How can solid organisation stop potentially dangerous situations arising? How can a goalkeeper be an option for back passes to help build an attack? The bullet point list (start of the chapter) shows areas that are fundamental to a goalkeeper's game, so being able to show real-life examples to reinforce a keeper's learning and back up coaching points is so valuable.

During matches I've moved the camera around to different positions to look at a variety of coaching points, (e.g. from 'side on' for positioning, 'closer to the goal' for technical analysis, or 'behind the goal' for defensive and team organisation observations). Obviously at grassroots level filming matches can cause issues when filming youngsters (e.g. child protection).

At grassroots level your club might well have a photography or video policy in place for matches. If you intend to film it's important to get the necessary permissions from those involved – opposition clubs especially – and state how you're going to use the footage. At higher levels video analysis is starting to become commonplace, especially at elite youth level; procedures should already be in place but it's always best to cover all angles and offer a DVD copy of the match to the opposition. From a training point of view always get permission from the players' guardians too. Explain how and why the footage will be used as it enhances 'buy in'.

Video Analysis in Training

A lot happens within a training session – there are so many actions the goalkeeper undertakes that, as a coach, a great deal can be missed. Video evidence can help bridge this gap.

This section will look at ways in which to examine a goalkeeper's technique and in what ways the footage can be viewed and broken down. Below is an image of two goalkeepers being analysed. Here we are looking at the basic set position, and hand shapes relating to the shot they are faced with (shown below using the Kinovea software).

Chapter 4

For training analysis, the 'session aim' is the most important factor in where to place the camera. Below are a few points to help explain this:

- To look for dive angle have the camera side-on to whichever way the goalkeeper is diving.
- For set position and body shape (before a shot) have the camera front or side on. From the front you can get a good picture of when the ball is struck.
- For technical dissection, zoom in so the goalkeeper is almost filling the screen.
- For positioning purposes you need the whole goal and shooter in camera.
- *A tip.* Leave the sound on the video, so you can hear when the ball is struck. This allows for a more detailed account of the movements of the goalkeeper.

It may seem obvious but remember to get good clear views of the technique you're looking for. In my early sessions I would often move the camera into a blocked position and have un-useable footage. Nowadays, I move the camera quite a lot during training sessions to get different views and angles to analyse with the editing and biomechanics software. The beauty of video is that it can pretty much do what you want it to. By that I mean you can set up the camera(s) pretty much wherever you want, either using a tripod or free hand – remembering that obtaining clear and useable footage is the most important thing.

Below are some other examples of using a hand-held camera, iPad and an iPhone to show how easily accessible the footage can be collected.

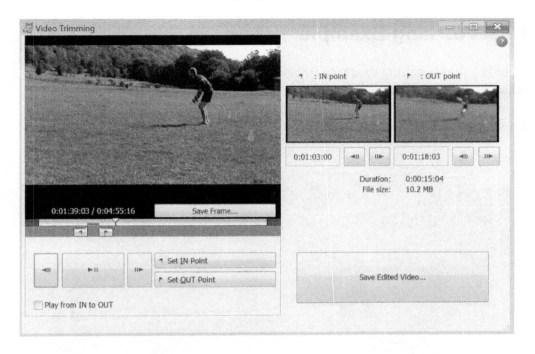

The two views below are examples of the type of analysis that can be done –
every coach will have differing opinions on technical points and what to focus on.
Here we focus on foot position.

Real Working Example

Here is a real coaching example (individual frames from a video) – examining what the coach will be looking for.

To start with – the goalkeeper is picking up the ball's flight from the server.

The keeper gets himself into line with the ball and has his hands forward to the ball.

When the goalkeeper takes the ball – look at his hand/saving shape to determine if he is looking through the back of the ball.

Another Example

We are looking at a keeper's initial movement to respond to a shot on their goal. With the sound 'on' you can pick up the point of server's contact. But here the main aim was to look at some close up technical points.

Here, we are examining what kind of position the goalkeeper is in to save the next ball – is he set and in a position to move in any direction from this shot?

The keeper has now made his initial movement(s) to save the ball. We can examine how they have responded to the shot – is his body moving into line? What kind of hand shape has he got?

Moving forward a frame or two – is the keeper looking at the ball? Is his body shape appropriate to the ball's flight and trajectory?

When the goalkeeper comes into contact with the ball - how has he reacted to it? Has he got a strong saving shape? Do his shoulders over rotate?

Although the above figures represent a slowed down and simplistic view of what videos can show, the idea is to identify the key technical points that the coach wants to adhere to. Coaches work to different technical points but the power of video is that you can coach retrospectively and provide evidence of practice.

Chapter 4

The iPad

In recent months the usage and application of Apple's iPad has become more widespread. Within my own coaching I use it to film mainly technical and tactical game play (when goalkeepers are with their teams) to get some key examples of the different KPIs that I'm looking for. Two crucial ones for game play would be: how are they playing out from the back, and what is their body shape and positioning when shooting opportunities are presented. For technical practice it is standard goalkeeping attributes with specific analysis done for each goalkeeper depending on their strengths and weaknesses.

When using the iPad, a typical session may look something like this:

- Before the session show the goalkeepers a 3-4 minute video that covers the main session topic. Focus on the key elements and critical features of the skill or action, asking questions on what is being viewed. I find this sets the tone and tempo for the session, and as a coach gives you something to refer back to whilst making coaching points.
- During the technical practice focus on one exercise or a couple of goalkeepers – the video is stored on the iPad and can be analysed using an app or as pure playback. A good time to show a few clips would be during a fluids break/rest period.
- When coaching goalkeepers within match situations (e.g. teams in small sided games) I often move between different sessions to get examples whilst verbally coaching them as well. The key would be to organise some specific clips and go through the points you want to make. Use relevant apps and software to code/tag actions and draw lines/highlight areas on the screen.
- After the session I would have a de-brief session of no more than 10 minutes to discuss the session and look through clips. This can be done either as a group or individually (more on this further on). The trick is not to burden yourself with having to analyse clips for five/six goalkeepers. Focus on a couple per session leaving the feedback rich and lasting. If you're fortunate enough to have them for more than one session per week you can rotate or use the analysis as most applicable.

Start by introducing this process in small parts then expand as you become used to the technology, and of course the goalkeepers become used to this process as part of their regular development.

The iPad is also great for match days. If, like me, you sometimes have to watch three or four games at a time it's easy to forget and miss what's happening so creating evidence is important. If additional personnel are available, ask them to film for you so you can move around and watch other matches. In some instances coaches who you're working with will also have iPads so there can be opportunity to obtain and share footage.

The over-riding factor here is the chance to use immediate feedback, without having to wait to download footage and analyse. Now we'll delve deeper into the feedback process, but first as a coach ask yourself a few key questions:

- What do I want to find from the video I have captured?
- Which examples best show the coaching points I'm trying to put across?
- How can I structure the feedback in a way to aid goalkeeper(s) development?

The next section will endeavour to help you answer these questions.

Developing Feedback

The importance of disseminating video footage from both training sessions and matches into usable and relevant information is paramount. Built into any goalkeeper's development programme should be a specific *time* for video analysis feedback. The higher you go up the professional game the more time and personnel are available for such structures. Being able to see swiftly where you've gone wrong is a huge advantage as a keeper, and in general supports coaching in so many ways.

Having a great deal of experience in the grassroots environment, I have found that one of the biggest hindrances in goalkeeper development is time. You might only have an hour a week with your goalkeeper(s) so, without question, getting the most out of these sessions is crucial.

When working with young goalkeepers it is good to set a structure behind video analysis. With younger goalkeepers it is important to maintain plenty of 'positives' even if that is on just one element of their game. The novelty of keepers seeing themselves on camera will, at first, be a barrier to overcome (believe me!) so make the video sessions short, sharp and concise for this age group. Don't overcomplicate the process, and focus on one area in the session, or even one coaching point. Channel their enthusiasm into a productive environment!

For a goalkeeper's all round holistic development, a keeper needs to be able to see and understand what they are doing. Looking at the four corner model, from the Football Association (found in all their coaching resources and which involves technical, physical, tactical and psychological development); you might want to target one area per analysis session. For example, look at how your keepers deal with balls over the defensive unit – this helps with the rationale of a particular analysis session (although of course as a coach you would want your session to hit all four corners).

With some younger goalkeepers the video work might be more focused on technical and physical areas as they are still learning the techniques required, but as you go up in age and ability the scope to focus on tactical and psychological areas becomes more prominent. Each area should be worked on, and experience has shown that variety is important. As a coach or analyst if you're focusing on the same area every video session – things get tedious and you will lose the effectiveness of the analysis.

Here are some suggestions for where to include the video analysis within the goalkeeper's weekly routine:

Grassroots

- Before a training session; if possible, arrange for your goalkeeper to arrive early and have your video session then, either looking back through a match or having a technical session.
- At the end of a session if you have limited time, get the keeper to stay back for 10 minutes which is enough time to do a short session.
- Of course, where possible, you can use the tips given within the iPad section.

Advanced

- The Monday following a weekend game is a good time to address the previous match, and then work on specific areas for the week. It's also a useful time to start preparation for the upcoming game.
- On a later weekday, review any training footage and highlight technical development.

- If you have the benefit of two training sessions on certain days, prepare footage from the morning session to either look through yourself for the afternoon session, or show the goalkeeper highlighted areas from the morning session giving feedback as to what they can do to improve a particular area.
- As discussed previously – using immediate feedback, subject to available equipment and personnel, can be a useful tool.

Familiarity and repeated methods reinforce learning and the ability to recall information.

The model below looks into how different sections of the analysis process link into each other within the match/training dynamic. The whole process looks at creating training sessions based upon match occurrences. Although designed for a team the coach can take this and mould it for their keepers. For example, highlighting positive and negative examples of actions can open a dynamic feedback process enabling the keeper to better understand their development and *why* they might be doing certain training sessions.

Dynamic Analysis Process (O'Donoghue 2006)

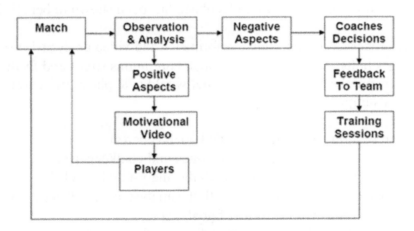

Whilst the above model is a dynamic analysis process, we can also look at things from a functional perspective. The functional approach offers clear themes that will shape training practices.

Chapter 4

Functional Analysis Process (O'Donoghue 2006)

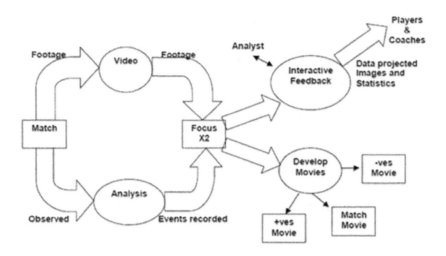

The functional model actually depicts the whole process by showing how all areas of the analysis process work together, and as you will see from the bottom right hand corner, it is important to provide movies that are both 'positive' and 'negative'; in turn, interactive video feedback has been shown to benefit learning.

This whole process looks into how performance and video analysis is used to aid a goalkeeper's holistic development through continuous structured feedback. The following are the types of sessions that would take place, from both matches and training examples:

- Video sessions with the coach and goalkeeper(s)
- Video sessions with the analyst, coach and goalkeeper(s)
- Video and statistical sessions with the analyst and coach
- Video and statistical sessions with the analyst and goalkeeper(s)
- Q & A sessions with a group of goalkeepers
- On the training pitch using immediate feedback sources

Feedback should be delivered in an appropriate manner relating to the skill and ability level of the performer. For advanced and elite goalkeepers you can really delve deeply into technical and tactical examples and question them so they take ownership of their development. Issues can be underscored such as understanding how fine margins can make the difference between a goal and a save. Ultimately finding out how any goalkeeper responds and learns best will depend upon their personalities and ambitions. Most of my coaching experience has revolved around retrospective feedback (after the training session has taken place). This allows for particular thought and structure to be brought into the process. On some occasions, however, immediate feedback has been used where a technical coaching point has arisen or positive re-enforcement can be shown.

Video feedback can only be useful if it is related to the problem addressed (versus just watching the performance and trying again). A previous study found that video-based performance analysis is predominately reactive; I advocate and use a pro-active outlook to find areas of goalkeeping that were either non-existent in terms of analysis, or which had academic value but no real way of practical application. This involved the use of augmented feedback.

Augmented feedback looks to reduce the discrepancy between actual and desired outcomes. An example of this would be comparing the goalkeeper's technical proficiencies with a desired execution, such as looking at *how* they dive to save a high ball and *breaking down* the relevant sections of this movement, i.e. initiation, take off, and ball contact (discussed later on). You can then compare these sections with the desired performance to build up a picture of what a keeper needs to do to reach a peak level of performance.

An effective way the coach (and analyst if available) can work together is to look through the training and match video footage and dissect performance in terms of technical, tactical and football related actions. As an analyst it's important to interact with coaches fully and determine what information they want and how you can tailor and structure the feedback most appropriately for *their* goalkeepers. The below model highlights how and what encompasses feedback within the goalkeeping environment.

Chapter 4

Goalkeeping Analysis Feedback Cycle

Because the ratio of coaches to goalkeepers is small (certainly compared to the larger numbers of outfield players) there can be constant interaction and dissemination of goalkeeper performance. The model shows how taking into account what occurs in matches (through video and statistics) can directly impact upon training sessions. For example if your goalkeeper is struggling constantly with playing out from the back then this would be an area to work on. Even as a goalkeeping coach watching a match it's impossible to recall every single action and event your goalkeeper is involved in. Hence video provides the evidence; relevant statistics can add further value to this.

I've seen numerous goalkeepers who are great in training by being brave, commanding and assured, but place them in an unpredictable environment (which a match is) and their technique does not always stand up to increased pressure. Therefore, the goalkeeping analysis feedback cycle, when coupled with analysis from training, can help a coach compare technical capabilities inside and outside a match situation; i.e. does your goalkeeper behave, move or act the same way as they do in a match? If there are differences, perhaps some psychological training and development would be of value?

A continuous feedback process allows for a flexible approach, so let's look at this in greater depth.

Feedback at the highest youth level can be used in a 'fast way'. A session can be filmed in the morning, the coach can watch the footage then design an afternoon session that meets the need to improve a certain technical point or performance in a drill. In this process the goalkeeper will be involved in watching the footage in-between sessions to see what's going to be worked on, or after both sessions where before-and-after comparisons can be created.

The type of feedback you wish to give will affect your video analysis set-up. For immediate feedback, coding actions/practices live (either through a camera or the iPad) allows you to get the information there and then. Whereas for retrospective feedback you can leave the camera/iPad in an appropriate place (as discussed) and then disseminate the content at a later date. Of course if you don't have the luxury of having someone film/code for you there comes a bit of organisation. Once the process of video analysis becomes more habitual, as a coach you can sit back and film/code the practice, then provide feedback there and then. Again it all depends on the type of feedback you want to give. Being able to disseminate the footage after the session will give you a more clean and thorough feel as you would have had time to look back in greater depth, but immediate feedback looks to 'solve' the problem there and then. I've found immediate feedback most useful when doing a practice in this way:

- Showing how the practice will be done
- Having a 'demo run' at the practice to gain familiarity
- Looking back through the footage highlighting to the goalkeepers the coaching points relevant to *that* practice (and physically demonstrating where necessary) then restarting the practice to seek that desired improvement or target for the goalkeeper(s).

Structures of Feedback

It is important that a goalkeeper can evaluate performances for themselves, as well as in group settings. This process should be relevant to the age, ability and personalities of the goalkeepers, taking attention spans and the ability to process information into account. This all relates to different learning styles. Some will respond best to watching videos or seeing images (visual), actually doing the practice or being involved (kinaesthetic) or simply reading and writing their thoughts and opinions down.

The Kolb cycle represents a model of learning that focuses on the learning process which involves the goalkeeper in the whole experience. Getting goalkeepers to reflect on how they're doing is a fantastic process. Examples could include: looking back on goals conceded, or looking at different goalkeeping skills in different situations.

The Kolb Cycle

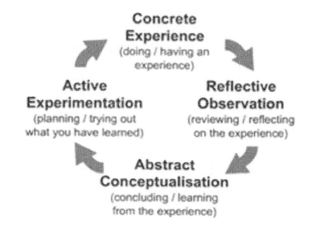

Of course, there is no one size fits all solution with feedback, and below are three different feedback approaches that can help keepers, both in matches and training.

Goalkeepers Video Analysis Spectrum

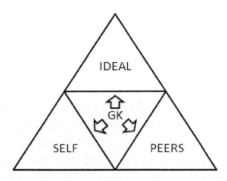

Ideal – watching and analysing an *expert performer* within one's field/job has always been a very effective way of understanding a skill or general performance. Therefore, laying on a video session that looks at an expert performer, on a specific topic each week, is a great way to generate discussion. I've used recent footage from the Premier League and the 1st team goalkeeper from one of my former clubs to look at different distribution styles. I've even used videos where goalkeeper errors have led to goals; these clips are designed to check goalkeeper learning through diagnosing errors then correcting them.

A really effective method I used a couple of years ago was to show the 9-12 year olds, at a professional club's Centre of Excellence, footage from the club's 1st team goalkeeper. This gave the analysis a real-life feel to it because it was a club they were all aspiring to play for – the engagement here was fantastic and I was able to ask many questions about different performance areas within goalkeeping. I would rotate age groups each week and found work with this age group most effective. With the older 13-15 year olds I focused on specific technical and tactical situations rather than more general goalkeeping.

Self – the goalkeeper reviews their own match and training footage. This is done either alongside the coach, or by oneself but provided with certain coaching points to look for, alongside specially designed sheets to complete. These points might consist of stating what technical point they need to work on in the future, or ranking how they think they did in a certain situation. However, simply looking through their clips can be done as well to gauge opinions. It is essential to check for a keeper's understanding after the session, though.

Peers – classified as peer learning. Looking at goalkeepers within their own group or club, a goalkeeper can start to review differing techniques and performances from people they can relate to. Group discussions can be generated by looking through different goalkeeping situations. Good examples include positioning without the ball and appropriate distribution methods.

Time and Type

How long an individual should spend on the various feedback methods should correlate to the ability level and personalities of the keeper, and (as discussed) the analysis time available with the goalkeeper. Some coaches watch the whole match and dissect every action, some pick out relevant clips (through software coding where specific clips are selected, see below) or spend 3-4 minutes looking at one or a small number of coaching topics.

Personally, I advocate a variety of the latter two (relevant clips, on a small number of topics). With attention spans limited, you need to engage the goalkeeper. Ask questions like 'How could you have improved there?' or 'How did that feel?' and have specific examples on hand to show what you want to discuss. When looking at training sessions have good examples and examples which highlight the need for improvements. A balance is needed. Knowing your goalkeepers you can do this by finding a way which works best. Trial and error is often needed to get up and running so experiment with the type of feedback you use. An analysis session is really retrospective coaching so being able to rehearse the session before giving it has been found to be useful. This isn't always possible of course. Sometimes, as a coach, you have to make the best of what you can!

In recent times, because of improvements in technology, it has been possible to offer immediate feedback on the training field (as discussed above). If a coach wants to stop the session and reinforce a coaching point or show an example, this can now be achieved easily. If used correctly, this type of feedback can prove fantastic. To be able to look at what a goalkeeper has performed within seconds of it occurring surely must be a crucial tool. When coaching (and I've experienced this myself) there is so much going on in a drill, or exercise, that being able to replay, even for yourself and not for the eyes of the players, what has just gone on is very valuable. Water breaks or a rest period is an ideal chance to reflect, for both the coach and/or players.

Coding

Coding/tagging is a process that enables you to highlight and label different sections of video footage to use as standalone examples rather than having to look back through a whole piece. This can be done by coding live (as the footage is actually recorded) which saves time and is ideal for immediate feedback, or after the session or match when you can highlight different examples to show your goalkeepers.

The coding process depends a great deal on the software available and is easier with advanced software (which does cost more). For a novice in video work or at the foundation or grassroots level, the process doesn't need to be advanced because you can cut and trim video footage after the session for feedback without the need for expensive software. Some free packages for creating video packages include YouTube Video Editor, iMovie for Macs, and Windows Media, all of which can be used to bring together different examples in a complete way.

With my own coaching I started off by simply trimming pieces of the video I wanted to show my goalkeepers on free software and the software that came with my camera – you can save this selected video into separate files (with a naming and numbering convention, e.g. kicked distribution_[date], thrown distribution_[date], etc) which creates a database of footage which means that if you want to find a particular clip; you do not have to go through hours of footage.

If you are coding a match, creating a goalkeeper specific code window is extremely useful. This can be as simple as listing the following:

- Goalkeeper Actions – when the ball is in and around the defensive third
- Goalkeeper Distributions – when they distribute the ball
- Goalkeeper Shots and Goals – when shots (on and off target) and goals occur

This is a simple way to separate footage. But of course the role encompasses a great deal more than the above. Referring back to the stated KPIs (above) can be used as a code window – this will allow for greater match feedback depth and role clarity.

When coding a training session I've used two main ways to separate footage. These are dividing the session up by name (when they are involved), and coding the individual drill or practice. You can have a personalised selection of a player's clips, and also compare different keepers within the same practice – I usually do one or the other.

Some of the above is done with a coach and analyst present. What if you're coaching on your own with the camera set up?

Coach as the Analyst

This section will look at how I've used video in my own coaching (i.e. as coach, not as an analyst). This would normally be done using a video camera set up so that I can concentrate on the session. If you have an iPad you can step back from the session to hold the device and film, whereas with a camera set up you can physically become more involved (i.e. put the camera on a tripod and get involved to serve or recreate coaching points). Although with the iPad you can get stands to place it on and film – all this depends on the type of feedback you wish to give as explained above.

To begin with, I would set up the camera in a designated area relevant to the session i.e. to the side of the goal to check diving angle, or in front to look for body shape. In the diagrams below, the arrows indicate the camera angle.

For an exercise in the goal area:

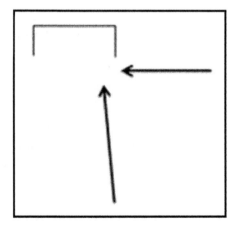

A game based exercise:

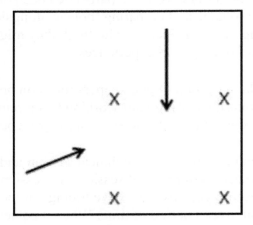

It goes without saying that without relevant and decent quality footage, filming becomes borderline useless, so the biggest piece of advice I can give here is to experiment with views. For goalmouth exercises, the best filming angle is determined by the session topic or aims. For example, if the coach wants to look at power steps or diving position 'side on' is best. For set position or general body shape then it's best to place the camera just left or right of centre. The beauty is that you can move the camera wherever you want during the session to create a variety of angles that raise coaching discussions.

Different filming approaches can be used:

- **Coach – Camera – No Computer** (coach and record but then load up the footage later for feedback before the next session).
- **Coach – Camera – Computer** (record directly onto the computer but have no coding done; which means a whole raw file is created. The coach can then highlight clips later on).
- **Coach – Camera – Computer** (operated during a live session, but often requiring sophisticated software, the coach/analyst stands by the computer and instructs the goalkeeper to carry out specific tasks as they code the footage in real time).
- **Coach – iPad** (the coach uses the iPad to film from various positions, either freehand or using a stand).

Note: It is often easier to record directly onto the computer, but if no computer is available (or if a computer impedes the filming process) then record and upload later.

Chapter 4

With all the video work, the extra burden placed upon the coach can be demanding at times. Obviously if you're a part-time coach or volunteer coach then balancing editing footage and preparing footage alongside your daily life sees time become a big factor. To people who think they might struggle with time, I have some tips from my own experiences.

- If you have a larger group of goalkeepers focus on one or two goalkeepers each session, thus decreasing your workload. But remember to rotate. Feedback sessions will be easy to structure if you choose to do individual feedback.
- If you get footage from a whole technical session and only focus on a couple of goalkeepers during that session (for session feedback), keep *all the footage* because you will now have footage of the other keepers (as well) spread out over a period of time. When it comes time to look at another goalkeeper you will have more than one session to generate feedback from.
- The more familiar you become with the software and the processes, the more efficient you will become. Create and refine ways of working, and new systems and procedures for yourself.
- As mentioned above, focus on a few key clips if you're looking at a larger group. It is better to have quality over quantity! More on this point at the end of the chapter.

As a coach or analyst finding what works for your group of goalkeepers is the key, find what engages them, and find the necessary ways of igniting their motivation for goalkeeping. It's key not to overload the video sessions or focus too heavily on one particular aspect of their performance as the coaching will lose its effectiveness.

Of course you may not want/need to film every single training session. Even in my most in-depth roles at clubs not every single part of every single session is analysed…this may be the next step however! But as a grassroots coach, delving into the video analysis world where necessary, appropriate or desired is rewarding. Perhaps the higher up the footballing ladder you work the more time and resources you'll have at your disposal.

A Working Example of Feedback

Here are a few examples to show the feedback that can be generated from analysis. The images have been frozen at certain points of the video (hence the blurriness) to provide coaching discussion points.

Talk to the keeper. Ask:

- Are both your hands behind the ball?
- Is your saving shape correct, coming forward to the ball?
- Are your head and hands forward?

- Is your bottom hand behind the ball?
- How can you be in a better position to make this save?

- How can you control your body more effectively in order to make a cleaner save?
- What can be done with your hands in order to make a better decision (catch, parry or deflecting hand shape differences)?

Summary

The first part of the chapter should help you find ways to extract visual information on your goalkeepers, and then convey this information in the best possible way. Being able to give tried and tested advice for coaches and analysts is so important. There's so much information to be obtained and much variety in overall game requirements that it's very hard to measure some areas. For example how do you measure communicational effectiveness, positional consistency and the 'best' technique in which to perform actions? Every performance analysis environment must be judged on an individual basis whether that be goalkeeper, game or instances within a game. Every goalkeeper is an individual and will therefore approach a situation in a different manner responding to analysis in a different way – it's up to us to find the most effective methods and this section should have sparked a few ideas off.

For positive re-enforcement showing the goalkeeper not only videos of their idols but indeed videos of themselves in matches (and training well) can lead to heightened motivation. At times even just before a match I've shown some positive examples to keepers so they start on a high. At half-time I have used footage to clarify some technical or tactical points (this is very short so as not to overload the goalkeeper).

Another tip would be to show footage before a session. If the topic is on crossing for example, show an example of these situations happening in one of *the keeper's* matches. This will help you as a coach explain why you're working on this topic and give the player a firsthand, relatable example to think about.

Video recording is so freely available in this day and age that the opportunity to get stuck right into goalkeeping performance has never been greater! Along with balls and cones I would always have a camera of some sort in my kitbag! So go out and seek the benefits of performance analysis and explore the potential it has to make the difference…!

5

Goalkeeping Performance & Video Analysis: Part 2

"There are lies, damned lies and statistics."

(Mark Twain)

With the Moneyball phenomenon, analytics in sport have never been so prominent, nor widely explored. Many different companies and organisations are using statistics to measure players, teams, results and the probability of events occurring.

Within goalkeeping I've seen little in the way of useable statistics from a coaching perspective, although there is definitely a place for them when put across in a relevant way. I prefer using more visual analysis methods, especially for younger goalkeepers as firing statistics at them isn't really conducive for their development. However my desire to try and create useable statistical information for goalkeepers is still a strong ambition and this section will look at some of the methods I've come up with and used on a day-to-day basis at varying levels of football.

In this chapter we will cover:

- Distribution systems
- Saving SnapShot
- Extra analysis support
- Age appropriate analysis.

Distribution Systems

The following section looks to show what distribution recording is, how it can be done, and provide examples.

If an outfield player had a pass completion percentage of 50-55%, would you deem that effective? Giving the ball away just under half the time would strike me, initially, as worrying. Although the statistics don't tell the whole picture, the below table shows a quick glimpse of the type of information that is collected at the highest level of goalkeeping.

Premier League Distribution 2010/11 (Opta)

Statistic	Edwin Van der Sar (Manchester United)	Petr Cech (Chelsea)	Joe Hart (Manchester City)	Pepe Reina (Liverpool)	Ben Foster (Birmingham City)
Total Passes	993	990	916	1,185	1,445
Accurate Passes	582	523	404	654	539
Pass Completion	59%	53%	44%	55%	37%
Chances Created	1	1	2	2	2

It would be useful to drill down into the numbers further, and the system that makes up the next section has been used successfully within various footballing environments.

Goalkeeper Distribution Analysis System

The Goalkeeper Distribution Analysis System was initially brought into the football world by Grant *et al*, from 2000 – *Goalkeeper Distribution Patterns in the Premier League*. This work was continued during the World Cup 2002 when Martin Thomas was accompanied by Jim Lawlor, Patrick Riley, James Carron and Mark Isaacson leading to the follow-up article: *Goalkeeper Distribution*.

Having realised the potential of measuring the distribution of a goalkeeper in a match, and the benefits on coaching, team tactics and performance, I modified the system to build a record of not only where the ball went from the goalkeeper but 'how' (i.e. if the ball was won, and whether possession was won back or retained by their team).

The system has been trialled and utilised at professional football clubs enabling coaching staff to go through the information and data available. Not only does it show if the goalkeeper is adhering to team tactics, it allows for analysis into what distribution method seems strongest, which one is used most frequently, and what areas of the pitch most balls are being won or retained in. The outfield players can be looked at subsequently, and research can be done into what areas are being successful from the goalkeeper's control of the ball and if the team set-up and formation is in line with where the ball is going. For example, if the team tactics are to play the ball short and build up play from the defensive third, and analysis shows that a high percentage of balls are going long and straight into the attacking third, the goalkeeper and staff must be notified of this.

The flip side to the example is where the goalkeeper is continuously playing the ball long, in line with the tactics, and the forward players aren't winning the ball. In this case, attention can be focused on the forward players. In turn, if they are winning most of the balls but possession is not retained then the players around them might be slow in reacting to their knock downs or passes, or may not be in a good position initially to receive the ball from the forward players.

There is a variety of different information available to be calculated from the raw data produced, including percentages of how many balls are won, lost and retained in each individual area along with a breakdown of which distribution method was most successful overall and into which area as well.

The beauty of the system is you don't need cameras or even computers to produce the data. A grassroots coach can take a blank template of the raw data and hand note the individual actions then produce the statistics and percentages manually. A coach can give immediate reflection on how the goalkeeper has influenced and even dictated play. These sheets can be looked at during training sessions and home study to work on the goalkeeper's tactical play alongside how the team can get the most success from their goalkeeper and build attacks.

I've found the pitch maps and statistics work well with younger goalkeepers and can be used to reinforce the importance of being able to distribute the ball effectively from a technical and tactical point of view. Young goalkeepers should be able to have a short, medium and long (depending of course on physical prowess) distribution game.

Below is an example of the system and an explanation to how it works, along with a breakdown of some statistics.

Explanation of Recording Sheet

The statistical system starts with the accurate recording of a match, and requires the analyst or coach to mark each play/distribution into five data columns. Generally speaking, when the goalkeeper has control of the ball, that would be considered a distribution. However, every *single* time the goalkeeper has the ball is not necessarily a distribution! An example would be if the goalkeeper receives a short back pass and has to clear it just as an onrushing striker bears down on him; this would be considered a clearance rather than a distribution.

Area

The first data column looks at the area analysis. The below illustration shows a football pitch that has been divided up into a grid, where each cell is a distinct area. The goalkeeper is located in the C1 goal, playing in the direction up to the higher numbered boxes (i.e. left to right).

L = Left   R = Right   C = Centre

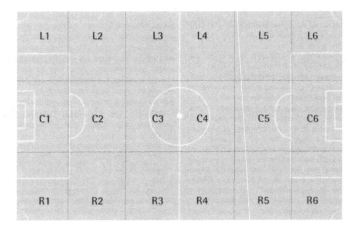

Action

The action column will record how the goalkeeper distributes the ball. The actions are divided into 5 different types.

A = Goal Kicks – when the goalkeeper takes a goal kick from their 6 yard box.

B = Free Play (Back Pass and Throw In) – where the goalkeeper receives the ball from open play and recycles the ball.

C = Ball in Hand (Drop Volley, Half Volley Kicks, Dribble & Drive, and Throws) – whenever the goalkeeper has the ball in their hand and distributes the ball.

D = Free Kicks – when the goalkeeper takes a free kick from any part of the pitch.

E = Header – when the goalkeeper uses their head to distribute the ball.

Chapter 5

Method

The method section only relates to action C above (i.e. only when the goalkeeper has the ball in hand) and is used to break down this action further to provide specific data.

FK = Floor Kick (Dribble & Drive Strategy) – when the goalkeeper places the ball on the floor form their hands and distributes.

T = Throw – when the goalkeeper throws the ball out.

HK = Hand Kick (Drop, Volley and Half Volley) – when the goalkeeper kicks the ball directly out of their hands.

To clarify: this data column is only added to when a Ball in Hand Action takes place.

Outcome

This is whether the initial play is initially won or lost.

W = Ball won   L = Ball lost

Retained Possession

After the initial challenge, the analyst coach needs to mark whether possession was retained. This has to be comfortable retained possession where the team can look to pass and build up an attack.

YES or NO

Example – if a long goal kick is initially lost but the ball is played directly out for a throw in or corner then this would count as outcome lost but possession won back as the team would have possession of the ball from this upcoming set play. Balls directly from the goalkeeper that go straight out of the field of play will be recorded as lost with possession also lost.

Example Recording:

So, we have covered each individual data column and the recording system would look like the following table. The data gatherer will work left to right for each play.

	AREA		ACTION		METHOD Follow up to Action C *Only*		OUTCOME	RETAINED POSSESSION
R1		A		FK		W		YES:
R2		B		T		L		NO:
R3		C		HK				
R4		D						
R5		E						
R6								
C1								
C2								
C3								
C4								
C5								
C6								
L1								
L2								
L3								
L4								
L5								
L6								

Now to record each distribution action I'm going to break this down step by step.

The first distribution action, labelled 1 as it was the 'first' play to be recorded, was played into area R1 on the pitch. It was a goal kick, so is recorded in the 'A box' and it was initially won and then retained after (W, and then Yes).

Chapter 5

This play would look like this in the recording table.

	AREA		ACTION		METHOD Action C Only		OUTCOME		RETAINED POSSESSION
R1	1	A	1	FK		W	1	YES: 1	
R2		B		T		L		NO:	
R3		C		HK					
R4		D							
R5		E							

The second distribution will be added to the first in the recording table. The second, marked as 2, was played into area R5, it was C (Ball in Hand) so we will need to mark the method column also (as a hand kick – HK). Unfortunately the ball was initially lost, but possession was subsequently won back. Both distributions would look like this:

	AREA		ACTION		METHOD Action C Only		OUTCOME		RETAINED POSSESSION
R1	1	A	1	FK		W	1	YES: 1	
R2		B		T		L	2	NO: 2	
R3		C	2	HK	2				
R4		D							
R5	2	E							

After every distribution has been recorded the data table would look like this from a whole match – to differentiate between 1st and 2nd half I would use a different pen colour for each.

Raw Data Example for a whole match

	AREA		ACTION		METHOD Action C		OUTCOME	RETAINED POSSESSION
R1		A	6, 12, 13, 17, 22, 25, 27, 28	FK	4, 5, 14, 16, 21	W	1, 3, 4, 6, 7, 8, 9, 10, 11, 12, 13, 15, 19, 21, 24, 28	YES : 1, 2, 3, 4, 6, 8, 9, 10, 11, 12, 15, 16, 17, 20, 21, 23, 24, 28
R2		B	2, 11, 18, 19, 24, 26	T		L	2, 5, 14, 16, 17, 18, 20, 22, 23, 25, 26, 27	NO: 5, 7, 13, 14, 18, 19, 22, 25, 26, 27
R3	18	C	3, 4, 5, 10, 14, 15, 16, 21, 23	HK	3, 10, 15, 23			
R4	15	D	1, 7, 8, 9, 20					
R5	23, 26	E						
R6								
C1								
C2								
C3	10, 13, 24							
C4	3							
C5	27, 28							
C6								
L1								
L2								
L3								

L4	1, 6, 11, 12, 14, 16, 17, 19, 20, 21, 22								
L5	2, 4, 5, 7, 9, 25								
L6	8								

A quick headline summary of the numbers shows 28 instances where the goalkeeper distributed the ball: 19 in the 1st Half, 9 in the 2nd Half.

So, let's take a moment to look at how percentages are calculated (using the example data table).

Won/Lost

The overall % of won and lost is worked out by using the overall number of actions won, then dividing this number by distribution actions to get a number. We then multiply by 100 to get a percentage. If you've worked out the 'won' figure the 'lost' figure will be the number that is needed to reach 100%.

e.g. 28 distributions overall, 16 of which were Won. 16 ÷ 28 x 100 = 57.14% won

Retained Possession

For calculating retention percentages, look at all the individual numbers in the won column, and the same numbers in the retention column. You can then see which numbers from the won column have been retained or not. Use the whole number of actions retained from the amount won, divided by the total number of actions won to get a %.

18 distributions (retained possession, yes box), out of 28 outcomes.
18 ÷ 28 x 100 = 64.28% retained possession overall.

16 distributions won (outcome column). 13 of the 16 retained (retained possession column).

$13 \div 16 \times 100 = 81.25\%$ retained

12 distributions lost (outcome column), 5 of the 12 retained (retained possession column).

$5 \div 12 \times 100 = 41.66\%$ won back

Pitch Area

The same methodology works for the pitch area. Use the individual numbers for each area to calculate the frequency. Remember to only use the numbers from the 'won' column to work out the % retained from the won column.

4 distributions Right: $4 \div 28 \times 100 = 14.28\%$ played right

Of the 4 distributions, just 1 distribution action was won. $1 \div 4 \times 100 = 25\%$

The 1 action that was won was retained. $1 \div 1 \times 100 = 100\%$ retained

3 actions lost were lost. 1 was retained. $1 \div 3 \times 100 = 33\%$ won back

Distribution Actions

For the individual action statistics use all the numbers in that column and use the same process as above.

9 Ball in Hand distributions. 5 won. $5 \div 9 \times 100 = 56\%$ won

Of the 5 won, 5 were retained. $5 \div 5 \times 100 = 100\%$ retained

Of the 4 lost, 2 were retained. $2 \div 4 \times 100 = 50\%$ won back

4 Hand Kicks, 3 were won. $3 \div 4 \times 100 = 75\%$ won

Of the 3 Hand Kicks that were won, 3 were retained. $3 \div 3 \times 100 = 100\%$ retained

Chapter 5

Displaying the Data

The numbers would be displayed like so if they were calculated from the example data table shown above. The numbers have been rounded up or down to the nearest whole number.

Overall

57% of the GK's distribution was initially won with 81% of that possession retained.

Of the 43% of the GK's distribution that was initially lost – 42% was then won back or possession was then retained.

64% of the overall possession was retained.

Specifics

Right – 14% was distributed here

25% of the GK's distribution was initially won with 100% of that possession retained.

75% of the GK's distribution was initially lost with 33% then won back / possession was retained.

Left – 65% was distributed here

56% of the GK's distribution was initially won with 80% of that possession retained.

44% of the GK's distribution was initially lost with 50% then won back / possession was retained.

Centre – 21% was distributed here

83% of the GK's distribution was initially won with 80% of the amount won then retained.

17% of the GK's distribution was initially lost with 0% then won back / possession was retained.

Let's now take a look at some example individual areas:

L4 – 45% initially won with 64% of that possession retained.

L5 – 33% initially won with 50% of that possession retained.

Distribution Actions

Goal Kicks

50% of the GK's distribution was initially won with 75% of that possession retained.

50% of the GK's distribution was initially lost with 25% then won back / possession was retained.

Free Play

50% of the GK's distribution was initially won with 66% of that possession retained.

50% of the GK's distribution was initially lost with 33% then won back / possession was retained.

Ball in Hand

56% of the GK's distribution was initially won with 100% of that possession retained.

44% of the GK's distribution was initially lost with 50% then won back / possession was retained.

FK = Floor Kick (Dribble & Drive Strategy)

40% of the GK's distribution was initially won with 100% of that possession retained.

60% of the GK's distribution was initially lost with 33% then won back or possession was retained.

T = Throw – No Actions

HK = Hand Kick (Drop, Volley and Half Volley)

75% of the GK's distribution was initially won with 100% of that possession retained.

25% of the GK's distribution was initially lost with 100% then won back / possession was retained.

Free Kicks

80% of the GK's distribution was initially won with 75% of that possession retained.

20% of the GK's distribution was initially lost with 100% then won back or possession was retained.

Pitch Maps

Translating this statistical data into a simple diagram is an effective way to get a good representation of the overall distribution from the goalkeeper.

Blank areas mean that no ball was directly played into that zone by the goalkeeper.

Entire Match

Chapter 5

First Half

Second Half

Additions

Something I have added to the analysis system since its creation is to time how long the goalkeeper spends with the ball in their possession from all types of distribution. This aims to look at the tempo each goalkeeper plays at and can be used to create benchmarks throughout different age groups.

Times are recorded as follows:

- Free Play – timed from when the goalkeeper receives the ball until they release it.
- Set Play – timed from when the keeper has the ball in his/her possession and takes the kick.
- Ball in Hand – timed from when the keeper claims the ball until they release it.
- Goal Kick – timed from when the goalkeeper brings the ball into the 6 yard box and can play.

All of these times are added up then divided by the number of distribution actions to create an overall average. For younger goalkeepers this is as simple as it needs to be but as you go up in standard you may also want to look at long and short distributions along with counter-attacking.

Another addition is to create a pitch map to show where the distribution is played into. Below is an example.

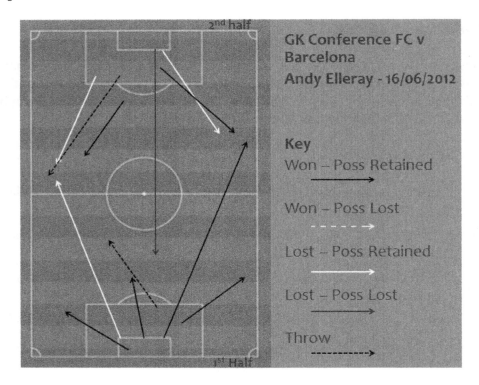

Without trying to overload the reader with information, the map shows a simpler recording of the system's information. In turn, the table below would be another version of the map, converted into percentages (a fictitious 3 game example is shown). This approach allows for easy comparisons between goalkeepers, teams, competitions or even home/away matches. (Initials in brackets are the keeper that played in that specific match).

Distribution Recording

Match + GK	GK Actions	Won	Lost	%	Retained	Not	%
Barcelona (AE)	12	8	4	67%	11	1	92%
Real Madrid (AE)	30	23	7	77%	20	10	67%
Ajax (AE)	27	26	1	96%	22	5	82%
Total	69	57	12	82%	53	16	77%

Summary of the System

All the above statistical information can be worked out using the raw data shown previously. By using different calculations you can really take an in-depth look into how successful a goalkeeper's distribution has actually been: hitting target areas, adhering to tactics, and more. In turn, coaching staff can identify areas of the pitch where the ball isn't being won or retained.

If you are an analyst, be aware that it is unwise to collect all this data and hand it straight over to a coach! Summarise the main points and what you want to portray – you may only need the overall main percentages. Only provide detail if it is needed.

Saving SnapShot

The Saving SnapShot was created in order to track where goalkeepers were making their saves from, and how they are dealing with shots on their goal.

I'm not usually a fan of save ratios, mainly because they don't tell the whole story (i.e. where shots are taken from etc,) each shot on goal should take on its own significance because factors such as ball speed, trajectory of the ball, player positioning, for example, are factors when a goalkeeper is facing a shot. Saying that, I have developed and used a system that produces some useable data.

The types of saves have been broken down into separate categories. The definitions are as follows:

Dropped – When the goalkeeper drops a ball that they go to catch.

Caught – When the goalkeeper cleanly catches a ball or pushes the ball down but still in control (i.e. a parry then claim).

Blocked – When the goalkeeper makes a blocking save with any part of their body (including feet).

Chapter 5

Goal – Where the ball goes in the goal.

Parried – When the goalkeeper parries a shot that stays in play.

Deflected – When the goalkeeper makes a save with the ball ending in a corner or throw in.

Due to the black and white content of the book, the Saving Snapshot has been altered. The coloured spot markings have been replaced with symbols. Full colour versions are available – see the Bennion Kearny website or contact the author for specific examples.

Saving SnapShot Front On: Goalkeeper A vs Team United – 10/12/2010

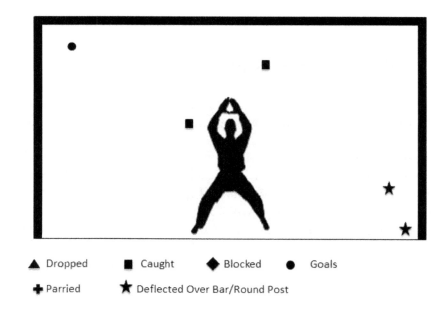

▲ Dropped   ■ Caught   ◆ Blocked   ● Goals

✚ Parried   ★ Deflected Over Bar/Round Post

Saving SnapShot Side On: Goalkeeper A vs Team United – 10/12/2010

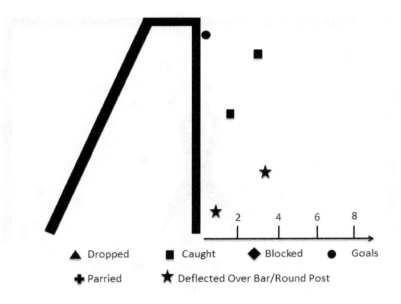

The SnapShot diagrams allow for a detailed perspective on how goalkeepers deal with the shots they face. These are done per match and can be used to create a seasonal representation. The main reason behind SnapShot was to get a better picture of saving analysis – of course having the visuals to support this adds a deeper analysis because you can see exactly how each keeper saves each shot.

Both front-on and side views are done to see the exact position of the save in the goal, and in relation to the goal line. Here is an example of a seasonal analysis of a keeper who played a small number of matches.

Saving SnapShot Seasonal Front On: Goalkeeper A Seasonal Diagram

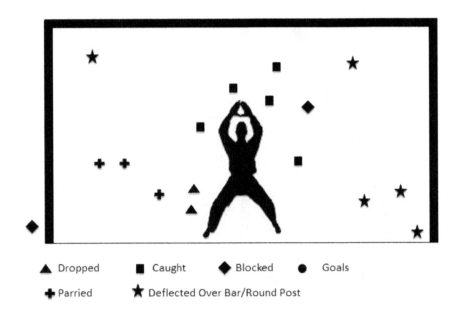

Saving SnapShot Seasonal Front On: Goalkeeper A Seasonal Diagram

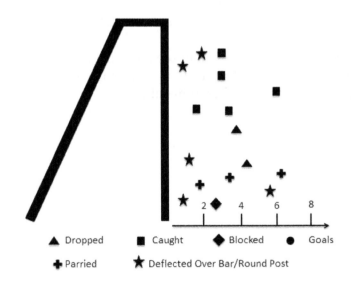

The seasonal diagrams for regular keepers can get a little cluttered. So I often plot each save type onto a separate diagram as shown below.

Saving SnapShot: Goalkeeper A, Parried Balls Front

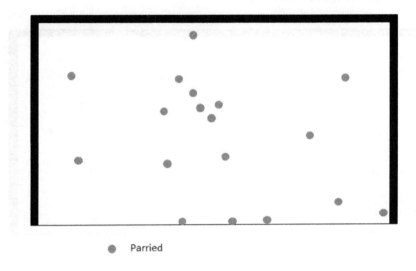

● Parried

Saving SnapShot: Goalkeeper A, Parried Balls Side

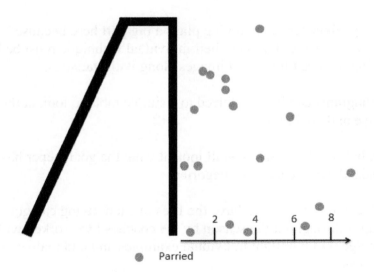

● Parried

The idea behind plotting each type separately is to look for trends, once again, into goalkeeper strengths and weaknesses along as well as making the data easier to comprehend. When conducting this in a real setting, having fewer numbers within each shape on the diagram (from both views) helps correlate the front and side views – by doing this you can see the exact ball from both sides rather than just a random clutter. This adds a bit of extra information.

Saving SnapShot Goals Conceded

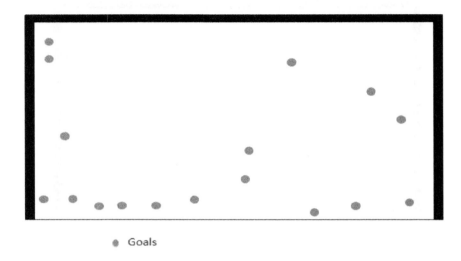

● Goals

The Saving SnapShot can also be used to indicate where the ball passed the goalkeeper before going into the goal.

Obviously the goalkeeper's positioning plays a big part here because if they're in a 'correct' position for the shot then their individual technique must be looked at, thus reinforcing the need for visual images along with statistics.

All of these diagrams can be transferred to a simple table to look at the exact number of save and goal ratios.

The 1ˢᵗ table, below, shows the overall look at what the goalkeeper has been faced with and breaks down the saving categories.

Something I've done before is to have the files of each saving category reviewed at various stages throughout the season by the coaches I've worked with. Having the video footage will highlight individual examples and add realism to the whole feedback process.

The save ratios give a benchmark and help for goal setting at the start of the season. For example if an Under-18 goalkeeper during the previous season had a save ratio of 60% from the shots they faced on target, the aim of the new Under-

18 might be to have a higher percentage than the previous goalkeeper.

Overall Season Statistics

Action	Number
Games	38
Goals	45
On Target	143
Off Target	167
Caught	43
Blocked	14
Parried	17
Dropped – Re Claimed	2
Deflected	22
Total	69% Save to shot on target ratio 31% Shot to goal ratio 310 attempts overall

The 2nd set of tables gives a comparison between two goalkeepers which allows for a discussion into how each goalkeeper performed throughout the season. Every match and occasion is different so a like-for-like comparison is not the fairest way of looking at the tables. But at least there's some useable data produced.

Chapter 5

Comparisons of two Goalkeepers

Goalkeeper A	
Action	Number
Games	19
Goals	12
On Target	61
Off Target	95
Caught	20
Blocked	10
Parried	9
Dropped – Re Claimed	1
Deflected	9
Total	80% Save to shot on target ratio 20% Shot to goal ratio 156 attempts overall

Goalkeeper B	
Action	Number
Games	19
Goals	33
On Target	82
Off Target	72
Caught	23
Blocked	4
Parried	8
Dropped – Re Claimed	1
Deflected	13
Total	60% Save to shot on target ratio 40% Shot to goal ratio 154 attempts overall

For grassroots goalkeeping coaches, a simple hand recorded method of obtaining game data is easy to accomplish. A simple tally of each shot can build up a good picture of how keepers deal with shots on their goal. Even if you don't use the SnapShot images, having the saving ratios will prove a useful resource.

These statistics have more value than just saying "a goalkeeper has a 70% save ratio". They can be used to drill down into what that really means. For example, what type of shots, where are they from, how has the goalkeeper dealt with shots, how many shots have they faced, etc.

Another area from a coach's perspective that can be opened up is whether the goalkeeper is saving every shot on goal. There is no way in which every shot on goal can be saved but by looking at the age and ability of the goalkeepers you're working with, something like the following diagram can be created.

Goals Conceded Target

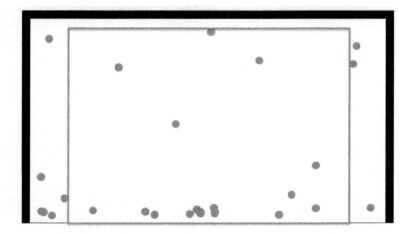

For a high ability goalkeeper you would expect them to save shots within the boxed area. The balls high and wide into the corners wouldn't be the areas of concern for a coach due to their difficulty to save. Obviously there are certain exceptions and this is where video backs up the snapshot a lot more.

The below map shows a boxed area which is more relevant for a young goalkeeper as their saveable goals target would be different due to size, experience, and ability. What this is trying to do is build confidence and set manageable targets: "Hey you're not going to save every shot you face, but the ones in this area are the ones we want you to save". With the example below as the coach you would want your goalkeeper to save balls within their arms' span for a younger goalkeeper. Of course every shot will take on its own story, as discussed previously.

These small targets can be tailored to the goalkeepers you work with as each have different abilities and needs.

Goals Conceded Target 2

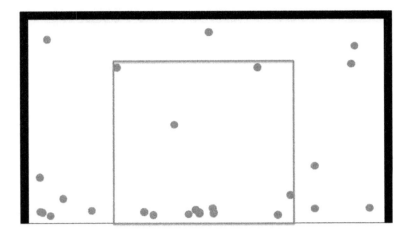

Ultimately statistics get used more and more as goalkeepers get older and the key is to focus on goalkeeper development. Don't go throwing stats around willy-nilly; make sure they have a purpose and reflect the message you're trying to get across. Some stats can be misinterpreted and not reflect what you're actually looking for. Work at 1st team professional level differs greatly from that at youth development level in that 1st team football is more results driven. Unless statistics help with goalkeeper development and game understanding then be careful of using too many statistical based analyses.

Extra Analysis…

Something that I've implemented into my own coaching is trying to get a better visual understanding of where my goalkeepers are 'at'… by which I mean a sort of grading system to check a goalkeeper's strengths and weaknesses.

The below table is a simple rating system of key attributes within goalkeeping. I used this during training and when I re-watched videos of sessions. It is useful to have examples on hand to justify certain ratings.

Although every coach will have a differing opinion when watching a goalkeeper, the table is also of value for a goalkeeper to keep a personal record of their attributes. Get the goalkeeper to rate themselves and compare the numbers – if there are obvious discrepancies in certain attributes then this can lead to discussion points. The psychology section covered more of this area – such as the performance profiles.

Goalkeeping Attributes	Rating out of 10	Psychological Attributes	Rating out of 10	Physical Attributes	Rating out of 10
Arial Ability		Anticipation		Acceleration	
Command of Area		Bravery		Agility	
Communication		Composure		Balance	
First Touch		Concentration		Co-ordination	
Handling		Decision Making		Flexibility	
Kicking		Determination		Jumping	
One On Ones		Off The ball		Natural Fitness	
Reflexes		Positioning		Speed	
Throwing		Teamwork		Strength	

One other thing I would advocate when watching matches (especially if video feedback isn't available) is to record match feedback. Here is an example, one that I've used as a coach and which I have asked goalkeepers to fill out:

Match Areas	Rating out of 10 and Comments
Command of Area	
Communication	
Defensive Organisation	
Handling	
Goal Kicks	
Back Passes	
Drop Kicks	
One On Ones	
Shot Stopping	
Support Positioning	
Throwing	
Game/Tactical Understanding	
Additional Comments:	

Age Appropriate?

This section will look into what types of analysis are appropriate for different goalkeeper ages. From my experience, at all youth levels, I will endeavour to offer suggestions of best and successful practice. The age ranges are set on the basis of what I've found to work best but, obviously, there will be exceptions and goalkeepers that respond better to video or general analysis work than others.

Dialogue between myself and goalkeepers has been important here. Finding out what works best for different goalkeepers, based upon feedback at different ages, and some of my own experiences in varying environments, has led to the following.

8-11 years old

Within this age range the main aim is to introduce goalkeepers to video in small doses – I very rarely (if at all) use statistics. I would use a small selection of clips focusing on only a few coaching points, potentially for 5-10 minutes. In turn, getting the players to understand *why* we're looking at video clips is important as it gives them a foothold into other ways in which they can learn – and not just on the football pitch. The novelty of the filming and seeing themselves on camera (as mentioned previously) is a barrier at first to overcome, but relating to the above point if players know *why* they are doing this then problems can be swiftly overcome.

As talked about previously, a good way in which to keep the video sessions variable and fun is to watch professional goalkeepers and show the youngsters examples of good practice. Letting them see that the top goalkeepers make the same movements and 'do the same things' as they do in a match is a powerful learning tool. The capacity to change behaviours within the age range is prominent so using the video session provides an extra dimension – the key is to balance quality vs quantity and to structure the sessions in a way which provides an enjoyable and ultimately a learning environment.

12-15 years old

This age range is where you can get into greater detail and start to produce comparison video examples, trend analysis, and more technical details. With their game understanding and maturity now increasing you can really get into using video to work on their technical and tactical understanding of goalkeeping.

The sessions can be longer due to the depth and level of analysis undertaken. To keep the goalkeepers' attention is important and research suggests that people 'check out' after 10 minutes. So, grab their attention by creating pieces of analysis rich in emotion – I've broken up individual analysis sessions by showing them a few clips of some of their best saves or some inspiring moments from a top goalkeeper. The clips that I've found to work best focus on the topic or coaching point being looked examined at that time, so if you are showing clips of goalkeepers taking crosses in training or matches have examples from a top goalkeeper. I've started introducing basic statistics to this age group (predominately distribution maps) but, as discussed, the importance placed on statistics within goalkeeping is not as important as the visual as every shot/situation is different in nature.

16-18 years old

When the goalkeepers reach this age you can really look in detail at fine technical and tactical examples. At the top end of youth football the importance of fine margins is extremely evident. From understanding the most appropriate technique to a shot, and when to set for 1v1s, to what impact a defender stepping up too early can have on the general team performance. If you're able to get match and training footage for grassroots goalkeepers you can really hit technical points.

Being able to translate training skills to match skills can be examined with video sessions, so you can analyse training ground performance against match performance. Does a keeper's technique change in the highly paced game environment? Do they look comfortable in possession? Are they seeing danger and attacks early? I would use statistics on this age range including the Saving Snapshot, save ratios and distribution maps. In fact, I would be especially keen to use the distribution maps due to the overall bearing on the team.

I've found that this age range (in general) can sit through a more detailed video session and talk through a larger selection of clips from both training and matches, with more structured questioning used and an emphasis on tactical play. Technically they are (if not already) reaching good levels of technical understanding and execution so tactically they need to be shown and told how they can positively affect the team dynamic.

The type of feedback and the way you use video and performance analysis methods will have an impact. Immediate or retrospective feedback I've found does have a bearing – not much in a session can complicate the process for the younger foundation age bracket – but with advanced older keepers you can trial any kind of feedback and video set-up you want. I've had great success with both.

The most important factor in all of this is to show the goalkeepers (at the earliest age you start to work with them) *why* and *how* performance analysis can benefit their performance. All goalkeepers respond differently to analysis but I've found that if you explain the benefits and what type of activities can be done you are 10 times more likely to create a fruitful developmental environment.

Coach Assistance...

A big positive for video analysis when coaching, either alone or with someone filming for you, is that when serving a ball or being involved in a practice you can accurately revisit events. If you're physically serving a ball it is virtually impossible to get your head up to see the goalkeeper's initial movements and to say with total certainty how they've dealt with a shot or other action.

When still playing at a good level and just about to enter the blind football arena I would film myself in training. I didn't have the know-how I've got now so I would simply look through the whole video and compare myself to the professionals, watching TV and live matches to see how they moved and made saves. Without a goalkeeping coach to guide and support me I would 'self-coach' and learned how to correct my technical issues using coaching books and DVDs that I purchased. The point being that as a goalkeeper you're in control of your game – you can be told what and how to do things but experiencing and learning goalkeeping for yourself by playing is so crucial. Using video as a recall method has proven to be extremely beneficial, so if you are reading this book as a player, ask your coach if you can implement video feedback methods.

Real World Analysis: Penalties...not again!

As a proud Englishman, the thought of a penalty shoot-out conjures up bad memories – Euro 96, World Cup 98... most recently Euro 2012 against Italy. But how can video help goalkeepers with penalties and penalty shoot-outs?

The simple answer is that video can show keepers how players took recent penalties. There's a well-documented occasion when Eric Steele (1st team goalkeeper coach at Manchester United) showed Ben Foster previous penalties from the Tottenham players (most notably Jamie O'Hara) before the 2009 League Cup Final, on his iPod. Manchester United went on to win the final 4-1 on penalties with Foster saving O'Hara's effort.

The 2012 European Championships was really the first time I had seen and heard a great deal on video assistance in penalty shoot-outs. The media were keen to find out goalkeepers' views and how they used video information. Joe Hart for example was asked at numerous press conferences if, and what, he was watching before the match. In fact, Hart watched his iPad on the pitch before the shoot-out although England went on to lose. Another example would be Petr Cech in 2012's Champions League Final where he saved one penalty in extra time and two in the shoot-out to help win the trophy. He studied, with the help of the other 1st team goalkeepers and goalkeeping coach, all of Bayern Munich's penalties from 2007 onwards, made notes, and went the right way every time.

For more information on penalties from an academic point of view I would recommend the research of Geir Jordet who has investigated in great detail reasons for players 'choking'– amongst other reasons – when involved in penalty shoot-outs.

Summary

Statistical analysis should try to give added weight to a coach's thoughts and opinions. I wouldn't say statistics are the be all and end all for goalkeepers but the distribution system allows for evidence to be provided into an individual's performance. The same with the Saving Snapshot. The more useful information that can be recorded the better – but only when used in the right and appropriate way.

Performance and video analysis is all about getting that extra insight and knowledge into whatever sport you're looking at. Football and goalkeeping are no exceptions. The chance to dissect goalkeeping actions, trends and techniques will ultimately enhance the understanding of how the goalkeeper works. Physically, psychologically, biomechanically and tactically. Their role in the team dynamic nowadays is very different to how it used to be and keepers have to be effective distributors of the ball, be highly organised and possess a variety of different movements responding to ever changing match situations. As coaches we need to give our goalkeepers all the tools to succeed…

The future of video analysis? I'm going to end these two chapters by including a few thoughts on where the video analysis environment can go. Since I've started writing this book, over a year ago, the advancement in different coaching software and 'apps' has come along a great deal. The iPad can be classified as a valuable tool for a coach with its ability to record footage and analyse actions 'there and then'. Relaying footage 'in the moment' has a big impact.

Apps such as *Coach's Eye*, amongst others, allow you to draw arrows and highlight areas of analysis – I've used these from a more technical viewpoint and it has proved very useful. The same can be said for other session planning apps where you can produce animations of exercises and take them out onto the training pitch with you. Apps for coding and tagging are also available.

By combining the above with free videoing apps that allow for the download of footage and you are good to go in terms of having the full package available – and all on an iPad. Search in the apps store for coaching and videoing – the possibilities are endless.

The way you use analysis can be as in-depth as you want. Exploring the possibilities is the key, whilst trying some of the ideas in your goalkeeping curriculum – see what works best for you and your goalkeepers.

6

Goalkeeping Practice

"Don't practice until you get it right. Practice until you can't get it wrong."

(Unknown)

It goes without saying that the type of practice the goalkeeper is exposed to impacts a great deal upon their development. In a nutshell, "If a skill doesn't get trained, it doesn't get played in a match situation." (Iñaki Samaniego).

Many training environments I've seen are structured similarly with regards to the types of exercises that are used, and the way in which they are ordered – for example a lot of technical shot stopping work.

I want my young goalkeepers to make mistakes, and to take them out of their comfort zones in a challenging training environment. That means avoiding drills and exercises set up to look organised or which play to their strengths most of the time. I want them to strive to save more balls and earn their saves, not give them to them on a plate. *Earn* the saves in training and in a match you'll see the rewards.

The type of practice you do as a coach paves the way for the type of goalkeeper that's produced. A goalkeeping philosophy is a good document I would recommend to every coach – think about how your teams play, and what key skills you want your goalkeepers to be proficient in.

Chapter 6

This chapter looks at how you can coach and train goalkeepers in different structures, and finishes off with some specific preparation examples and some further reference on the importance of distribution, showing some unique exercises.

In this chapter we will cover

- Goalkeeping specialisation
- Practice environments
- Training structures
- Preparation
- The importance of distribution

Coach, When Should I Be a Goalkeeper…?

The discussion surrounding early specialisation in goalkeeping is a strong one. I've heard both sides of the debate from different coaches and clubs; some start general goalkeeping at 8, others not until 12/13. One key factor is that everyone is of the impression that a player's 'general game understanding' needs to be started as soon as they start playing the game.

As goalkeeping is a specialised position, the demands placed upon player coaching and development are very specific. Some research suggests that *early* specialisation is associated with a range of negative consequences affecting physical, psychological, and social development. On the other hand, some researchers have proposed that an early diversification approach does not disadvantage athletes in acquiring expertise, and is important for the development of intrinsic motivation and skill transferability. We shouldn't pigeon-hole children wanting to play football into positions too early but is there a proven 'right age' yet? No.

It is said that by the age of 11 a person's neural pathway is 95% complete, meaning it becomes more difficult to learn new movements and mechanics. This phase, also called 'concrete operations', applies to sport in general, not just goalkeeping.

Repetition is seen as the best way to get movements into your muscle memory, so repeating technical drills (diving, catching, and jumping techniques amongst others) and breaking them down so they become autonomous should be an effective way of working with your goalkeepers, although this repetition should be structured in such a way that a range of skills can be developed.

Some American goalkeeper coaches (amongst others no doubt) have found that many expert professional goalkeepers they coach have played a variety of sports in their younger days including Basketball, Baseball and American Football. There is a belief that playing these other sports can help develop hand-eye co-ordination alongside movement skills that can transfer directly over to goalkeeping.

Combine this thinking with the fact that some high level goalkeepers don't start playing in the position until they are 14-15 years old. Joe Hart still played outfield for his school until he was 16.

There will always be exceptions within goalkeeping development as goalkeepers come from all sorts of different environments – but what I'm trying to do is to suggest a balance. Could you argue that game understanding can be taught more easily than physical and technical requirements? When your goalkeepers reach 15/16 should you work on technical elements? Wouldn't more training time be better suited to tactical and game play environments? Both are poignant questions but, looking at the former, you would hope that a player's technical game would be of a good standard thanks to early career training. Of course, a focus on technical training often highlights a lack of specific coaching and knowledge for goalkeepers at an early age.

The consensus from research (and my experiences) is that combining specific technical training with general footballing/game understanding and tactical training, complimented with a range of motor movement exercises (such as games based theory and other sports) would be ideal for overall biomechanical and physical development at an early age.

Specifics

When watching a match people get a general outline of what types of movements the goalkeeper makes – but my question is do we actually *observe* what happens in the match? And do we then translate this over to the training pitch? There is often a discrepancy between what is coached and what actually occurs in a match. One could argue that: "Cones and equipment around the goal mouth are a map to make saves – but in a match there are no maps or guidelines. We're left to our own devices and to find out what works best for us."

Does two feet through a pair of cones, round a pole into a pre-determined save reflect a save in a match? You could suggest that it's getting the goalkeeper's feet shifting then moving them across the goal, but surely it's better to stick to a clear penalty box where the goalkeeper has to decide for themselves what foot movement is best for the situation and how to best react to the play in front of them?

Practice…Practice…Practice?

There are various types of practice in the sporting world – here are some main examples:

Blocked – a practice sequence in which the same task is repeatedly rehearsed.

Random – a practice sequence where there are a number of different tasks in no particular order. This avoids or minimizes consecutive repetitions of a single task.

Constant – a practice sequence where only one variation of a given task is rehearsed during a session.

Varied – a practice sequence where a number of variations of a given task are rehearsed during a session.

Within goalkeeping blocked and constant are the main types of practice used due to the 'drill' type nature of goalkeeper training. There can be variations in footwork and handling with technical drills. For learning, gaining familiarity or maintaining a skill this type of activity is great as it is structured and the performer can train knowing the actions and movements they are faced with. But the higher up the ladder you go the more varied and un-prescribed the goalkeeper's training should become, because no two saves are exactly the same and no two situations in a match are the same.

Although repetitive practice is seen as beneficial for learning skills, there still needs to be a large portion of goalkeeper training devoted to random and reactive practices, or the goalkeeper will become mechanical and robotic, expecting the same movements every time. Varied practice enriches the flexibility or adaptability of movement production, allowing the performer to apply what they have learned in practice to similar actions they have not attempted before. So the goalkeeper is prepared for situations they face within a match.

A goalkeeper's movements and actions don't follow a linear path. They are exposed to quick abrupt changes and the athlete needs to be a dynamic. An example of this could be for a goalkeeper who is say 15 and has played in the position for a number of years; they play at a good level and are looking to progress. Why do we tell them where the ball is going in technical drills? "Johnny, what you're going to do for this next drill is jump over this hurdle, touch the post and I'm going to serve you a ball that's on the ground to your left."

Does the goalkeeper have to make a decision here? The drill has been mapped out for him so his brain is already thinking 'Okay I need to move here and do this.' If goalkeeping really is a reactive and decision based position this wouldn't challenge a keeper. At a novice level or possibly for a short warm up to get into the mindset for the session then yes. As Dan Coyle says in his latest talent book - the 3 Rs - "Reading, Recognising and Reacting" - drills make sense for goalkeepers. But do training sessions allow for the goalkeeper to *read* different situations, *recognise* the most effective way of dealing with a match scenario, and then *react* accordingly? If not they should! All this begs the question do we coach and train a particular 'drill' in that setting or actual goalkeeping?

The picture above shows the first part of a drill. The working goalkeeper knows where the ball is going and his body is already going the way of the ball. One could argue that the keeper is learning to read body shape but players are skilled enough to whip the ball across their bodies into the opposite corner.

By knowing where the ball is going, the goalkeeper will save this ball no doubt, because if you look at their set position their body weight and momentum is going that way already – so could this be considered cheating?! There is a case for this type of practice to build confidence and familiarity with younger keepers, but as competence increases this type of training should decrease. This type of training will create very good technical goalkeepers for sure but robotic and mechanical in nature. The key is to make them explosive and reactive.

One thing I always say to myself, and advise others, is: "Does this exercise replicate the movements the goalkeeper makes in a match?" Thinking more widely, one might argue that using other sports (as advocated above) in their rawest form might not be considered replicating a match state – but this isn't the point. The point is that other sporting actions *overlap* into goalkeeping and can be more effectively taught in different settings.

A couple of things I've used when doing a penalty box exercise is to have a keeper walking into the goal mouth before they face a shot or situation – this reflects matches because the goalkeeper spends most of their time walking (physiology chapter) so starting like this is realistic. Another one is to move backwards in some exercises – it's amazing to see how many times the goalkeeper has to drop off, then come forwards, and then drop off again.

Goalkeeper Training Spectrum

The Goalkeeper Training Spectrum is a blueprint or structure that enables a coach to add their own ideas into training sessions – specifically goalkeeping skills, actions, and movements. This is something I have developed in order to assist a coach in deciding upon session content. I use this on a regular basis in my coaching environments. Every coach is different but being able to meet the demands of the position in every session should be of high priority. If you're fortunate enough to train your goalkeepers more than once a week then there is opportunity to really focus on some specific technical areas, so the weighting of each section may well be different.

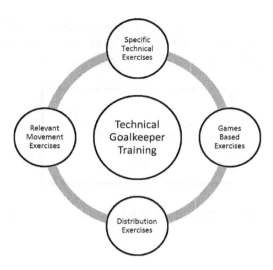

Let's look at each section in turn.

Specific Technical Exercises: Elements of a session that work solely on one technical situation or action. More structured for younger goalkeepers and less prescribed for older and higher ability goalkeepers.

Games Based Exercises: Part of the session works on a particular topic or theme using games based activities, exercises or individuals simply play other sports.

Distribution Exercises: With a large majority of the goalkeeper's match actions involving distribution in some way, it is crucial to work on engineered situations where the goalkeeper can work on distribution methods for a good period of a session, outside of any team based training. Being comfortable on the ball can be worked on during every session no matter what the session topic, or the number of goalkeepers in the session. After the goalkeeper has saved and held the ball (in a practice) get them used to looking to distribute – this will breed the habit of quick thinking…turning defence into attack within seconds.

Relevant Movement Exercises: These exercises should contain replicated match movements, i.e. dropping off to come out for a through ball, re-adjusting position after playing out from the back, recovery saves and walking exercises. Exercises that emphasise motor movements would fit into this category along with isolated movements such as quick passing and support play. Mobility exercises that enhance and promote these two areas of physical training are relevant. Activities such as plyometrics are a great way to build up different ranges of movement. See the physiology chapter for specific exercises.

The image below shows a quick example. The Goalkeeper (GK) would play a 1-2 with each player and support their pass. Vary this between 10 and 20 yards. P1 and P2 would be other goalkeepers in a technical session.

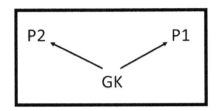

Again, see the athletic development chapter for specific exercises on movement.

Examples

Using something similar to the above, I've included a couple of examples that can be used with different age groups, in different settings. The following session structure examples are ones that I have used with great success. Ultimately each coach will work differently but these are some evidence based examples.

Within a goalkeeping specific practice session for Under-13 goalkeepers, I like to use the following:

A one hour goalkeeping session, with the topic of the session being reaction saves.

- 10 minutes warm up – involving mobility, flexibility and footwork exercises
- 10 minutes on the session topic
- 10 minutes possession based exercise – i.e. playing out under pressure
- 10 minutes on the session topic
- 10 minutes handling games based exercise – possibly handball or a game from my games based catalogue
- 10 minutes on the session topic with a competitive element

I might structure a session like this because the sections are short, sharp and intense. The session topic is worked on during three different periods because the goalkeepers will have to 're-learn' the topic, so to speak, and this has been shown to be an extremely effective way of acquiring a skill. Age, ability and time for the session will each play a factor but it's good to put in a session structure that meets the needs of your goalkeepers.

An Under-9 session could look like this:

A 45 minute goalkeeping session, with the topic of the session being diving technique.

- 10 minutes game based warm up – involving all the core motor skills
- 10 minutes on the session topic
- 10 minutes game based handling or possession exercise
- 10 minutes on the session topic
- 5 minutes competitive diving technique game.

Of course, after any session don't forget an effective cool down.

This particular session topic with this age group works on diving technique to build up confidence and familiarity with the necessary movements, although this should be done in a realistic and creative environment.

Another general transferrable age range structure that could be used, on the topic of 1v1s:

- Practice 1 – prescribed exercise on 1v1s to build technique, confidence and familiarity
- Practice 2 – distribution based exercises
- Practice 3 – 1v1 exercises that focus on the random, varied and unpredictable aspect of this goalkeeping topic
- Practice 4 – reaction based goalkeeping handling exercise
- Practice 5 – games based exercise on 1v1 situations

If time is of the essence and you have a short session and want to focus on 1v1s then take out practices 2 and 4. Another structured approach would be to start and end with a games based or variable exercise, and in between work on a technique in isolation. This is particularly good for those goalkeepers who are familiar with a technique but looking to groove and consolidate it.

Something I've found that works well is to break away from the session topic and do a totally different skill, providing a physical and mental rest. If working on 1v1s do some distribution work in between practices – this relates to having to re-learn the skill. All of the above can, of course, be tweaked – for example, you could focus your session on one main topic but have different practice types within it.

As there has been a big focus on the use of video within the book, I feel it would be quite useful to show an example practice structure that includes the use of video and the feedback process where accessible. The timings are an example and would be changed depending on numbers, time available and video analysis.

Using the analysis breaks up the session and allows for the goalkeepers to rest and take things such as fluids. The analysis and psychology chapters will have mentioned most of the below. It is based on a one hour session.

1. Warm up exercises/mobility/ball familiarisation (10 minutes)
2. Specific handling warm up (5 minutes)
3. Practice 1 (10 minutes)
4. Video feedback and target discussion (5 minutes)
5. Practice 1 re-visited (10 minutes)
6. Practice 1 progression – possibly a game based progression (10 minutes)
7. Video and feedback de-brief (10 minutes)

The video turnaround is quite quick so this would be used for a more experienced coach using video, or an analyst looking for immediate feedback. What this practice structure allows is for the coach to focus on maybe one particular topic. The advantage here is that corrections, or indeed mistakes, can be addressed *there and then.*

A parting question for this section. Should we practice how the goalkeeper deals without the ball in specific goalkeeping sessions, or wait until they're in their team based training sessions?

Skills

Ever heard the term *hard* or *soft* skills? Well, hard skills are things that are consistent such as a repeated movement (like a golf swing), whereas soft skills are more about being able to respond in different ways when there is more than one technique to deal with what is coming. Goalkeepers need a mixture of both; core motor skills are crucial but these soft flexible, agile skills give the goalkeeper variation so they do not need to rely on one type of technique or movement pattern.

Skill acquisition is a huge area in itself. Examples within this chapter and the biomechanics chapter will serve to aid the acquisition of skill, but without over-crowding the chapter I just wanted to recommend an example book I've found quite important. For reading on how the brain learns and develops skill I would highly recommend a book called *Brain Rules* by John Medina – information on this book is in the reference list and further reading.

Being Prepared

With all sports, a full warm up is crucial. The warm up allows you to physically become ready for match actions, and gets you psychologically prepared for the occasion.

The warm up should include more than just kicking endless balls at the goalkeeper as: a) this doesn't meet the holistic needs of match requirements and b) if the goalkeeper spends his time picking balls out of the net from a continuous shooting exercise they will be fatigued and their confidence going into the game will be diminished. Following on from the broad themes of this book, building more 'decision based activities' into a goalkeeper's warm up is something I would advocate. A goalkeeper should feel adequately prepared rather than going through the motions if you like.

I've seen many different ideas fed into match warm ups. When I was playing I wanted a quick 15-20 minute warm up: a few shots, a feel for the conditions taking crosses and through balls, then finally some distribution methods. Others want a 45-50 minute warm up that includes shots from different angles and with different paces, alongside a selection of match scenarios.

If a player is fortunate enough to have a goalkeeping coach on match days, take guidance as to what the warm up should include. Ultimately, the warm up is designed to make a player *feel* ready for the match. If a player wants to include something to make them *feel more ready* they should ask the coach. In the same way, if there is an exercise that is not felt to work then communication with the coach is needed.

Coaches should ask their goalkeepers to design a warm up that they feel is good for them and which prepares them best. This is much easier for older goalkeepers as they understand their games needs better, so for younger ages a more constructed and coach lead approach would be more effective, although they would still need to comfortable with this.

Chapter 6

Little Tips

- In the warm up, serve balls with both feet – this way the goalkeeper gets used to a variety of shots and through balls from both left and right feet (should apply in training too).
- Don't be worried about serving a few shots wide – this way the goalkeeper can judge the goal area and different paced shots.
- Along with getting the goalkeeper used to general shots from different angles, as well as crossing, through balls and distribution methods, try doing an exercise where the goalkeeper has to make some decisions and adopt different starting positions. Examples of this can be to get the goalkeeper to touch a coloured cone on your call then moving to save a shot, as shown below. You could change the position of the cones as well to get the goalkeeper moving backwards and sideways.

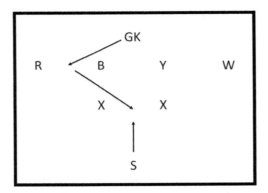

In reality, most young goalkeepers will not get a fully sufficient warm up due to the fact that, outside the professional game, the presence of a goalkeeping coach on match days is scarce. Being physically prepared is very important, but being switched on psychologically and fully ready to play is an area that rarely gets as much attention as it should. Without repeating myself, the psychology chapter will give ideas on how to approach match preparation.

Warm up examples – without a goalkeeping coach

Here are a few tips that you can do if you don't have a goalkeeping coach or a designated coach/parent to help you warm up.

- Go for a walk around the whole pitch with a ball (not around the perimeter but the whole area) – this will allow you to see the state of the pitch. By bouncing the ball and having the ball at your feet you can see the run along with any uneven areas. Passing the ball in front of you can show you the speed of the pitch. **5 minutes.**
- Now do the same but pay extra attention to the penalty area (use the one you will warm up in; this can also be done before the second half starts). Stand in the six yard box and rehearse playing out from the back, goal kicks, taking crosses and coming for through balls – do this without the ball. This will help with becoming used to the goalkeeper movements on this particular pitch. **10 minutes.**
- With a ball perform familiarity exercises like moving the ball around your body and passing the ball between each arm. **3 minutes.**

If you can use a substitute player then do the following:

- Get the goalkeeper to stand in the centre of the goal, about three yards out, and get the substitute player (who's about 12 yards out) to pass the ball aiming past either post at a steady pace. The keeper should take a touch and pass the ball back to them. After six passes each side change the activity to moving your hands into line with the ball and rolling it back. Change the angle by doing this from the left and the right. Like so:

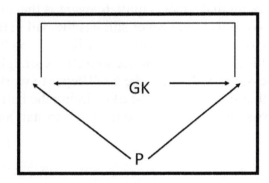

Although the above is a simple exercise, it will get the goalkeeper used to moving across the goal and past the post, allowing them to judge the width of their goal more accurately.

The Importance of Distribution

The research chapter will show hard evidence of the importance of a goalkeeper's distribution in a match. Without harping on about the make-up of the modern day goalkeeper they MUST be comfortable on the ball – either playing short or long, when being closed down, and when having more than one option to play to. Key coaching points would be to keep the ball moving, not get the ball caught under the foot, make sure the passes/throws are appropriate to the situation, and make the distribution easy for the outfield player to deal with. Something quite effective when asking your goalkeeper to play the ball out would be to explain their choices in possession if received from wide.

1st – look to switch the play (invariably where most of the space will be)

2nd – look centrally to pick a pass

3rd – play back the same way, or clearance

Every situation will be different, for younger goalkeepers getting them to scan the play and outline their choices is very effective. Ultimately it's about getting the goalkeeper in a position to play, and then making appropriate decisions.

Here I'll offer some practice exercises that work on different distribution methods. Combine these with traditional work on techniques in the penalty area and team based training (phases of play and small sided games). There should be no excuse for not having exercises that work on distribution.

One key practice point that I feel is quite relevant is that after making a save or dealing with a cross, if the goalkeeper still has the ball in their control make them distribute the ball to a player or target. This will work on the keeper being able to develop the transition of turning defence into attack straight away. Specially laid on practices, or sessions, will allow the goalkeeper to work on their train of thought when in this situation. Instead of claiming the ball, admiring a clean save or well caught cross, the keeper will be prepared to start an attack.

Some examples could be:

- Practice a distribution method back to a server
- Have a target area in a wide position of the playing area (playing to feet or space)
- Build in catch then distribute exercises (the games based exercises have plenty of these)

All the upcoming practice exercises have no grid dimensions. This is because they depend on the number of participants and the particular method of distribution will vary the dimensions required – it's up to the coach to tailor the practice to their needs after reading the explanation.

For younger goalkeepers, or ones being introduced to pressured distribution, give them a 'safety zone' or 'time limit' within the practices where they can control the ball without getting tackled or pressured. This will build confidence and familiarity, but it's important to identify as a coach when to progress them. Usually when they are comfortable. Try dipping in and out of this to see if they can handle a more pressurised environment – if not, simply revert back.

Within each practice session, work on both feet, both arms, and at different speeds. Within a match the goalkeeper might have to think quickly and distribute fast (play quick but don't rush) whilst they may also have more time to pick out the most appropriate and effective option. Something I see all the time is younger goalkeepers putting the ball down for a goal kick and moving back four/five yards to kick the ball. Of course if a long ball is the best option then fine, but initially stand by the ball and look for a shorter option – by the time they've come up to engage with the ball the picture in front of them has changed. The same with the ball at their feet, if nothing is on or there's a lack of movement, then touch the ball either side – this can help change the picture and engage one half of the pitch.

Now let's look through a selection of small practices. The fundamental technical and tactical points will apply throughout, but place great emphasise on verbal and visual communication.

Chapter 6

1. Each goalkeeper has a ball in the grid and must dribble a ball, emphasising the use of both feet.

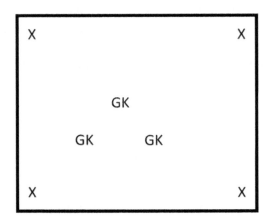

Progressions:

- The predominant use of a certain foot
- Emphasise verbal and visual communication
- Goalkeepers will interchange balls with each other
- One ball can be used for different lengths and angles of passing – one touch, two touch, chipped pass, driven pass. Advocate the use of appropriate distributions based on the distance of the receiving goalkeeper
- The same as above but with throwing – underarm, javelin and overarm
- Still using one ball, have the goalkeepers dribble and clip the ball into other goalkeepers' hands. Once caught, the receiving keeper will then practice the dribble and drive by placing the ball at their feet

2. Each goalkeeper will have a ball at their feet and will move around the grid. When they come up to a hurdle, they will flick the ball over the hurdle and then re-control it on the other side. This exercise works on close control.

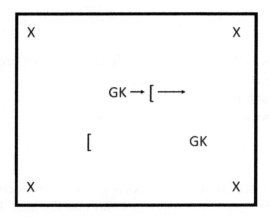

Progressions:

- Add other obstacles such as cones, rebound boards or one-twos with the coach to add variety
- Have a goalkeeper working round the outside with a ball swapping this ball with the goalkeepers working inside the grid

3. The working goalkeeper (GK) will start with the ball. They will pass the ball to GK1, who then supports this pass and plays the ball to their right, or if in a penalty area outside the line of that post. The working goalkeeper then plays a diagonal pass over to GK2 – and the same process occurs. Be sure to work on these diagonal passes with both left and right feet because, depending on the pass, the working goalkeeper might have to re-adjust. This movement and distribution pattern is common with teams playing out from the back. I would usually start this practice with the serving GKs outside the penalty area or 18-20 yards out.

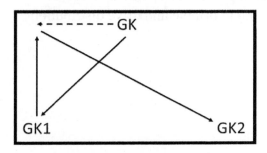

Chapter 6

Progressions:

- Have GK1 and GK2 closing down their pass to put pressure on the working keeper
- Work one touch passing
- Change the position of the serving GKs

4. A very simple practice where the working goalkeeper receives a shot and then distributes the ball to one of the goalkeepers around the area. Each goalkeeper rotates in a clockwise direction – use this practice for working on throwing techniques over different distances.

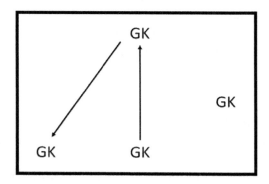

Progressions:

- Change the service to a shot or a high ball or even a through ball
- Have the receiving GKs act as moving targets
- Change throwing to dribble and drive distribution

5. Maybe the most simple of short, sharp distribution exercises. One goalkeeper (GK1) closes down the others trying to get the ball while the others play between each other.

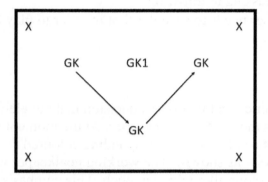

Progressions:

- Limit everyone to one touch play
- After ten successful passes everyone must use their weaker foot only
- Change to throwing rather than using the feet

6. The working goalkeeper (GK) will start outside a marked goal or an actual goal post. GK1 will start with the ball playing a one-two with GK. GK will move into the goal. Carry out the exercise with the GK moving in opposite directions to practise both sides.

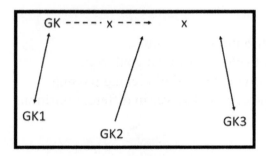

Progressions:

- When receiving the ball from GK3, the GK should control the ball and play it into a pre-determined target around the training area
- Change the passing to throwing
- The goalkeeper needs to save the shot in order to play the final one-two with GK3

7. A distribution practice that involves a decision making element. A server will play the ball towards the working goalkeeper. At the moment the ball is struck that server will shout a colour (the corresponding coloured cone will be placed next to receiving GKs – as shown). The working goalkeeper will then have to play the ball to this colour after taking a touch. This emphasis is on quick thinking and action. This exercise works best if the working goalkeeper has a good number of distributions before switching.

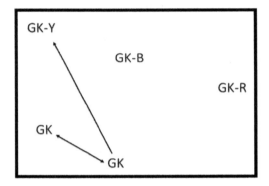

Progression:

- Make the distribution one touch
- Use someone to close down the goalkeeper
- Change to throwing instead of kicking/passing
- Start the goalkeeper and server in different positions

8. This practice has two groups working simultaneously but on two different topics. The inside grid will work on one touch. Due to the smaller size the focus will be on quick feet and being on the balls of your feet to move the ball on. The outside grid will work on two touch play, where they will look to switch play –

the focus here will be on a first touch that enables them to play quickly and scan the play.

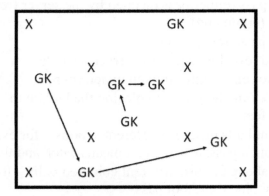

9. This practice has quite a few different set-ups. The group will work around the inside cones in a clockwise or anti-clockwise direction. The GKs working in the middle will rotate to each server performing a different action.

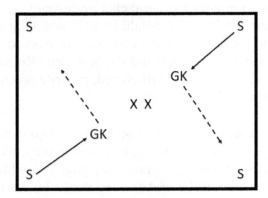

These actions for the working GKs can be as follows:

- A one touch pass (either pass dictated by the server (respond) or by the working GK (command)
- A two touch pass (same as above)
- A control and lofted pass into the server's hands
- A caught save (any height) into an underarm roll
- A caught save (any height) into placing the ball on the ground and playing a pass to the feet
- Have different balls meaning different actions – for example a size 5 ball means one touch pass, a size 2 ball means catch and through back
- Same as the above but use different coloured balls – for example white is left foot pass, blue right foot pass
- Put a save in, for one of the servers, to break up the distribution servers

Some Other Thoughts…

Instead of ending a session with a general chat or de-brief, give the goalkeepers small tasks for the next session. This might include watching a professional goalkeeper on TV and focusing on the technique you worked on that week – so for example watch a Liverpool match and see how Pepe Reina deals with 1v1 situations. You can even set them a written task to write down their thoughts on a particular goalkeeper or skill in a match.

A prominent thing I see in training and matches is that goalkeepers get attracted to the ball very easily, overly eager to get involved in play, like a hummingbird to a feeder. Quite often they leave their immediate goal area which sees them out of position, decreasing reaction times and causing confusion in defence. Having to react to a striker's touch and the visual cues involved is common, If the striker has the ball under control, they are in control, so holding your feet or standing your ground and setting is vital. When the striker is moving the ball then look to creep – but again be aware of the visual cues of the striker's control, backlift to shoot, or body position.

I've not done a section on positioning because there are numerous theories on which method is better – getting down the line of the ball and narrowing the angle, closing down the time the opposition has, or staying closer to the goal line to increase sight and reaction time towards the ball. Whatever your personal philosophy it's important that the goalkeeper stays composed, leaves the goal when necessary and doesn't overcompensate to either side leaving it easy for the opposition. A prime example of this is when a goalkeeper moves too far outside the line of the near post when the ball is close to the by-line or at a crossing angle – this exposes the whole goal, like so:

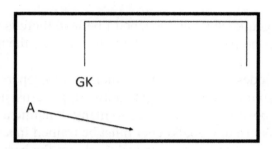

Of course the goalkeeper needs to engage the attacker at the front post, but over-compensating leaves recovery back into the goal very hard as the ball will move faster than the keeper. This over-attraction occurs regularly with through balls and 1v1s. Keepers need to defend the goal first and foremost; tell your young keepers to think clearly and not become too keen to get involved. Yes…anticipate…but over-anticipation can be risky, especially at the higher levels of football. Be aggressive and engage at the right moment – it's all about decision making.

Relating to the above, a number of people have two rules of thumb – a goalkeeper should claim every ball in the six yard box, and should never get beaten at their near post. Now to generalise here is unfair, because every cross and shot is different. Different trajectories, different speeds, different attacker's body angles and different positioning of players. So analyse every situation on its own rather than generalising or employing a one size fits all reasoning.

An element within practice that can be overlooked is the size of goals the goalkeeper trains in. Of course the facilities that are actually available are a major influence, but an experience of mine is that when training a group of goalkeepers at a club, they only trained in 5-a-side goals (this was a few years back). I found that when it came to matches, when they reverted to their normal size goals (full size and three quarter size), they set very low – this might well be because they were so used to defending a lower sized goal where they needed an advantage to get down earlier, and more frequently. This showed in the type of goals they were conceding, which were mostly above their eye-line (Saving SnapShot recorded this). This experience is potentially something to think about!

Summary

Looking at the way goalkeepers are coached I believe there is more we could add to practice that better prepares them for the main event… the match.

This preparation includes training the movements that keepers are likely to make in a match rather than traditionally taught footwork patterns, and prescribed handling drills. The position encompasses so many dynamic and irregular body positions that the modern day goalkeeper must be trained in a more varied environment where *they* can be creative and work out the best way to deal with any given match situation. Remember every shot, or event, is different in some shape or form.

When to work on different goalkeeping topics and how far in advance to plan a development programme are common discussions. Should coaches plan every week, every 4 weeks, every 6 weeks, every 3 months, or even plan the whole season? Every coach will have a different cycle of working. What I would say is keep it flexible and focus clearly on what each goalkeeper at your disposal needs in order to develop fully as a player and as a young person.

A lot of training environments I've seen in the past, or at times been a part of playing-wise, are too comfortable for the goalkeeper and don't leave them striving for improvements – leaving very limited or non-existent decision making opportunities. For young goalkeepers and novices the environment could be a bit more structured at first, but as skill and proficiency levels increase challenge them – take them out of their comfort zone. In training they should make mistakes – if you're learning a new skill or movement this is expected. Finding the balance between quantity and quality is also crucial.

Coaches can get caught up in a methodical manner: "The ball goes there – make this save; the ball goes there – make that save." In reality, goalkeeping is far more complex than this, hence training should incorporate a large proportion of reactive and anticipation natured exercises. In turn, don't be scared by spending a short period of time in a session on the basics (to get a goalkeeper's eye in, during the warm up).

Some of the time, I see a jovial atmosphere where the coach has laid on 'easy to coach' drills, where they know which technical points to teach – and when. I ask you to open your eyes and… *observe* and tailor your training programmes to what happens in a match, making sessions realistic, relevant and appropriate.

7
Goalkeeping Research

"Think Different."

(Apple)

Numerous stories and theories have been talked about so far in this book. But where can the world of goalkeeping go? And how can you implement your own concepts and ideas within goalkeeping?

The vision for this book has always been to provide something different… to show some 'outside the box' thinking.

The chapter will show a few examples of goalkeeping research in a variety of different settings. A dissertation study highlighted the need for further research into goalkeeping – many of these chapters have been off the back of this, with the need for further understanding of the position in general and how it's trained.

Research involving goalkeepers has mainly been focused around penalties and how the goalkeeper responds and anticipates to different kicks. There have been biomechanical measures, but from an academic standing there has not been a whole host of specific testing.

For further information on these studies and whole presentations, contact me.

In this chapter we will cover

- Goalkeeper Analysis Applied Reserach
- World Congress of Performance Analysis Research
- TGfU Based Research – relating to the Games Based Chapters

Goalkeeper Analysis Applied Research

During a placement with Liverpool FC's Reserve and Academy Team in 2011, I was looking to investigate how analysis can help aid the coaching process by filming training sessions and matches from solely a goalkeeper's perspective. The aim was to reflect on the technical and tactical aspects of goalkeeping and feedback took a few different forms:

- Comparison clips between actual and desired performance and actions (using the Kinovea editing software).

- Compilation DVDs that showed how what was being worked on in training reflected scenarios in a match and vice-versa.

- Statistical analysis on distribution using the system detailed in the Analysis chapter.

- Sessions with myself, the coach and selected goalkeepers to float suggestions and perform Q & As.

Working alongside the coaches, footage was prepared that enabled us to build up a portfolio for each goalkeeper we worked with. The focus was mainly on the two Under-18 and one Under-16 goalkeepers but we also managed to get match and training footage of every goalkeeper from the Under-10s to the Reserve team.

Seeing a Match from a Goalkeeper's Perspective

One of the main ideas was to film all matches from behind the goal to get the goalkeeper's view of the game. This type of approach has often been neglected and was designed to open the position up to examine positioning without the ball, angles of support, actions without the ball, flight and trajectory of the ball and general play when in direct involvement. The reasoning behind this view is that the traditional 'TV' view misses out so much action involving a goalkeeper.

During a match a goalkeeper only directly touches the ball, or is directly involved in play, a limited amount of time so looking at the above areas allowed for a more holistic evaluation of goalkeeping performance. For example, if a keeper's starting position was too deep this would ultimately affect their ability to deal with a through ball.

The Feedback Loop

The model (below) illustrates the type of process we were looking to achieve - with continual feedback being given and every point of contact being inter-linked. Everything we did was flexible. (The performance analysis chapters explain this model in more detail).

From the footage captured during training (which included a number of additional angles to the above) one main area was identified for each keeper that he was to work on over the subsequent three weeks. The three goalkeepers actually had very different areas that they needed to improve upon so this gave scope to investigate ways in which the software and footage could isolate different goalkeeping actions.

ISPAS (International Society of Performance Analysis of Sport) World Congress – 2012

The World Congress of Performance Analysis of Sport was held in Worcester, England, in July 2012 and brought together performance analysis experts from around the globe to present the latest research and discuss new ideas.

ISPAS stands for the International Society of Performance Analysis of Sport – an organisation which was founded to improve international cooperation in the analysis of sport. Further information can be obtained at *www.ispas.org*

The following paper illustrates some of the research presented.

Analysis of English professional goalkeeper match actions over two competitive seasons – Implications for the coaching process.

Andy Elleray and Gareth Jones
University of Worcester, Worcester, UK

Introduction

Traditionally the goalkeeper's contribution to a football game has been associated with handling skills such as shot stopping and catching crosses. Previous studies within goalkeeping have predominantly focused on activity profiles (Di Salvo et al., 2008;) diving techniques (Spratford et al., 2009), penalty kicks and defensive technical actions within major tournaments, (Bar-Eli et al.,2006). However, as part of their new goalkeeping initiatives, FIFA have investigated goalkeeper's 'interventions' (FIFA, 2012). The study has scrutinsed forty three high profile competitive matches, discovering that 66% of the goalkeeper's interventions involved their feet e.g: distributions from dead ball situations, back passes and kicking the ball from their hands.

Very little research has been carried out in this area of goalkeeper match profiling and therefore it is the aim of the present study to further add to the limited evidence available and to consider implications for the coaching process.

Method

Match analysis: Ninety two games of a professional English Football League Two level team, over two whole seasons, were analyzed and the following parameters considered: Interventions with feet (Dribble and Drive; Goal Kick; Back Pass; Hand Kick); Interventions with hands (Save; Dealing with Crosses; Throw Out; Through Ball).

Training analysis: A typical week of professional goalkeeper training was also examined through observation. The various training activities were monitored and the time allocated to each area calculated as a percentage.

Results

Match analysis: Goalkeepers intervened over twice as much with their feet as with their hands. Results for the 2009/10 season were: Interventions with feet 69% (Dribble and Drive 7%; Goal Kick 16%; Free Play 24%; Hand Kick 22%); Interventions with hands 31% (Saves 16%; Cross 8%; Throw Out 2%; Through Ball 5%). The following season 2010/11 results reported: Interventions with feet 70% (Dribble and Drive 6%; Goal Kick 14%; Free Play 29%; Hand Kick 21%); Interventions with hands 30% (Saves 14%; Cross 7%; Throw Out 5%; Through Balls 4%).

Observational training analysis: The 'typical week's training' included time spent in the following activities: Intervention with hands specific training (specific shot stopping and handling sessions, 36%); Interventions with both hands and feet (Team based shooting, phase of play sessions, team shape and small sided games, 36%) and gym based sessions (28%).

Discussion

It is evident from the results that there is a clear discrepancy between what the goalkeepers actually do within a competitive situation and within training scenarios. Implications for coaches include: structure of the training sessions need to reflect time devoted to specific match actions in order to create more realistic training environments; Further emphasis required on certain areas of the game (distribution as opposed to shot stopping and reaction training).

References

Bar-Eli, M & Azar, O.H. (2009) Penalty kicks in soccer: an empirical analysis of shooting strategies and goalkeepers' preferences. *Soccer & Society*, 10, (2), 183-191

Di-Salvo, V., Benito, P., Calderon, F.J and Piozzi, F. (2008) Activity profile of elite goalkeepers during match play. *Journal of Sports Medicine & Physical Fitness*, 48, (4), 443-446

FIFA. (2012) The Special Ones. *FIFA World Magazine,* (26), 53-55

Spratford, A, Mellifont, R & Burkett, B. (2009)The influence of dive direction on the movement characteristics for elite football goalkeepers. *Sports Biomechanics, 8,* (3), 235–244

ISPAS Presentation Explained

Here follows a write-up to some applied research that looked to compare the type of events a goalkeeper is faced with in a match, versus what they do in training.

A FIFA study from 2012 recorded the 'interventions' a goalkeeper made during a match, and looked at 43 different matches encompassing various different leagues and competitions at elite Champion's League and domestic level.

The results are depicted in the below graphs which outline the interventions the goalkeepers made.

FIFA Study Graph 1 – Overall Results

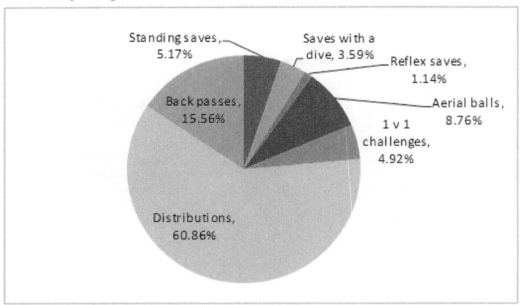

Chapter 7

FIFA Study Graph 2 – Intervention Breakdown

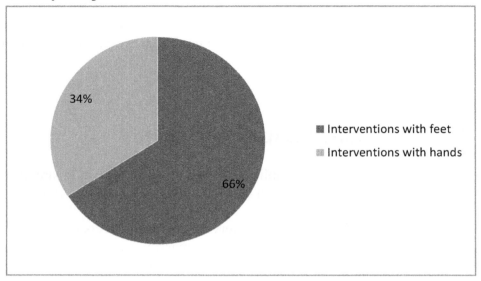

FIFA Study Graph 3 – Situation Breakdown

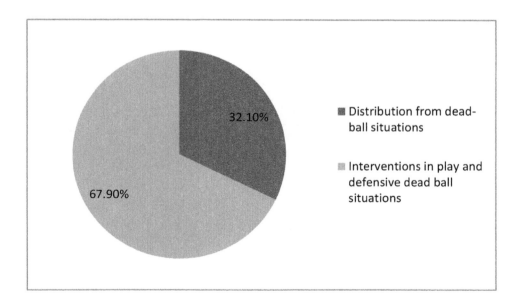

The overall results show that just over 76% of goalkeeper interventions involve distributions or backpasses. It is evident that goalkeepers used their feet almost twice as often as their hands in these analysed matches.

The findings from the FIFA study resonated with a previous study I had conducted 6 months earlier which looked at match actions over two whole seasons and 92 matches using the same team, with the same goalkeeper.

My definitions differ from the FIFA study but on the whole compare quite noticeably – although the exact FIFA definitions weren't available at the time. In turn, although this study takes into account that a goalkeeper can save the ball with their feet(!) a 'save' was classified in the hands section.

Intervention Definitions

Action	*Definition*
Save	Goalkeeper generally makes a save with any part of their body
Cross	Having to deal with a crossed ball
Through Balls	When the goalkeeper deals with a through ball or an over hit pass into the penalty area
Dribble and Drive	Goalkeeper will place the ball on the floor to distribute when the ball is in hand
Thrown Out	Goalkeeper has thrown the ball out
Hand Kick	Goalkeeper kicks the ball out of their hands
Goal Kick/Free Kick	Goalkeeper takes a goal kick or a free kick
Free Play	Goalkeeper has been presented with a back pass to deal with, or receives the ball in free play.

Chapter 7

The results of this study are shown in the graphs below.

Comparative Study – Season 2009/10 Breakdown of Interventions

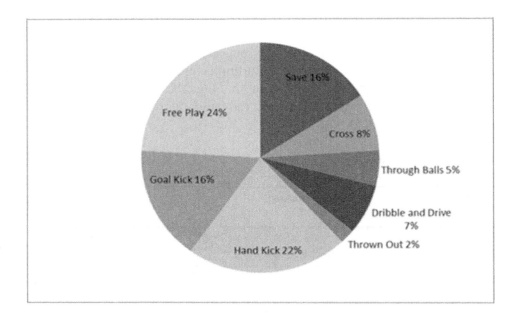

Comparative Study – Season 2009/10 Overall Interventions

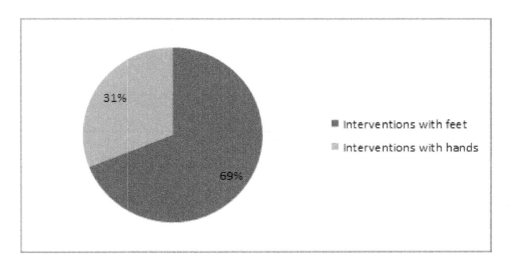

Now let's take a look at the next season:

Comparative Study – Season 2010/11 Breakdown of Interventions

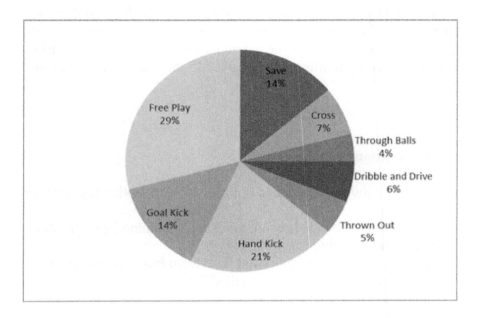

Comparative Study – Season 2010/11 Overall Interventions

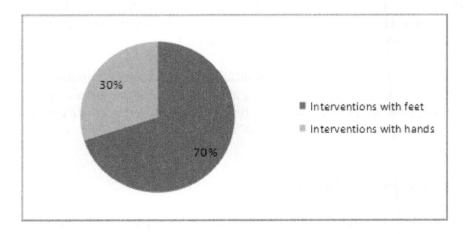

It is evident that both studies produce similar results.

Chapter 7

To deliver a clearer picture and see if there were noticeable discrepancies between what the goalkeepers were performing in matches compared with training sessions - training observation was conducted.

This was achieved by examining designated training schedules looking at goalkeeper sessions, team based sessions, and gym based sessions. The timings of the sessions varied slightly but the average timings worked out to just under 50 minutes for goalkeeping training and just over 45 minutes for team based training.

Training Observations

The 'typical week's training' included time spent on the following activities:

- Intervention with hands specific goalkeeper training (specific shot stopping and handling sessions, 36%)
- Interventions with both hands and feet (team based shooting, phase of play sessions, team shape and small sided games, 36%)
- Gym based sessions (28%)

Those working in football will appreciate that no working week is the same but through looking at, and recording sessions, an accurate percentage was calculated. The technical sessions would have included the goalkeeper using their feet as servers and acting as an occasional shooter.

*As a side note, younger goalkeepers should practice their distribution in handling exercises by serving the ball – although the argument amongst goalkeeping coaches is that this can at times compromise the quality of sessions.

Practical Training Implications

It is evident from the results that there is a clear discrepancy between what goalkeepers actually do within a competitive situation and within training scenarios. And that the vast majority of their match action involvement is distributing the ball and using their feet.

Implications for goalkeeping coaches include:
- The structure of training sessions needs to better reflect time devoted to specific match actions in order to create more realistic training environments.
- Further emphasis required on certain areas of the game (distribution as opposed to shot stopping and reaction training).
- A goalkeeper's involvement in team based training and tactical sessions is of paramount importance.
- Based on the results the goalkeeper initiates the play a large amount of times. They are the first point of the attack. They are a playmaker and a leader of the team.
- Variability of practice should exist to ensure that all match actions are practiced.

A main point from the FIFA article about goalkeeping is worth noting: "It's a very specialised position and the goalkeeper has a very important role in modern football", (Alex Vencel, FIFA Goalkeeper Instructor, 2012)

Overall Conclusion

The amount of time spent training the shot stopping capabilities of a goalkeeper usually takes up the vast majority of a technical session at present, with team related exercises and specific fitness taking up the other part.

If goalkeepers are taking 45-50 distribution actions a match do they need to be physically conditioned differently? Yes, they should be. Most goalkeepers might not be physically prepared for this much action and appropriate practice should address this. A games based approach uses both handling and footwork skills in training exercises, reduces this discrepancy, and is a good way of utilising a variety of goalkeeping skills.

You could further investigate the types of saves the goalkeeper makes within a match to see which are the primary ones – this research could potentially have an impact on the amount of time focused on each type of save.

A goalkeeper is judged on the number of clean sheets and saves they make and it is the primary role of a goalkeeper to keep the ball out the net. So the importance of being able to effectively and consistently cope with the ball is not under question. However, if every goalkeeper in every professional league in the World was analysed through a season I'm certain each would produce a different range of percentages due to the way in which teams play. Victor Valdes at Barcelona would have totally different results from say Thomas Sorensen at Stoke City, based on factors such as team shape, tactics, and opposition and league demands. The statistics, as always, wouldn't tell the whole picture but it makes you wonder are we making training match specific enough for goalkeepers?

TGfU Based Research

I'm now going to introduce some new research into the TGfU (Teaching Games for Understanding) coaching philosophy (to be discussed in detail in the next chapter).

The games based approach promotes more touches of the ball and more goalkeeper involvement compared to that of traditional drill-based training. But can this be proved? Although practical in nature this research is not academically based or formally structured like some of the previous sections – it's merely an observational analysis during selected training sessions.

Aim

The study was designed to see whether the games based theory actually achieved what it set out to achieve. The study was a simple comparison. Was maximum productivity being achieved in terms of the goalkeeper's actions (i.e. keepers having more saving and distribution opportunities)?

Method

The evaluation consisted of 6 games based sessions and 6 drill based sessions from my own coaching, in addition to 6 random sessions from other coaches within various coaching setups.

The 3 topics across sessions were general shot stopping, 1 v 1, and distribution. These sessions could combine other sub-areas of goalkeeping but for the purposes of this study these umbrella terms were used.

The data was collected using hand notation along with videoed sessions where possible; coding software wasn't available to me at the time of the study. For the external sessions I hand notated live.

The time of each session was 45 minutes (+\- 3 minutes for every analysed session). This time did not include the warm up or cool down just the main bulk of the sessions topic exercise.

*within the session there will be factors that affect the time of actual training – factors such as collecting balls and interacting with coaches would be included here. Alongside the above, recovery saves and rebounds were included in the overall number of saving opportunities in the overall numbers.

The participants

My Coaching

- Development centre ability
- Age range 9-12
- Games Based – 4.5 average number of goalkeepers
- Drill Based – 4.3 average number of goalkeepers

External Coaching:

- Age range 8-12
- Drill Based – 5.5 average number of goalkeepers

Results

The results have been broken down into the following tables. The numbers are for every goalkeeper that was in the session, leaving an overall number of opportunities. This number could vary slightly for each goalkeeper but dividing the overall value by the number of goalkeepers across sessions gives a mean value.

Chapter 7

Definitions:

- Saving Opportunity – whenever the goalkeeper is given the chance to make a save that reflects what they would be faced with in a match. Examples include shot catching, shot stopping, and 1 v 1 exercises.
- Distribution opportunities – whenever the goalkeeper performs an action replicating distribution in the session; serving volleys count alongside passing, throwing and set conditions such as goal kicks.

Table 1 – Shot Stopping

	Games Based	Drill Based	External Coaching
	Saving Opportunities	*Saving Opportunities*	*Saving Opportunities*
Session 1	289	148	109
Session 2	306	164	125
Session 3	302	155	128
Session 4	276	139	133
Session 5	265	150	159
Session 6	256	163	131

Table 2 – 1 v 1

| | Games Based | Drill Based | External Coaching |
	Saving Opportunities	*Saving Opportunities*	*Saving Opportunities*
Session 1	301	112	89
Session 2	323	105	78
Session 3	285	89	101
Session 4	259	103	97
Session 5	301	140	95
Session 6	314	133	108

Table 3 – Distribution

| | Games Based | Drill Based | External Coaching |
	Distribution Opportunities	*Distribution Opportunities*	*Distribution Opportunities*
Session 1	228	106	114
Session 2	247	123	136
Session 3	244	97	138
Session 4	198	148	88
Session 5	204	148	120
Session 6	234	131	117

Chapter 7

Discussion

In every session, where games based exercises were used, the number of opportunities for the goalkeepers to be directly involved were higher than for drill based sessions. The numbers of participants in drill based training will affect the number of actions the goalkeeper has; the lower the number of goalkeepers, the more saves and distribution actions.

As discussed in the games based chapter, being able to perform under pressure and keep good habits with regards to decisions about what techniques to use in a given situation is critical to modern goal keeping, alongside how to react to ever changing stimuli.

The study was conducted around the key development phase of 9-12 year olds within football. With outfield players, there should be an emphasis on more touches of the ball and more game understanding... and goalkeepers should be no different. Getting as many saves or desired actions as possible in the time you have is great for development.

The study looked at sessions comprised solely of either games or drill based activities. As discussed in the practice chapter - incorporating a mixture of both games based and other techniques have been seen as beneficial.

Summary

Study one showed how a performance analyst can help support coaches in a specifically designed environment. The main aims of the study were to explore feedback methods with goalkeepers and build video analysis into a daily coaching environment. The more you are able to work with expert and highly receptive coaches, and try out new ideas and gain knowledge into goalkeeping performance, the better. From my perspective, the findings and experiences here helped shape the analysis chapters.

Study two evaluated what actions goalkeepers performed in matches in comparison to training practice. The results provide big implications for the coaching process as studies show that a goalkeeper's most frequent interventions are with their feet, and in distribution situations.

The third study was a simple observational analysis that compared how many saving and distribution opportunities a goalkeeper would be exposed to if a session included just games based practices. The number was far greater than for traditional practice (my own and also external coaching). Within foundation development phases, games based learning can been seen as crucial in getting more contact with the ball and more general game interaction. Not just for technical skills but decision making skills as well.

All the studies look to offer practical findings and give solutions that complement and add to youth goalkeeping development. I would like to think that despite the academic nature they can resonate with coaches and players alike.

8

Games Based Goalkeeper Training

"There's nothing more realistic than unpredictability."

(A.R.E)

In my career I've had the privilege of working with a host of different ages and abilities, not just within goalkeeping and football but also across numerous other sports. I would say - like most coaches - that my experiences have helped shape the way I approach my coaching and the philosophy which I endeavour to follow.

Having taken numerous coaching courses in football, handball, and basketball to name but a few, the content of these courses have given me a platform to build my approach utilising different drills, skills, and techniques from each.

From the outset I will stress that standard technical drills *still have an important role to play in goalkeeper development*. What this coaching concept aims to do is offer an alternative to the drill based sessions - *not replace them*. Training must replicate match situations for a number of reasons but most importantly for decision making – the concept takes specific skills for goalkeeping into different environments whilst still building up skill acquisition and familiarity. A key aim of the training theory is to produce skilful goalkeepers, not just technical goalkeepers. By this I mean that we should be training keepers not to simply be proficient in handling, footwork and positioning in isolated situations, they need to adaptable, reactive, and able to utilise different goalkeeping skills within different match specific scenarios.

It is important, from a physical viewpoint that games are played in a short, sharp and intense manner. Some of the games can be quite chaotic, so make sure there are good rest periods just as players would face within a match – periods of inactivity with good amounts of physical recovery time.

My games-based approach can perhaps be likened to the goalkeeping version of Futsal, where the player receives more touches and time on the ball. Futsal is a fantastic game for goalkeepers for working on close control, being pressured on the ball, playing as a sweeper, and shifting the ball with sharpness - not to mention enhancing reactions through quick fire shooting and saving the ball (not just with hands). Some games involve the goalkeeper without the ball, which has been established in previous chapters as extremely common in matches. The necessary concentration must be applied in these environments!

The games based methodology has been used successfully within many different environments. From grassroots novice goalkeeping centres right up to elite youth level – each level of coach will be able to take certain games from the ones shown with beginner coaches (in my experience) using the games to develop basic goalkeeping skills.

So, let's crack on and get this ball rolling…

In this chapter we will cover

- What is Teaching Games for Understanding (TGfU)?
- Why the concept complements current training methodologies
- What games are there, and how can we implement them

An Introduction into Teaching Games for Understanding

One method of teaching I was exposed to early on in my University life was that of TGfU (Teaching Games for Understanding). Brought to light by Bunker and Thorpe in the early 1980s and perfected by people such as John Allpress (The FA) and Lynn Kidman, this philosophy is focused around the game (or sport) being the teacher with the participant taking a direct involvement in learning. The way this works is that the coach sets up the environment and lets participants make decisions for themselves rather than orchestrating proceedings directly. The coach does so by asking specific questions and setting up game-specific scenarios which often seem chaotic but which aim to replicate a match situation. These questions might include: "How can you be in a more effective position to save that ball?", "By changing your position can you help the team?", "What technique might be more appropriate to save the ball?", or "What commands does your teammate need in this situation?"

For some of the games, lists of potential coaching points that may arise have been included. Although not every single coaching point has been written down – the ones included should give you a good basis to start the games, providing cues as to what situations might arise and staying aware of the goalkeeping demands within the games. Along with these, a few suggested starting points are included, for some of the games, that are designed to put the coach in a position to organise matters effectively.

This way of learning is different to most current goalkeeper training which involves technical practices isolated in the goal or penalty areas. These TGfU games (if *purposeful*) offer an alternative approach that complements current goalkeeping work. Specific drill work which focuses on a topic or movement is still useful when the situation requires it, but it is important to remember that athletes learn better when the environment is realistic.

Much of game based goalkeeper training is designed for coaches who have a large group of goalkeepers to work with. With large numbers it is very hard to do small technical practices in goals, because of space constraints and having so many goalkeepers not working (or only working as servers or passive players).

Game based goalkeeper training combines physical, psychological, technical, tactical and social skills in small situations that a goalkeeper will face in games. These include 1v1s, communicating with the defence, decision making, shot stopping, and more.

Goalkeeping is not just about going in goal and someone kicking a ball at you. There is so much more to the position in the modern game: a goalkeeper must be able to use their feet, communicate effectively with the team as a whole, have an in-depth understanding of football, and prove able to read the game situation. Goalkeepers will be working on areas of their game relevant to their position without even knowing it because they will be made to think quickly and do what comes naturally to them. They will be learning to cope with new and challenging situations in these games and how to work as a team to win points or solve a problem.

It should be noted that most of these games are inclusive for all keepers in the training environment as most of them only require balls, cones, bibs and a coach with a creative and imaginative mind. The other equipment is easily replicated if certain pieces cannot be found; cone substitutes are a more than useful replacement for many situations.

Chapter 8

The Games

For each game listed, the purposes are referenced in the accompanying explanations so coaches can tailor their sessions accordingly. The set distances, diameters and lengths are not usually stated because it will be up to the coach to decide this through identifying their goalkeepers' needs.

If working on short reaction saves then decrease the length of the working zone, and do the opposite for long range work. If there are a large number of players then make areas bigger and add in more goals. All the games are flexible and adaptable depending on the age, ability and number of goalkeepers in the group.

Knowing your goalkeepers' needs is very important, so if you wish to challenge them - make goals bigger, areas tighter, and apply stricter rules such as deducted points/goals or lives for basic errors. This is especially applicable for advanced players, but it is up to the coach, or at times the goalkeeper's themselves to choose the appropriate scenarios.

To make the games easier - simply make the goals smaller, increase target areas or make exceptions for good play to build up a goalkeeper's confidence.

At the end of the day goalkeeper enjoyment, development and progression are all extremely important and through the games in this chapter and subsequent chapters you will find that all goalkeeper areas will be worked upon in a fun and safe environment. And in a good learning atmosphere!

The games will be broken down by name, explanation, the areas of goalkeeping worked on, and finally the setup. Let's begin!

Goalkeeping Bulldog

Explanation

The aim of this exercise is for the runners to evade the bulldogs and to get to a designated area of safety or a target. The bulldogs have to tag the runners, or remove a bib tucked into the runners' shorts or trousers. This is a non-contact exercise.

Goalkeeping Bulldog benefits goalkeepers because it gets them moving and warmed up both mentally and physically for the session ahead.

When running this game - overloading either side can make life more challenging for the bulldogs. Giving the runners a ball to get across to the other side will also test the participants' teamwork and communication skills.

Within the game certain tactics can be used; for example assembling a wall to block the runners which can relate directly to a match situation with free kicks. Goalkeeping Bulldog is also excellent in 'new sessions' where it can be used as an ice breaker to get to know everyone in the group.

Areas Worked

- General agility
- Speed/quick footwork
- Decision making
- Communication
- Teamwork – when teamwork is mentioned, within games, it implies that goalkeepers are working towards a common goal. The coach could ask questions such as "How can your positioning here benefit your team?" or "If you were to pass there, how can your team build up an attack?"

Chapter 8

Typical Setup

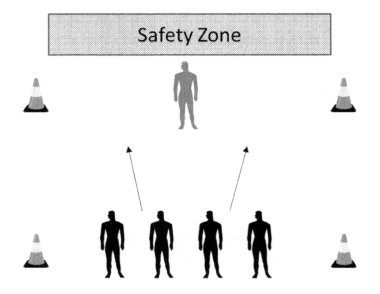

Alternative Setup

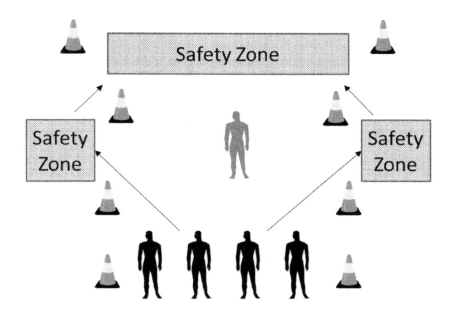

American Goalkeeper

Explanation

The aim with American Goalkeeper is for the team in possession of the ball to reach the opposition's end zone (or to reach an area on, or beyond, the end of the grid). It's a non-contact game. As in a match situation, only 6 seconds are allowed with the ball in hand whilst no running is allowed with the ball - only a pivot step in all directions.

There are many variations of this game, for instance you can use:

- Different sizes or types of ball
- Only allow certain types of throw to be used
- Have someone permanently in an end zone (organising the team)
- Play with end zones scattered around the pitch
- No overhead height
- Use feet instead of hands (no pivot involved)
- If the ball is dropped then turnover ball (working on handling)
- Put a dividing line half way across the pitch – this will make one goalkeeper stay back orchestrating the team

Areas Worked

- Basic handling
- Communication
- Ball distribution
- Reactive agility
- General motor skills
- Communication (specific to goalkeeping)

Potential Coaching Points

- Hand shapes on catching the balls
- Weight, accuracy, and appropriateness of passes
- Diving technique
- Tone and directness of communication
- The challenge of high balls (body position and approach)

Chapter 8

Game Starting Positions

- Coach starts with the ball and plays to one of the teams (varying heights)
- Team who is scored against restarts the play
- If the ball goes out on the side-line the team who didn't touch it last restarts

Typical Setup

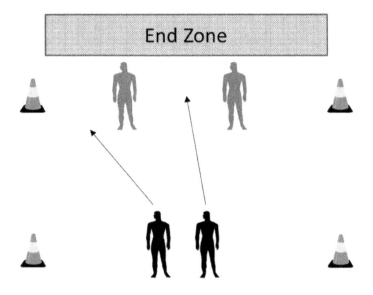

Alternative Setup

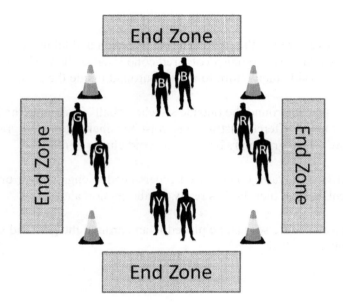

Coloured Cone Games

Explanation

Each goalkeeper moves around the grid changing direction and taking small short steps like a goalkeeper would move. When a coloured cone is called they will go and touch that cone as quickly as possible then return to moving around inside the grid.

There will be balls placed around the outside so when "ball" is shouted the keepers will dive on the nearest ball. Different instructions must be adhered to in the grid, such as "jump" or "get low". Two grids may be used to avoid clutter in one.

This is very effective as a warm up because keepers need to engage their brains alongside physical movement and get their bodies ready for the session ahead.

Additional hurdles and exercises can be placed in and around the grid and specific goalkeeper movements called.

Areas Worked

- Reaction time
- Decision making
- Quick feet
- Power movements

Typical Setup

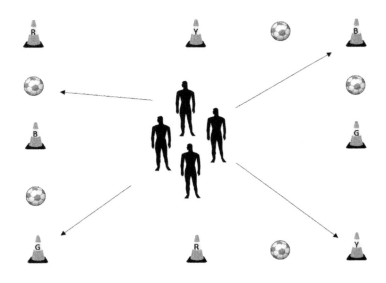

Dodgy Keeper!

Explanation

Like the traditional Dodgeball game, the goalkeeper has to dodge the ball and make it across a designated area.

Areas Worked

- Reactions: With balls flying everywhere the keeper needs to be able to react to catch a ball, move sharply to avoid it, or use the ball in his hands to deflect it away.
- Decision Making: The keeper needs to decide when to throw the ball and how to do it, when to avoid the ball or catch it, and how to organise the team (defence).
- Footwork: To get in line with the ball when catching, to avoid the ball, move towards the opponent when aiming. It is also valuable for getting around the pitch quickly, effectively, and with purpose.
- Handling: The basic catching of a ball doesn't change in any sport - you need to have a basic stance and catching shape to hold the ball.
- Communication: To organise a team as the keeper would organise a defence.
- Agility: In Dodgeball it's imperative to be quick around the area, much like goalkeeping, whether it is saving a shot or coming off the line quickly to gather up a through ball. This game will help develop being able to change direction quickly.
- Distribution: Different types of throws, like those used in a match, should be used - for example: the javelin, or the overarm throw. Aiming at an opponent is just like aiming at a team member, it has to be accurate and precise.
- Concentration: Keepers need to keep their eyes on the ball at all times like goalkeeping.

Chapter 8

Typical Setup

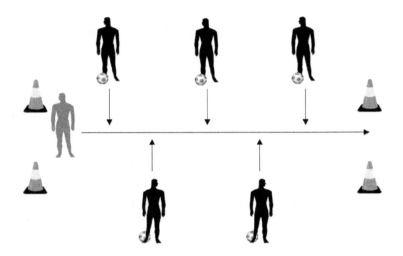

Circuit Training

Explanation

The idea of circuit training is to give goalkeepers a variety of small drills and exercises that will benefit their performance. Exercises like skipping, reaction work, speed and intensity work with balls, will enable goalkeepers to work on their all-round game and fitness.

Have as many different stations as you need to meet the group's requirements as well as any other exercises. Possibly hurdles, speed ladders or resistance methods.

Areas worked

With circuit training exercises, the focus will be on:

- Footwork
- Speed
- Intensity of practice
- Handling
- Varying exercises

Chapter 8

Typical Setup

Each exercise will last for thirty seconds to a minute before moving on to the next. There will be two or three sets done depending on the physical state of the goalkeepers or time constraints.

1. Skipping.

2. Side to side diving saves. The GK sits down and saves the ball from a sitting position.

3. Rest and recovery period.

4. Cone reaction work. The GK has various cones spaced out around them, when a colour is called they will touch/dive on it then return to a standing start position.

5. Jumping and agility work.

- 10 x right leg hops
- 10 x left legs hope
- 10 x tuck jumps
- 10 x star jumps

6. Rest and recovery period.

Goalkeeper's Volleyball

Explanation

Using a volleyball or badminton net - goalkeepers should be separated into two teams. If a net is not available then cones are an adequate alternative.

The aim of the game is to land the ball in the opponent's half, with the ball touching the floor in the designated area.

To restart play a serve is taken which is an underarm throw or drop kick from the back of the court. No 'lets' will be played and if the serve is out, hits the net, or doesn't reach the other half court - the opposing team gains control of the ball. Teams can score on their own serves or the opposing team's serve. Any body part can be used throughout the game, although catching is not allowed. A minimum number of passes between a team will be another progression along with a time limit to get the ball back over the net.

Different variations can be put in place such as:

- Every team member must touch the ball
- You can only score off your team's service game
- Different sizes and types of ball can be used
- Target scoring areas put around the pitch for punch or kick accuracy

Areas Worked

- Handling
- Communication
- Team organisation
- Decision making
- Game awareness

Potential Coaching Points

- Not stretching for the ball – control the body, move into line, and play back over
- Strong wrists and hands
- Timing of jumps and movement patterns

Chapter 8

Game Starting Positions

- Coach plays the ball into the area
- Teams serve back in, after a point

Typical Setup

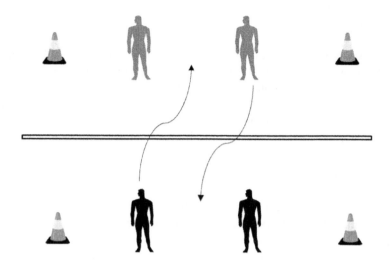

Goalkeeper's Tennis

Explanation

Different types of ball should be used with the objective of throwing, then passing, the ball through the coned goals. Different coloured goals are created with different coloured cones. Each goal will offer a varying number of points if scored through.

Two teams are needed, one either side of the dividing line. Each team has to stay in their half so collecting rebounds and recovery saves/recovery lines will be important. As in a football match the goalkeeper will have six seconds with the ball in their hands.

The game can be restarted by the coach or a side-line ball from where the ball went out. If the coach (standing on the side line) scores a goal against a team - they will be deducted a point. Usually because of obvious poor positional play.

The winning team will be whichever team scores a certain amount of points first, or whichever team has accumulated the most points in an allotted time.

Areas Worked

- Distribution techniques (short/long passes, different types of throws)
- Basic handling techniques
- Diving saves
- Positional play
- Communication and organisation
- Concentration

There are also some variations to the game:

- Different balls
- Points for good play
- Specific methods of distribution, for example only using one type of throw
- Make one team's area smaller than the other team's and see how this affects positioning and tactics

Potential Coaching Points

- Changing position when the balls move (side to side, advance or drop)
- Saving the ball back into play (dangerous areas)
- Not committing too early on dives or other movements

Chapter 8

Game Starting Positions

- From Coach
- Player who's scored against

Typical Setup

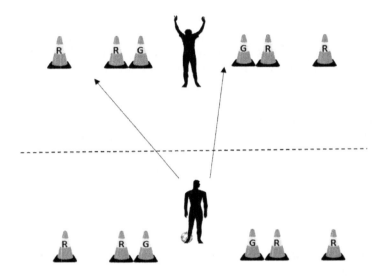

Goalkeeper's Tennis (No Hands)

Explanation

The same principles as volleyball should be used but the net will be considerably lower (or a coned substitute). The goalkeepers will only be allowed to use their feet and are limited in the number of touches they have (depending on what rules are used). To score a point you have to bounce the ball on the opponent's side.

All serves will take place in the serving area; this will be a drop kick into the opponent's area. Two small games of this should be done with players in designated teams but split into equal numbers if possible. The games will be the best of three sets with each set being the first team to 11 points; if the scores are tied at 10-10 then each team will have to win by two clear points.

For progression, target areas can put around the pitch for extra scoring points. Also if the group is advanced, or you want to challenge them, then say that every player on the team needs to touch the ball before it goes back over the net, or that keepers need to use their weaker feet.

Areas Worked

- First touch
- Ball judgement
- Pass weight and accuracy

Potential Coaching Points

- Too soft or too firm passes
- Stretching for the ball
- Not being on toes ready to receive
- Changing position in relation to the ball

Game Starting Positions

- Coach starts by playing the ball in
- Team starts with a serve into play

Chapter 8

Typical Setup

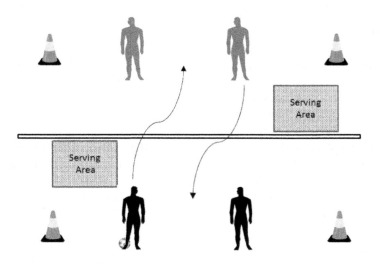

Keeper Combat

Explanation

This game is just the same as a normal small sided football practice except the goalkeeper can pick the ball up and use their hands to pass and score. All players can move anywhere on the pitch.

The rules that can be enforced are:

- Six seconds with ball in hand
- You can bounce, kick up, and punch the ball
- Any team who hits the ball outside the grid loses possession
- After a goal is scored the team who was scored against restarts with the ball or (for a changeup) the team who scores keeps possession
- No rugby style tackling
- The ball can be run with for two seconds

Like a lot of the games here, the rules can be tweaked at your discretion.

Areas Worked

- Decision making
- General motor skills (jumping, catching, kicking, etc.)
- Co-ordination (using different balls; i.e. tennis balls, rugby balls, or futsal balls)
- Communication and organisation

To break up the game, a traditional small sided game can be played with all the goalkeepers acting as outfield players to enhance their game understanding, and ability with their feet.

Potential Coaching Points

- Not moving in accordance with the ball
- Committing too early (especially on a small pitch)
- Players making themselves big on reaction saves
- Commitment to saving the ball

Chapter 8

Game Starting Positions

- Coach starts with a shot, high ball, or pass to either team
- Team who didn't touch last touch the ball, before it went out of play, starts on the side-line

Typical Setup

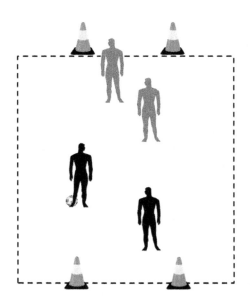

Basket-Keeper

Explanation

The same format as Basketball. If you have an indoor or outdoor pitch available – great. If not - trade the basket for a goal or equivalent. Use your imagination. I've used players as a target to catch the ball instead of a basket before!

Areas Worked

- General handling
- Quick dynamic movements
- Jumping
- Communication
- Organisation
- Decision making
- Footwork

Once again you can add in relevant rules such as six seconds on the ball, and having everyone touch the ball - so every goalkeeper will get the chance to use their skills.

Typical Setup

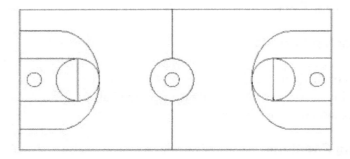

Bench-ball

Explanation

There are two teams with one member of each team on the opposite bench to their team. If you don't have a bench use a coned off area. The objective is to get the ball to the person on the bench and whoever does this will join the person already on the bench. The team that gets all their team members on the bench first will be the winner. If a bench isn't used the elevated advantage is lost – so if using a coned area a greater emphasis would be placed on jump height and timing.

The opposition team can gain control of the ball by intercepting it. When a team gets a person on the bench the ball will go to the other team. If the ball goes out of bounds the team who didn't touch it last will get the ball. Again different balls can be used and the six second law can be enforced so goalkeepers get into good habits with the ball in their hands. This exercise gets goalkeepers used to timing their jumps off both legs - both to intercept and to catch the ball above the opposition.

Areas Worked

- Jumping
- General handling
- Decision making
- Team organisation

Potential Coaching Points

- Timing of the jump
- Adaptable movements in accordance with the ball
- The decision of punch or catch

Game Starting Positions

- Coach plays the ball into the area to restart at any point

Typical Setup

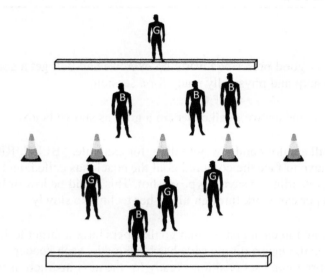

Face and Dive

Explanation

This game is a very good prescribed warm up exercise and will get a goalkeeper psychologically sharp and physically ready for a session.

It can be done with one or two goalkeepers in a grid, as shown below.

The coach will call a colour and a way to dive, for example, "BLUE, RIGHT". The goalkeeper will have to face the coloured goal the coach has called, and then dive in the called direction pretending to save a type of shot. This could be low or high and without a ball the goalkeeper can work through his or her technique slowly.

A ball will be located in each goal so that goalkeepers have a target to fix their eyes on when facing the goal. Once a diving save has been made, each keeper will recover quickly into an upright and set position - ready for the next instruction from the coach.

This exercise can also be done with servers at each goal working the goalkeeper in the grid. This will work both the goalkeeper and the server psychologically as the servers will also have to concentrate and respond appropriately to the coach's call to produce the correct serve.

If there is a group of six, have the goalkeeper *not* in the exercise doing ball familiarity exercises and keep swapping the servers and the working goalkeeper.

Areas Worked

- Diving technique
- Concentration and attention
- Reaction time

Typical Setup

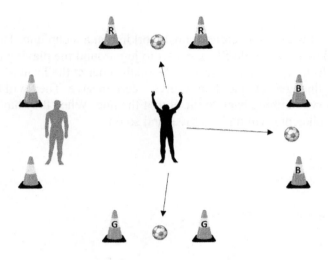

Follow the Keeper

Explanation

Again this is a good warm up exercise whilst working on a technique. The working goalkeepers will line up in single file and start to jog around the playing area. When "GO" is shouted from the coach, or server, the goalkeeper at the front of the line will advance from the line, get set, and then receive a certain save. They will then throw the ball back to the server and jog back to the end of the line. When they have completed this action the next goalkeeper will make a save, and so on.

Typical Setup

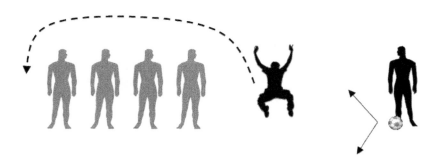

Lines

Explanation

The aim of the game is to work on diving technique when saving low shots, making collapse saves and high handed saves.

The goalkeepers will be lined up facing one working goalkeeper, who will then proceed to work along the line receiving a diving save (the direction is up to the server) all the way along, and then on the way back.

For the coach the key thing is to get the working goalkeeper to stand up quickly and set in line with the next ball. Because the working goalkeeper doesn't know which direction the ball is going they must not anticipate and gamble.

Typical Setup

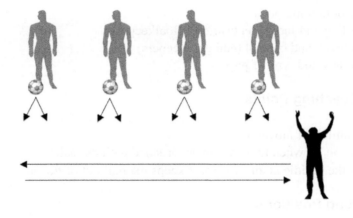

Piggy in the Middle

Explanation

The goalkeeper at either end must get the ball over to the goalkeeper at the opposite end, using one method of distribution at a time. For example, it could be ground kicking a stationary ball, throwing, or a moving ball where a lay-off would be provided by the goalkeeper in the middle. The goalkeeper in the middle will have a designated area to stay in.

The goalkeeper in the middle will try and stop the ball; if they succeed they will get one point. If the goalkeeper at either end gets the ball over to the opposite side this is again worth one point. The winner will be the goalkeeper with the most points once everyone has been in each position. For progressions you could change the position of the middle goalkeeper's area plus increase or decrease the size of the grid.

Areas Worked

- Distribution methods
- Handling and judgement (middle goalkeeper)
- First touch and control (end goalkeepers)
- Accuracy and type of passes

Potential Coaching Points

- The timing of movements
- Decision on when to move, in accordance with the ball
- How the middle goalkeeper best keeps the ball out of the net

Game Starting Positions

- Coach plays the ball to either end player
- Goalkeeper in the middle starts with the ball, plays to either end player (underarm roll or pass), and has to react off their first touch

Typical Setup

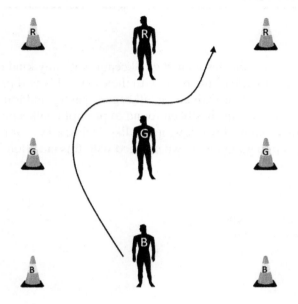

Back Ball/Knees

Explanation

The aim of the game is for the designated goalkeeper, with any kind of ball, to touch their opponents on the middle of the back with their ball. This will promote staying 'face on' to the ball at all times. Alternatively, goalkeepers can try and touch each other on the knees, both front and back. This has been found to prompt goalkeepers into getting into a lower stance with their hands down low, much like facing a 1v1, or a close range shot. This will get keepers into good habits when faced with this situation in a match.

Areas Worked

- Concentration/awareness
- Different set positions
- Quick feet

Typical Setup

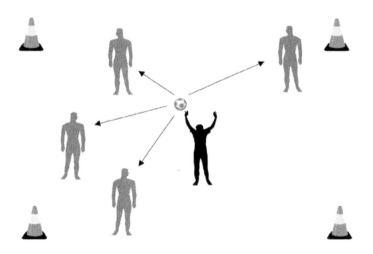

Further progressions are that a ball can be added for the team to pass or throw around while the goalkeeper who is 'in the middle' is trying to go about his job. Another progression sees each goalkeeper having a ball and trying to 'tag' each other on the back or knees.

Keeper's Union

Explanation

This mini game is a great way to finish off any session! The group is divided into two sides with one occupying each half. The idea is to try and score as many goals as possible in a set time. This can be done by whatever means necessary as long as each team stays in their own half. The goalkeepers on each team can pass between themselves if they desire (changing the angles and distances) or they can go straight for goal once they produce a save. A group of balls will be placed by either goal to ensure a quick turnaround with each team taking alternate shots.

To keep things interesting you can introduce uneven teams (2v4) or change the distance in one half by making it shorter or longer.

Areas Worked

- Decision making
- Shot stopping (parrying, deflecting and catching)
- Concentration
- Appropriate positioning
- Reactions

Potential Coaching Points

- Moving into line with the ball
- Staying square onto the ball
- Can the goalkeeper make an early decision on how to deal with the ball
- Commitment of wanting to keep the ball out

Game Starting Positions

- Coach takes a shot at either team
- Coach plays a pass into a team who controls and shoots
- Coach plays a high ball into either area
- One team starts with the ball, and plays it over to the other team who then start the game after their first touch

Chapter 8

Typical Setup

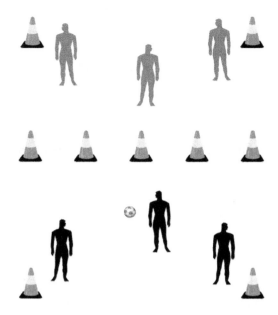

Alternative Setups

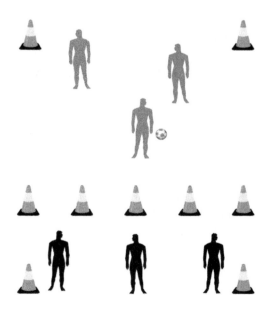

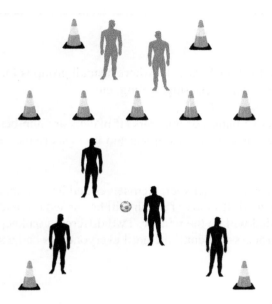

The winning team is the one that scores the most goals in the time allowed. Alternatively the winning team could be the one that produces the most saves, it's up to you!

Mini Match

Explanation

Mini Match is similar to "Quick Attack" where a small group is located in an end grid performing an exercise such as passing, saving, etc.

When the coach calls two names or numbers (if players are numbered up) the keepers must advance together towards the two goals and try to score past either of the goalkeepers.

These two 'attackers' can pass between themselves and have a maximum of six seconds to have an attempt on goal. Rounds of seven will be carried out and the goalkeeper with the least goals conceded will be the winner. Two different goalkeepers will be selected to go in goal, and this process will continue until everyone has had a spell in goal.

Areas Worked

- Decision making
- Shot stopping (parrying, deflecting and catching)
- Anticipation
- Positioning in relation to the ball

Potential Coaching Points

- Does the goalkeeper take up an appropriate position in relation to the ball
- Are they on the front foot when the ball is being played around in the grid
- Handling techniques
- Skilful saves
- Being hard to beat

Game Starting Positions

- Game will always start with the players in the grid passing the ball around

Typical Setup

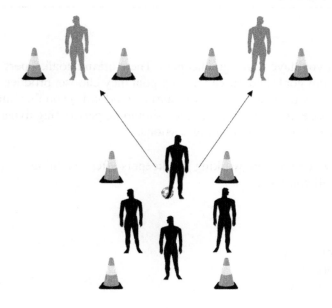

A progression of this game can be where there is one attacker and one defender from the grid, thus adding a communication and organisational element to the game. Also only one goal might be used so the working goalkeeper has a chance to work closely with one defender. However, this would work better with a smaller group so each goalkeeper gets more turns being in goal and can practice the skills mentioned earlier.

Warm Up Goals

Explanation

A great exercise if you have four+ goalkeepers. The working goalkeepers will start in the middle of all the mini goals and move into any goal they choose, produce a save (one that has been stated by the coach before the start or randomly) and then move onto any other goal they choose. In between saves they should be performing dynamic stretches and movements relevant to the upcoming sessions.

The servers will switch with the working goalkeepers after two minutes (for example) and this process will continue.

Areas Worked

- Cup, W, or Scoop
- Low handed dive
- High handed dive
- High ball
- Pass into left or right foot
- Control volley back to server
- 2 diving saves (1 each side or 2 consecutive)
- Dynamic stretches and movements

Typical Setup

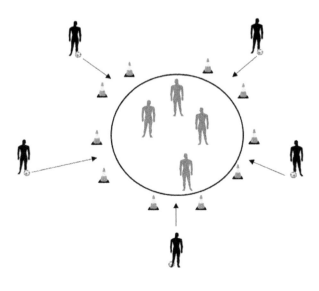

Touch Rugby

Explanation

Each team attacks an end trying to place a Rugby ball down on the ground behind an end line. If anyone is touched during the game whilst holding the ball they must place the ball on the ground and pass the ball back between their legs to another team member.

The ball is not allowed to go forward, if this occurs the ball will be turned over. A ball going out of play will result in the ball being given to the team who was not in possession last. The ball is also not allowed to be kicked at any point.

The winning team at the end of the allotted time will be the one with the most points.

Areas Worked

- Basic handling
- Quick explosive footwork
- Communication
- Decision making
- General motor skills

Potential Coaching Points

- The timing of movements
- Acceleration with the ball (speed)
- Is the goalkeeper's feet quick when moving
- Can the goalkeepers mirror movements and get into line with the ball

Game Starting Positions

- Either team starts with the ball
- One team plays the ball to the other and the game begins
- Coach plays a high ball in that's contested between both teams

Chapter 8

Typical Setup

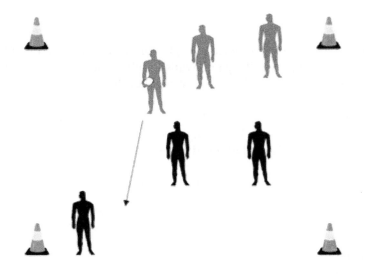

Keeping with the Hands

Explanation

On a small pitch (depending on numbers) goalkeepers will be placed in even teams attacking the opposite goal. The only difference between this game and a standard small sided game is that tackling is done with the hands. When the ball is won the goalkeeper must place the ball at their feet and try to score in the opposition's goal.

Each team will have a designated goalkeeper in their goal that rotates at the coach's discretion, or players can move freely wherever they please. Side-line and goal kicks are taken with the hands using an under-arm roll. The team with the most goals wins, or alternatively the team who makes the most clean 1v1 takes will win.

Areas Worked

- 1v1 situations
- Building confidence and timing
- Decision making

Potential Coaching Points

- Not committing
- Staying big and delaying the attacker
- Moving in accordance with the ball
- Can the goalkeepers use controlled aggression

Game Starting Positions

- Coach starts with the ball and plays to one of the teams (varying heights)
- Either team starts with the ball
- If scored against, that teams starts with the ball
- Side-line balls start with the team who did not touch it last

Chapter 8

Typical Setup

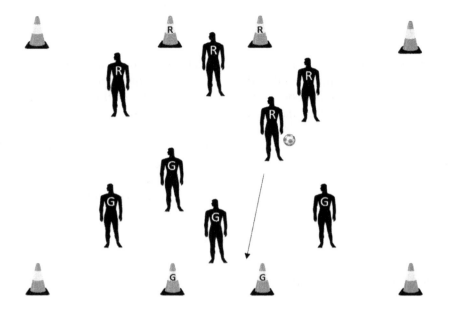

9

Games Based Handling and Shot Stopping

Handling and Shot Stopping will be the main focus of the games in this chapter although other areas of goalkeeping will be worked on throughout. These will be listed in the 'Areas Worked' sections.

Four Goal Game

Explanation

The aim of the game is to score as many goals in the opposition's goal(s) as possible. One goal scored equals one point. The goalkeeping group will be divided into four teams each defending a coloured goal. If you have a team of four players then one goal per keeper can be used. If you have an odd number of players, assign two goals to individual players.

You score by throwing or passing the ball on the floor, into the goal, although it may be preferable to choose just one method at a time to avoid confusion. Whoever concedes a goal will restart with the ball between their goals. You may handle the ball anywhere on the pitch. A good way to start the practice is to say that a goal can only be scored by dribbling past the goalkeeper – this way the participants will get a feel for the environment.

If the ball goes out of play then the ball will go back to the coach or the person who retrieves the ball. Double points can be scored at the coach's discretion, for example if he asks for a certain type of throw to be used. If the grid is made small then reaction saves can be worked on; when a goalkeeper gains control of the ball in such a small area they should be told to shoot early and from close range.

Different types and sizes of ball can be used to keep the goalkeepers on their toes. Tennis balls are good to use for this game because the emphasis will be very much on assured handling and control.

Many or fewer goals can be used depending on the number of goalkeepers or equipment available.

Areas Worked

- Basic handling techniques
- Positioning
- Short distribution
- Reactions
- Concentration

Potential Coaching Points

- Reaction saves
- Positioning
- Reaction off the attackers' first touch
- Not committing on 1v1s
- Recovery saves after initial contact
- Concentration when ball is in play

Game Starting Positions

- Coach plays to one of the goalkeepers who starts the game
- Coach shoots at any of the goalkeepers
- Coach plays a high ball to one of the goalkeepers
- Coach plays the ball into the middle for a contest
- Coach plays a pass to one goalkeeper, who then has to pass to another goalkeeper with the game starting off their touch

Typical Setup

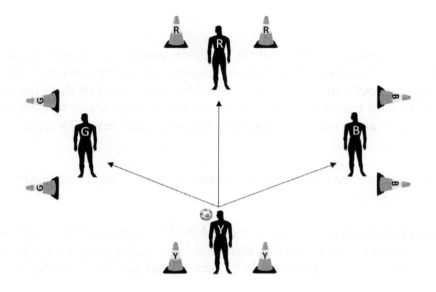

Triangle Goal Game

Explanation

The coach will call a coloured goal for the goalkeeper to move into – to save a shot. When a save is completed the same process will be repeated until the working goalkeeper's turn is over; this could be any number of shots depending on the intensity of the exercise and the numbers the coach wants to work with. Also, to keep practice realistic (especially for older goalkeepers) keep the service varied.

Different sized balls can be used once again so the goalkeeper has to adjust their technique accordingly.

Along with coloured cones, the coach could decide to rename the colours with things associated to that colour, for example, in the below diagram the blue goal could be called 'sea', the green could be 'grass', and the yellow could be 'sun'.

As another progression the coach could name the goals as things that are *not* associated with that colour to really test the goalkeeper's thinking and decision making skills, for example the blue goal could be called 'car', the green could be 'train', and the yellow could be 'plane'.

This game can also be set up with more than three goals, with the same principles and setup used. Remember to keep this game short and sharp – with no more than a minute of action. For younger keepers you might want to slow the game down to focus on particular technical coaching points.

Areas Worked

- Reactions
- Basic handling techniques
- Low/high diving save
- Short explosive movements

Typical Setup

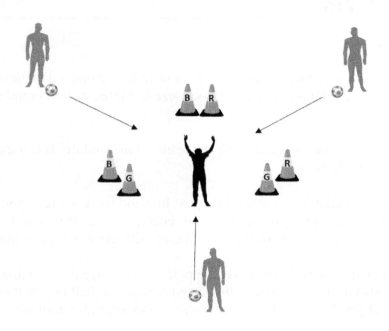

Double Team

Explanation

There are three teams with varying numbers of team members depending on the group's size. Two team members is a good size but three or four could also be used.

Two teams go into the end goals with the team 'in the middle' being the main shot stopping workers.

An end team will take a shot from their goal line and try to score against the middle goalkeepers; if they do so they will receive a point. If they also manage to score against the team in the opposite goal they will receive three points.

The middle goalkeepers will receive one point if they save the shot and parry it outside the grid into a safe area. If they keep hold of the ball before it goes out then they will get three points. Any recovery saves after an initial save will count as well.

The coach or goalkeepers can decide the target time in the middle and how far apart the goals are. If an aim is to work on reaction saves then bring the goals closer together.

The two end goals can be a real goal net with the middle goal being cones. If cones are used then head height rules will apply in the middle. If cones are only used then head height (or a pre-determined height) should apply to all goals.

The team with the most points after each team has been in the middle will be the winner.

Areas Worked

- Shot stopping/parrying/deflecting
- Reaction saves
- Recovery saves
- Top hand saves
- Kicking
- Concentration

Potential Coaching Points

- Are the goalkeepers' saves effective
- Positioning in relation to the ball
- Reaction off the attackers' first touch
- Concentration when team at the opposite end has the ball
- Can the middle goalkeeper be brave and aggressive
- Stay chest on to the ball in middle

Game Starting Positions

- Coach plays to one of the end teams for a shot
- Coach shoots at one of the end teams who then start with a shot
- Coach plays a high ball to the end teams, they claim then take a shot
- Coach plays a pass to middle goalkeepers who then pass to end goalkeepers, reacting off their touch

Typical Setup

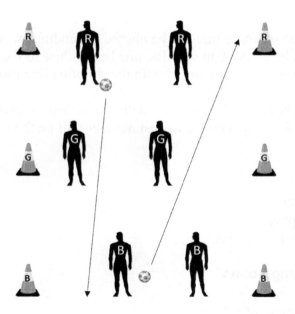

Quick Attack

Explanation

The aim for the goalkeeper in this game is to get into the correct position to save an oncoming shot. The goalkeeper should work on getting into line with the ball and set when the attackers are preparing to shoot.

The game works with the non-working goalkeepers in a grid either passing the ball between themselves or performing handling exercises (for example, scoop saves or low handed saves). When the coach calls a colour, the working goalkeeper in the goal area will touch that cone and move into position in relation to the ball and the middle of the goal - ready to save a shot.

When the colour is called the goalkeeper with the ball in the grid will become an attacker and when the working goalkeeper is in position will have four seconds to score a goal. This can also be done without the coloured cones, perhaps making the game more realistic, as the goalkeeper does not come out of position to start with.

The position of the shooting line can be altered depending on what the session topic is. 1v1s can be worked on with the line being close to the goal, or long range shot stopping can be attempted with the shooting line moved far back.

The working goalkeeper will be rotated with the number of goals conceded recorded. The goalkeeper with the lowest number will be the winner.

Areas Worked

- Positioning
- Shot stopping
- Parrying into safe areas

Potential Coaching Points

- Re-adjustment of position
- Can the goalkeeper take up an effective position
- Being set and balanced upon impact of the ball

Game Starting Positions

- Game always starts from the grid

Typical Setup

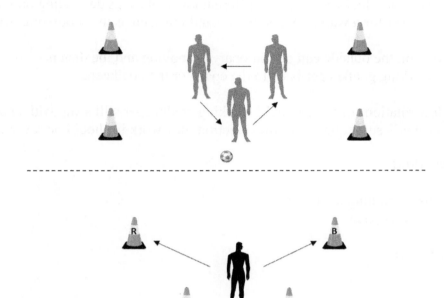

The shooting line can vary as discussed above.

The Circle of Saves

Explanation

There will be one goalkeeper in the middle and the others in a circle formation around him or her. The working goalkeeper will go around the circle either clockwise or anti-clockwise making different kinds of saves depending on the session topic (or for a warm up, just basic handling such as the scoop or cup).

The servers on the outside can be stationary or moving and the distance away from the working goalkeeper is up to the coach or the goalkeeper.

After a few rotations of the circle the working goalkeeper will swap with another. On any keeper's subsequent turn the direction they work in should be reversed.

Areas Worked

- Basic handling techniques
- Recovery saves

Typical Setup

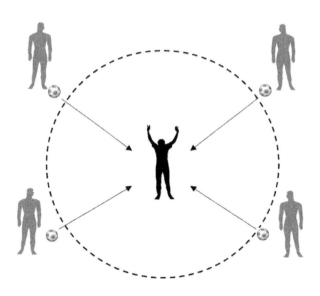

Team Keeper

Explanation

Each goalkeeper will start in a goal but is free to move around the pitch and use their hands in the whole area. However, they are not allowed behind their goal into the area 'in-between the goals'. This area will be cordoned off by cones in the middle.

The outfield players will be aiming to score, and if they do so they will get a point. They will be passing between themselves, changing angles and distances, but keeping the tempo high at match pace. If the goalkeepers claim the ball or make a save that goes outside the grid (or is of high enough quality to merit a point) then they will gain one point.

The ball is only dead when the goalkeeper has two hands on the ball or the ball leaves the playing area. If a goal is scored, for example, and the ball is kept in the playing area - the game continues.

If any goalkeeper enters the coned off area, they will be deducted a point. It's up to the coach to determine what points total will be the target for both teams.

The example setup has three goals and five outfield players but this can be adapted to more goals if there are more participants. Alternatively the coach can overload the attackers to make it harder for the goalkeepers.

Areas Worked

- Set position
- Reaction saves
- Concentration
- Appropriate positioning
- Footwork

Chapter 9

Potential Coaching Points

- Does the goalkeeper take up appropriate positions in relation to the ball
- Are they committed in making saves
- Can they claim the ball where possible
- Does the goalkeeper chase the ball, or prove too eager to commit at the outfield players' feet

Game Starting Positions

- Coach plays the ball to an outfield player
- Coach plays the ball to a goalkeeper who then passes to an outfield player – having to react off their first touch
- Outfield players play a number of passes to each other before the game is live
- First pass can be free between outfield players

Typical Setup

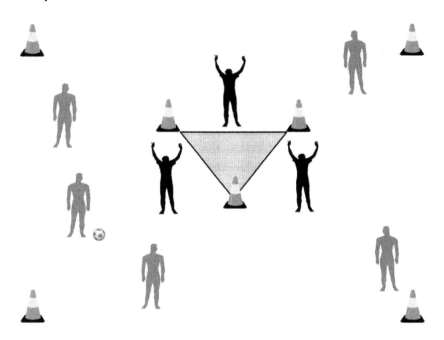

Own Goal

Explanation

There are two teams, each of which has the objective of eliminating all members of the opposing team. This is done by scoring a goal against a goalkeeper which results in them losing a life; all players start with three lives, for example. The setup is shown with six goalkeepers but more or fewer goals can be added alongside different goal positions.

Each goalkeeper will have an allocated goal which they have to defend, however they are allowed to move freely around their own side of the pitch.

Shots will be taken using the feet or the hands depending on the session, but not both in the same game. Goalkeepers can't move with the ball in hand but may throw to a team member. Passing may be done within any team to change angles and shot distances.

If a goal is scored, the beaten goalkeeper will start with the ball, but if the goal means a keeper is eliminated then the attacking team will have the ball back. When out of bounds the coach will restart the game.

The goal height will be up to the coach depending on the age, ability and equipment available but the head height rule is a good way to go to clear up any confusion.

The winning team will have eliminated all opponents.

Areas Worked

- Decision making
- Concentration
- Shot stopping
- Reactions

Chapter 9

Potential Coaching Points

- Can the goalkeepers make reaction saves
- Are keepers set in, and around , their goal area
- Does the goalkeeper attack the line or stay on the goal line
- Head and hands forward

Game Starting Positions

- Coach plays a high ball to either team – they then place the ball down and play
- One team plays to the other who then look to attack
- Coach takes a shot at a particular goalkeeper from varying positions outside the playing area

Example Setup

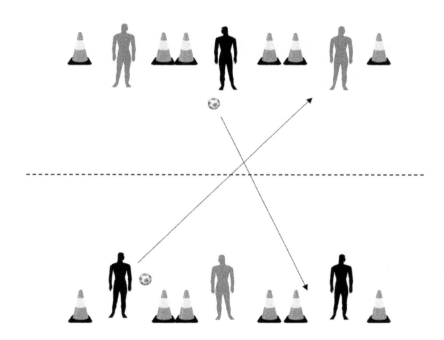

Zones

Explanation

This game can be played on a number-of-lives basis or by a simple scoring system (one goal scored equates to one point). The position of the goals can change; for example, on an angle, close to the line, or further away to vary the type of shots being received. Goalkeepers must stay in their zone. If they enter the opposing zones they will either be deducted a point/goal or give one to the other team. The game can work on the basis of two teams (each side of the dividing lines) or alternatively each keeper against each other.

The rules are the same as "Own Goal" but a target score should be set. Have every goalkeeper rotating zones so they get a taste of new angles and situations.

Areas Worked

- Decision making
- Concentration
- Shot stopping
- Reactions
- Teamwork (if the game is setup as one team vs another)

Potential Coaching Points

- Can the goalkeepers make reaction saves
- Is the goalkeeper in position in relation to the ball
- Is the keeper set in, and around, their goal area
- Does the goalkeeper attack the line or stay on the goal line
- Head and hands forward

Game Starting Positions

- Coach plays a high ball into either team – they then place the ball down and play
- One team plays to the other who then look to attack
- Coach takes a shot at a particular goalkeeper from varying positions outside the playing area

Example Setup

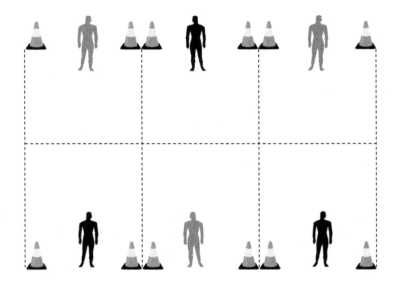

Outnumbered

Explanation

The idea with "Outnumbered" is that there are players/servers (each with a ball) located around a designated area, each of whom takes various shots at the working goalkeeper.

When the shot is saved then the goalkeeper must throw the ball back to the server in order for the game to be continuous (and to practice distribution after claiming a ball).

The outside servers can be stationary or moving. These players will be defined as numbers, colours, animals, etc. to keep the goalkeeper alert. They will take a shot, one at a time.

This game can also be done in pairs with goalkeepers receiving alternate shots.

The serves can be along the floor, throws, or drop volleys depending on the goalkeepers – you might start with throwing for a warm up and then progress to moving balls.

Once again the distance and shape of the area can vary depending on the topic - a small area for reaction work, large for long range, or a circle so shot angles will change.

Areas Worked

- Reaction saves
- Getting into line with the shot
- Decision making

Chapter 9

Example Setup

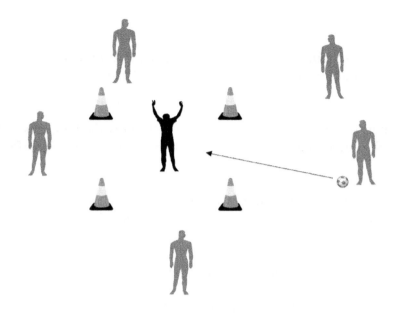

Multi-Goal

Explanation

There are three separate goals in the designated playing area that three goalkeepers have to defend. The attackers will be trying to score by working together to beat the goalkeepers. Play starts from the coach or a floating player outside the playing area; they may play the ball in wherever they wish to vary the angles and types of play.

Goalkeepers score a point for a save and attackers for a goal scored. When one team reaches a certain number of points the goalkeepers will switch so everyone has a turn in goal. The positions of each goal can be changed to create alternative scenarios and to mix the play up. This would include perhaps placing a defender within the practice.

Something that works well is if the coach starts with the ball at their feet and shifts the ball out, in any direction, such that goalkeepers will have to change their position in the goal in accordance to the position of the ball. Here you can work on the front foot start, and re-positioning, after a phase of play.

Areas Worked

- Shot stopping
- Positioning
- 1v1 situations
- Crossing

Potential Coaching Points

- Are the goalkeepers on the front foot
- Do the goalkeepers shift into line
- Appropriate handling techniques
- Desire and commitment to keep the ball out
- Only moving when the ball is not under the control of an outfield player

Chapter 9

Game Starting Positions

- Coach plays a ball into the goalkeepers, who then distribute to an outfield player reacting off their first touch
- Coach plays the ball to the outfield players
- Coach varies their position outside the grid, and plays a ball to be contested by both the goalkeepers and outfield players
- Outfield players play a one-two with the goalkeepers, the game is live after the outfielders' touch
- An outfield player passes a ball to a goalkeeper, the goalkeeper then plays the ball to another outfield player, the ball is then live off their touch

Typical Setup

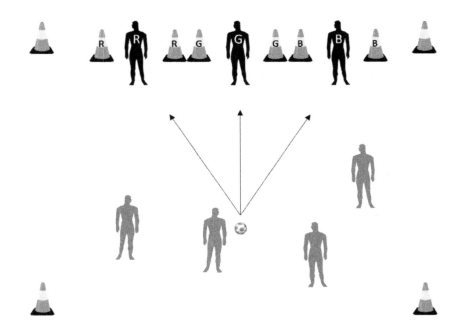

Get To The Next One!

Explanation:

The goalkeeper will work his or her way through a series of goals. The servers must wait until the goalkeeper is set before shooting (or to keep the practice more realistic the goalkeeper will have to set based upon the visual cues they receive from the shooter). The working goalkeeper will have to get to the next goal as quickly as possible. Once they have completed the set everyone will change positions and rotate. Although a speed orientated game, don't let the quality diminish.

Areas Worked

- Shot stopping
- Speed
- General agility
- Footwork
- Decision making

Example Setup

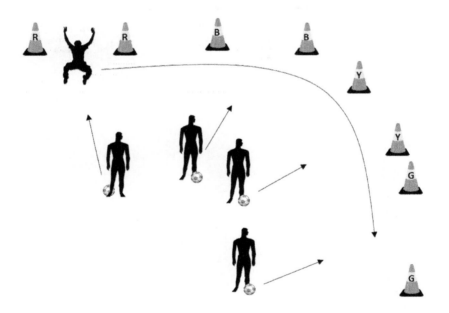

Chapter 9

An alternative set up can be arranged so that, like the first set up, the goalkeeper has to get to the goals as quickly as possible. However this time the coach can call a specific goal the player has to get to. These goals can be defined by colours, numbers, player names, or trigger words to get the goalkeepers used to making quick split second decisions.

The working goalkeeper must return to the starting cone before the next shot.

Alternative Setup

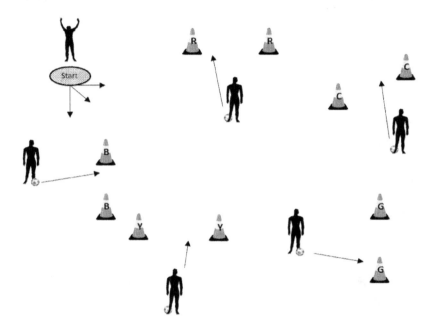

Backwards and Forwards

Explanation

In the example shown below, the goalkeeper will receive shots from all four servers at the first line of goals. He/she will then carry on receiving shots at the second line from the servers (over a longer distance). Once completed, the keeper will move onto the third line of goals. The working goalkeeper should receive a total of 12 shots from three different ranges.

This exercise can be done going backwards or forwards, hence the name.

The types of shots the goalkeeper can receive are varied but in a higher ability group they should all be diving shots working in either direction for varied practice.

For a progressive competitive element the aim will be to concede as few goals as possible - these shots should really test the goalkeeper.

Areas Worked

- Speed
- Agility
- Power
- Basic handling techniques

Chapter 9

Example Setup

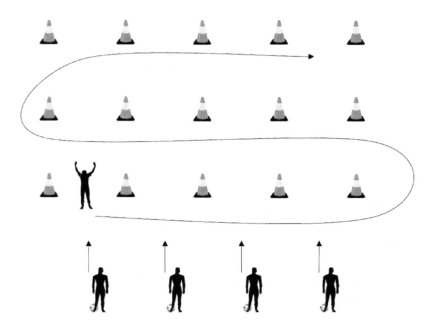

Goalie-Ball

Explanation

Goalie-Ball is a game that has been taken from blind sport and adapted for the world of conventional goalkeeping. It's a simple game where the ball must not go over a goal line following a shot from the opposing team. The teams will score points for a goal scored and the winner will be the first team to a certain number of goals.

Shots can be taken with the hands or feet. Both methods can be used in the same game, or separately. When a goal is scored the team who has conceded a point will have control of the ball. The ball is not allowed to be passed between the team so the goalkeeper who makes a save or pounces on a rebound must distribute the ball. Team zones can also be added to keep things fresh.

Areas Worked:

- Distribution methods
- Shot stopping and handling

Potential Coaching Points

- Saving shapes on each shot
- Explosive, dynamic movements
- Moving up and down the line of the ball

Game Starting Positions

- Coach plays the ball to either team
- The ball is passed between each team, the coach will then show a coloured cone or shout a command, after this the ball is live

Chapter 9

Typical Setup

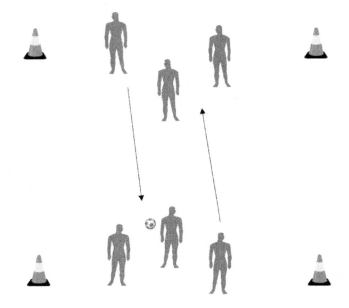

The Pit

Explanation

All the goalkeepers will start in 'The Pit' where they will pass a ball to each other using feet or hands, do ball rotations, or move around without a ball doing actions such as skipping and high fives.

Every goalkeeper will have a number, when this number is called they will advance into the goal and face two challenging shots; if they save both they will move to the winners area, if not then they will go back to 'The Pit'. Depending on the group's size, the number of shots at each goalkeeper could be reduced to one.

At the end there will be one goalkeeper left and they will have been left in 'The Pit'. The game could also continue by having an overall winner through the elimination of the losing goalkeeper every turn. Once there are two goalkeepers left in 'The Pit' at any one time they should both have the opportunity to go into sudden death for a fairer game.

Don't get stuck in THE PIT!

Areas Worked

- Decision making
- Quick thinking
- Shot stopping

Potential Coaching Points

- Watching the ball all the time
- Being set despite maybe being out of position
- Keeper reacting to their name being called
- Does the goalkeeper show quick, explosive movements
- Does the goalkeeper show desire to keep the ball out
- Watching for effective, maybe at times, unorthodox saves

Chapter 9

Game Starting Positions

- Games always start in accordance with the explanation

Typical Setup

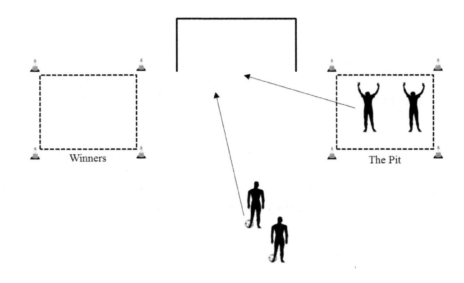

Choices

Explanation

The working goalkeepers (labelled "1") will start by the starting cone and the coach will call a colour. The goalkeeper must then get to that coloured goal as quickly as they can. A time limit (depending on the ability of the goalkeepers) will be in place until the serving goalkeeper can shoot.

Teams of two keepers will be set up and turns will be alternated. The team with the least number of goals scored against them will be the winner.

Teams will rotate, For example, if there are six goalkeepers two would be working, two resting and keeping mobile, and two serving. More goals and bigger teams can be put in place if required. Each goalkeeper will receive the same number of shots; a good number would be five each - then they will move to the rest zone after working intensely.

Areas Worked

- Shot stopping
- Decision making
- Responding to verbal commands

Chapter 9

Typical Setup

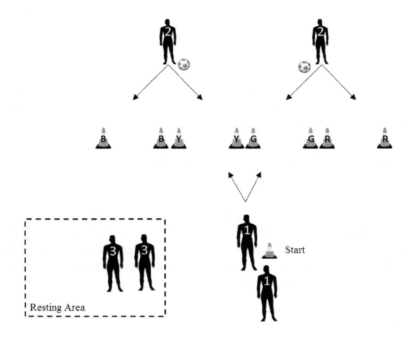

Back to Back

Explanation

The diagram shows two netted goals turned back to back and a small pitch created around the outside. The aim of "Back to Back" is for the players to score in either of these goals, and they can do this by playing the ball anywhere on the pitch. This could be over the goals, around the goals, etc.

The goalkeeper's job, as usual, is to stop the ball going into their goal.

Goalkeepers can work as a team against the attackers and score a point for a save with the attackers scoring one for a goal, or they can work against each other and the one that concedes the fewest goals in the allotted time will be the winner and get to stay on while the other goalkeeper is swapped.

If a goal is scored against a keeper, he/she can restart by kicking the ball onto the pitch wherever they want. If a ball goes over the side-line then the ball re-enters from that spot.

Players can move freely anywhere on the pitch but the goalkeepers must stay in their respective goals. Outfield players, despite being goalkeepers, aren't allowed to use their hands.

Areas Worked

- Reaction saves
- Positioning
- Concentration

Potential Coaching Points

- Being big and brave
- Is the goalkeeper always on their toes, ready to move into line with the ball
- Being skilful and adaptable in keeping the ball out of the goal

Chapter 9

Game Starting Positions

- Goalkeeper rolls a ball out to an outfield player (who cannot score against them)
- Coach plays the ball in, anywhere within the playing area
- Coach plays the ball to an outfielder who starts the play

Typical Setup

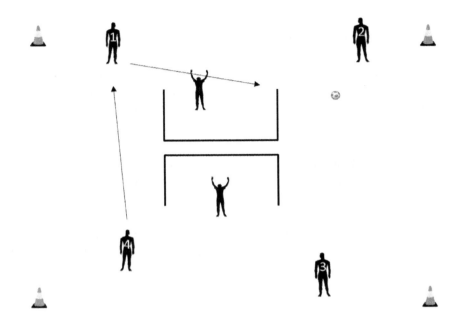

Inside Out

Explanation

All goalkeepers will be located around the main grid but outside the small coned-off grid. They will either pass or throw the ball between each other using a variety of different methods. While this is going on the coach in the blue coned-off grid will call a goalkeeper's name, and the keeper will have to get to the nearest blue cone, go around it, then produce a diving save. As the middle grid is a square, it represents four mini goals. As the game progresses the coach can test the goalkeepers more and more by adapting the outside group's activities.

Areas Worked

- Concentration
- Dive technique
- Basic handling
- Speed (body and mind)
- Distribution methods (outside grid)

Typical Setup

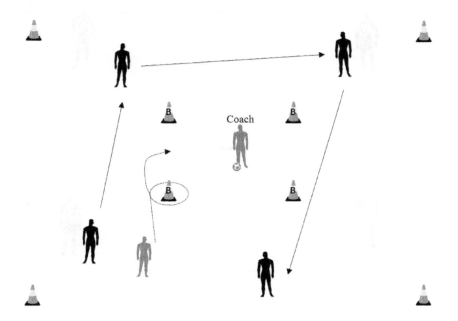

Testing the Angles

Explanation

When a goalkeeper has control of the ball (in this case the green goalkeeper) they can score in either of the other keepers' goals.

To start with, this exercise should be non-competitive, just working on angles, positioning, and basic handling using a drop volley service. But if used later on in a session it might be a game scenario with a point scored for each goal. Varied service can be used if desired but allow the goalkeepers no longer than six seconds with the ball before they must shoot.

Areas Worked

- Positioning
- Basic handling techniques
- Concentration

Setup

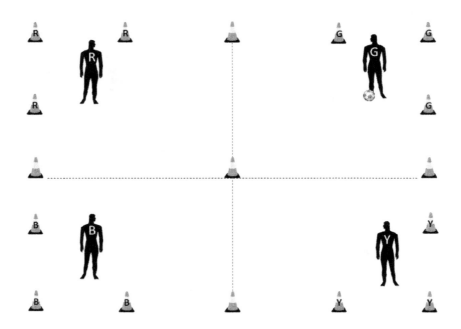

Boomerang

Explanation

Just like a Boomerang it keeps coming back to you!

The game starts with one team receiving the ball; their objective is to score in one of the coloured goals shown. This is done by either taking a shot or dribbling into the goal depending on the topic. Alternatively both plays can be done.

The attacking team are effectively outfield players so can't use their hands at any point. The goalkeeping team can use their hands anywhere. The attacking team can also pass the ball between each other.

Once a goal has been scored, or a save performed, that team then gains control of the ball. They then attack, and the game carries on back and forth, hence the name "Boomerang".

The attacking team can either attack straight away trying to catch the goalkeeping team off guard or they can wait until they have recovered into their goal area, this is up to the coach.

After the allocated time or points target, the game is finished with a winner crowned. Red Goal = 1 point, Blue goal = 2 points, Yellow goal = 3 points.

Areas Worked

- Positioning
- Decision making
- Concentration
- Shot stopping
- Parrying/deflecting techniques

Potential Coaching Points

- Does the goalkeeper make appropriate decisions in terms of their saves, movements, and positioning
- Can the goalkeeper turn defence into attack quickly (transition of play)
- Keeping eyes on the ball at all times
- Being aware of when a pass is played, or when a shot is being taken

Chapter 9

Game Starting Positions

- Coach plays a ball to be contested
- Coach plays the ball to either team
- Coach plays the ball to one team, who then passes the ball to the other – play is live off their first touch

Setup

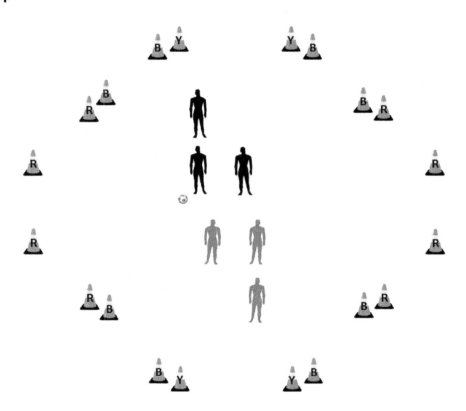

Alternative Setup

In this setup there is only one goal area and the goalkeeping team stay in for a certain number of attacks. Once they have been completed the sides will switch.

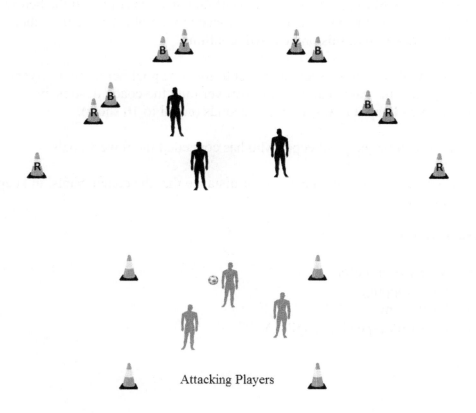

Attacking Players

Back 2 Goal

Explanation

With "Back 2 Goal" the working goalkeeper will always have their back to the next goal. The working goalkeeper will start facing a server (red in the below example) and when the game starts will proceed to the blue server first, then green, then back to red; this process will continue.

The keeper will have three seconds to get to the next goal before that server shoots at goal. This game can last for however long the coach desires, but for quality's sake - keep it to less than 30 seconds (equal to 10 shots).

The winner will be the goalkeeper who has conceded the fewest goals.

The servers can shoot from any angle or distance that the coach wants, in keeping with a session's theme.

Areas Worked

- Set position before shot
- Shot stopping
- Positioning
- Footwork (speed and agility)

Setup

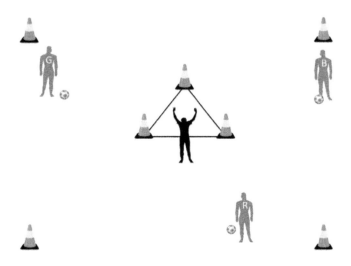

Stay in Control!

Explanation

This game involves the shooting goalkeeper (in the coned area) receiving a throw, volley or ground kick from one of the two serving GKs (in their respective circles) who will aim for their hands or feet. The shooting keeper will then either shoot at goal using a drop or half volley, or a shot off the floor if received with the feet.

The ball is continually recycled from these servers in the circles. The working goalkeeper will stay in the goal as long as he or she does not concede a goal. If a goal is conceded then the working keeper moves to a serving position and one of servers becomes the shooter. Everyone continues to rotate when a goal is scored. The winner will be the goalkeeper who stays in the goal for the greatest number of shots.

A progression of this game is to change the position of the shooting grid or to make the grid smaller so the servers have to be more accurate.

A great way to end a session!

Areas Worked

- Shot stopping
- Distribution methods

Potential Coaching Points

- Does the goalkeeper show commitment in wanting to stay in the goal
- The distribution accuracy of the goalkeeper in the circles
- Being set upon impact

Game Starting Positions

- Ball starts from the players in the circles, as mentioned above

299

Setup

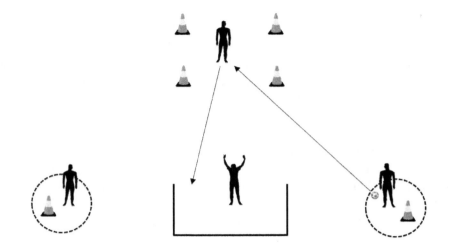

Beat the Goalie

Explanation

The game starts with the first goalkeeper receiving a shot on goal from either server. If they don't concede a goal they will return to the back of either line. If they do concede a goal they are out of the game.

The next designated goalkeeper will then move into the goal, position themselves, and receive a shot.

The servers will take alternate shots (raising their hand and calling) - giving the goalkeepers ample time to get set and into an appropriate position for the server's ball. The serves can vary from a stationary ball, to a shift-out-of-their-feet-and-strike, or even the servers playing a pass to each other and then shooting at goal.

The last goalkeeper not to concede a goal is declared the winner.

Areas Worked

- Shot stopping
- Positioning
- Moving into and down the line of the ball

Setup

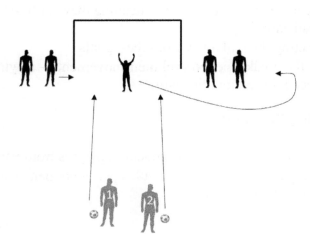

Ball Out!

Explanation

The working goalkeeper has to defend the blue coned goal while the outside players try to score through it. The goalkeeper has one minute to concede as few goals as possible. The players on the outside must shoot from outside the red area and are not allowed to pass to each other. If the goalkeeper claims the ball they should play the ball back to the player who shot at them, but if they parry to save the shot - the nearest player should fetch the ball and then shoot.

Due to the quick-fire nature of this game the outside players should be encouraged to shoot on sight and fetch balls quickly. To aid this, plenty of balls should be located around the playing area. After all the players have had a turn working as the goalkeeper the one who has conceded the fewest goals is the winner. If a tie occurs a sudden death 30 seconds can be operated.

Areas Worked

- Concentration
- Shot stopping
- Positioning
- Quickness (feet and mind)

Potential Coaching Points

- The goalkeeper committing – meaning they can't get back into position if the ball stays in play
- Deflecting the ball away from their goals
- Does the goalkeeper control their movements – staying composed and balanced throughout the game

Game Starting Positions

- Coach plays the ball to the attacking players from varying angles
- Coach plays the ball to the goalkeeper, who then passes to an outfield player to start the practice

Setup

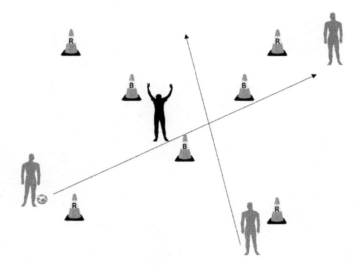

10

Games Based Footwork and Distribution

Footwork and Distribution will be the main focus of the games in this chapter although other areas of goalkeeping will be worked on throughout. These will be listed in the 'Areas Worked' sections.

Obstacle Course

Explanation

An obstacle course can be made into a game where teams see how quickly they can complete the course (whilst keeping the correct technique of course). While one group is doing the obstacle course another can be doing simple drills of possession passing or handling.

This exercise is mainly to work on goalkeeper fitness which is short sharp bursts of movement. This includes jumping, quick foot movements, sharp changes in direction, and power jumps. You can add anything into the course - from using a ball throughout, to climbing over obstacles and footwork ladders. Keep the practices short (maximum a couple of minutes) and have goalkeepers walking before they perform a quicker more dynamic exercise – this will reflect the type of physical activity they have in a game. Make sure they work 360 degrees rather than just forwards, backwards and side to side.

Chapter 10

Areas Worked

- Speed
- Agility
- Athleticism

Suggested Setup

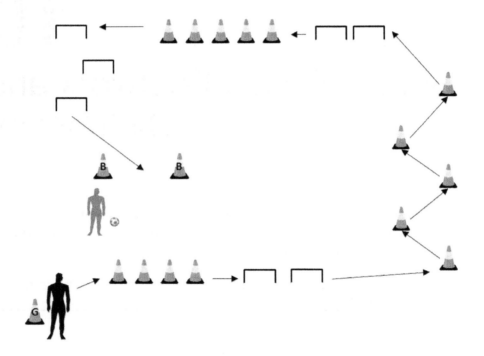

Slalom

Explanation

In the slalom run each goalkeeper will take it in turns to produce diving saves on a stationary ball on the ground; the aim is to work on diving technique for low balls and to get the body shape correct.

Once the keepers have progressed through the ball arrangement - footwork exercises will be done (any footwork can be done; e.g. hurdles, squats or lunges), the goalkeeper will then re-join the back of the line. After the front goalkeeper has done the first two sections of the slalom the next keeper will go. The emphasis should be on correct techniques and not purely on speed.

Areas Worked

- Power
- Agility
- Speed
- Strength

Typical Setup

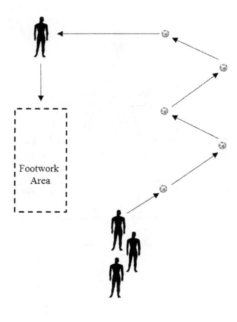

Moving Goal

Explanation

The aim of the Moving Goal game is to test a goalkeeper's footwork within a shot stopping setting. This exercise can also be used to build up power and strength through recovery saves.

The goalkeeper will receive a shot of the coach's choosing; if basic handling is being worked on then shots 'at' the goalkeeper but if diving, collapsed saves or high handed saves are focused on - 'away' from the keeper. Serves can be tailored to fit the needs of the group. Keepers will then perform a series of footwork exercises in between receiving shots from the servers. This can be done with two working goalkeepers each starting opposite each other.

Areas Worked

- Power
- Strength
- Agility
- Basic handling

Typical Setup

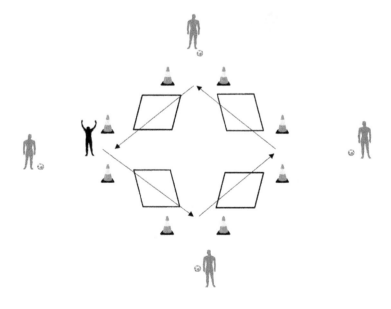

The 'Footlympics'

The aptly named "Footlympics" is designed to test the goalkeeper's footwork in a variety of situations that replicate match situations, for example being quick off the line, and using small steps to move into position.

All the games are timed in some way and a points scoring system can be devised to determine who the overall winner is (e.g. 1st = 10 points, 2nd = 8 points, etc.).

Footlympics: Jumping Circuit

Explanation

The opening game is a test of speed and endurance with a small bit of throwing rolled into the equation.

Aim To roll as many balls through the gate, in one minute, as possible.

The participating goalkeeper will proceed from the start cone then:

- Do a two footed jump over the first hurdle
- Do another two footed jump over the left hurdle
- Retrieve a ball and repeat the process in the opposite direction
- Once over the final hurdle roll the ball through the gate cones to complete a set

Once this is done the participant will then go to the station in front of them and then finally to the right-hand station. Once this is done - repeat the same order until the time is up.

Once the ball crosses the gate line - that will constitute a point; if cut off mid-set – the run will not count. The winner will be the goalkeeper who scores the most points (balls through the gate) in the allotted time.

It is worth putting at least two balls, if possible, by every station, or have someone collecting the balls behind the scoring gate.

Chapter 10

Setup

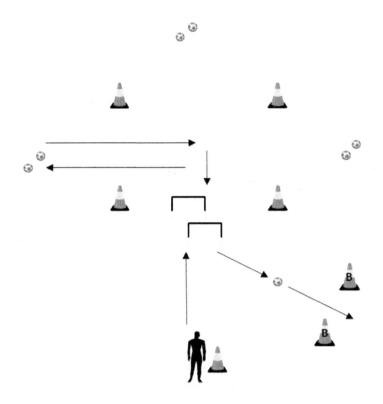

Footlympics: Get The Ball

Explanation

This event will test a goalkeeper's quick feet, and getting into line with the ball.

Aim To catch and return as many balls as possible in one minute.

The working goalkeeper will start at the blue cone and work his or her way around the grid using sidesteps and lateral running. When they are facing a server they will get set, gain control of the ball, then return the ball back to that server. This will be done as many times as possible in one minute.

When a complete circuit has been done the goalkeeper will touch the starting cone then proceed onto a new circuit.

Setup

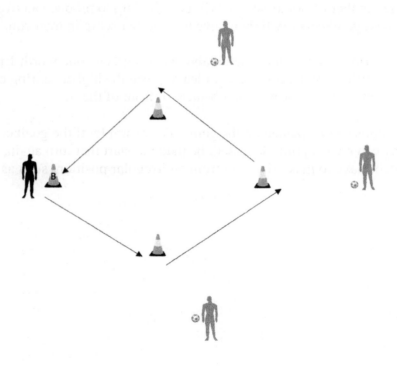

Footlympics: Coloured Feet

Explanation

The main focus of this game is to improve a goalkeeper's quick feet. "Coloured Feet" can have many variations, and adaptations can be easily moulded into more complex and intense periods of training.

Aim To score as many points as possible in one minute.

Within the setup a point scoring system can be implemented to encourage quick and efficient footwork, an example of which will be explained below.

To start - the goalkeeper will receive a drop volley. Once claimed and thrown accurately back to the server the keeper will go and touch a coloured cone as quickly as they can, then proceed to re-enter the goal and receive another drop volley. This cycle will be completed as many times as possible in the allocated time and the number of points scored will be added up to produce an overall score. The next goalkeeper will then have to beat that score in their run.

The points scoring system on the setup above has a green cone worth 1 point and a blue cone worth 2 points. It is a good idea to place the higher scoring cones further away, at an angle, or with an obstacle in front of them.

Other conditions can be placed on the game. For example, if the goalkeeper drops the ball they can have a point deducted, be made to start that turn again, receive a harder shot, or have to make the save from an irregular position, such as on their back.

Typical Setup

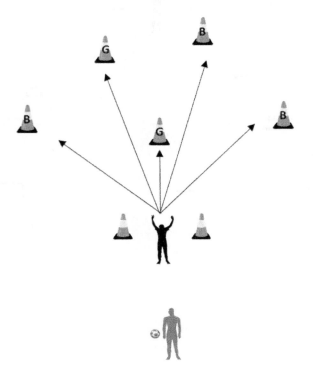

Alternative Setup

The alternative setup is designed to make the goalkeeper work forwards then backwards - as if they were recovering - to tip a shot over the bar or to get back into position.

The red cone in this setup is worth three points but has a hurdle in front requiring more effort to pick up the higher points. The goalkeeper will have to think of tactics and a strategy to gain the most points possible – so this is an exercise that also works them psychologically.

Footlympics: Andy Agility Meter

Explanation

The 4th event of the Footlympics will test the goalkeeper's speed and, as the name suggests, their agility.

Aim To complete the course in the quickest time possible.

The procedure is as follows:

- The goalkeeper will start by lying down with their hands behind the start line.
- The first part of the exercise will be to go in and out of the line of cones (facing at a 45 degree angle) changing from left to right as they go through.
- Once they have completed this they will then work back through the poles any way they wish.
- The ladders are next, and both feet must be placed in each segment or this part will be done again (and the keepers head must be kept up, of course).
- Next the goalkeeper will perform a collapse save and touch the cone with two hands before moving onto the next one. This will be done three times and is indicated by the right hand zigzag cones.
- Through the finish gates to end the course.

Setup

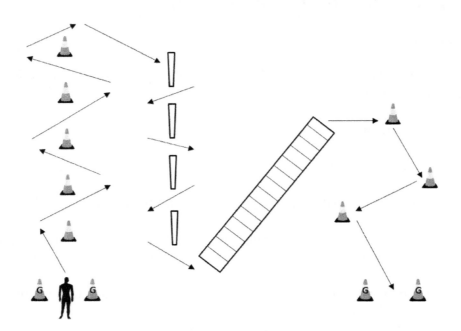

Footlympics: Coloured Batak

Explanation

The final Footlympics event will test a goalkeeper's footwork whilst moving into different positions around the goal.

Aim To accumulate as many points as possible in one minute.

There are two variations to this event using the same setup.

- The coach will call out what coloured cone the goalkeeper will go to.
- The goalkeeper can decide what colour to go to, but they must call the colour before they advance to it.

The goalkeeper will start in between their goal and in front of the starting cone. The coach or the player will call a coloured cone then the goalkeeper will advance to the left firstly, touch this cone then recover dropping off to the appropriate side. They will then touch the starting cone and do the same to the front set of cones. Once this is done the right side will be worked and the same procedure repeated over and over until the time has elapsed.

The points scoring system goes as follows:

Red = 1 point, Green = 2 points, Yellow = 3 points, Blue = 4 points.

The further away the cone from the starting cone then the higher the points value, apart from the forward facing cones which are all the same value because they are equally spaced from the starting cone.

This event will test a goalkeeper's decision making when it's up to them what colour to go for as well as, of course, their physical speed out of their immediate goal area. When the coach makes the decision for any keeper then it might be deemed unfair if some participants always get the chance to go to the higher value cones - but this will be up to the coach.

The ball is located where it is so that goalkeepers are encouraged to focus on it, making this event as game realistic as possible - and to practice not turning their back on the ball.

317

Chapter 10

Setup

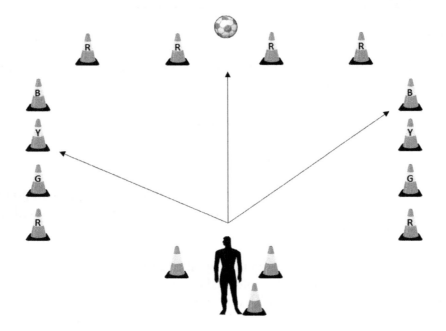

Back Pass

Explanation

The aim here is for the goalkeeper to play the ball through the highlighted areas when receiving a back pass. When the defending team wins the ball they must attempt to play the ball straight back to the goalkeeper, either directly or by passing to create the opportunity.

If the ball leaves the field of play a kick in shall be performed. Goal kicks and corners are included and the goalkeeper has the opportunity to hit target areas with a goal kick. After a goal or distribution by the goalkeeper the coach can decide who and where the play will be restarted to vary the situations faced. If the goalkeeper claims the ball with their hands they can either throw or drop kick through the target areas.

The attacking team will score a point for a goal and the goalkeeper a point for the target areas. Extra points can be awarded for the further away target areas if desired. Also a goal against a keeper could result in a point deduction for the goalkeeper.

The circular area is a small sided game, using the other goalkeepers (or outfield players if available).This is usually 2v2 or 3v3 so the working keeper will get plenty of exposure to backpasses.

The target areas are located where they are to encourage the goalkeeper to look wide. The areas could be moved depending on your team's tactics or other specifications. Remember – when leaving the width of your goal posts make sure there is eye contact with the player who is playing a back pass to you.

Areas Worked

- Back passes
- Support positions
- Distribution in general
- Tactical understanding
- Verbal/visual communication

Chapter 10

Potential Coaching Points

- Are the goalkeeper's support positions appropriate in relation to the ball
- Is their communication effective and informative
- Does the goalkeeper pick the most appropriate options of distribution – in terms of tactical decisions and technique (accuracy, weight of pass)

Game Starting Positions

- Coach plays the ball anywhere into the area – from varying angles
- Let the defending team start with the ball

Example Setup

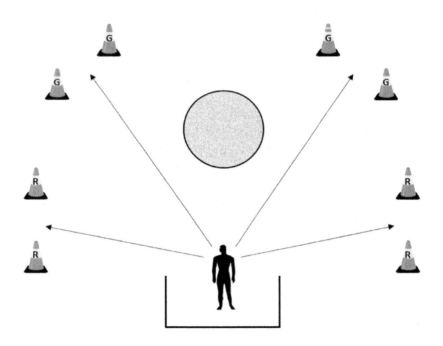

No Bounce

Explanation

The aim of the game is to avoid the ball bouncing in your zone. The team in control of the ball will aim for the opponent's zone (marked out by cones) using an agreed method of distribution. This could be throwing, drop kicks, stationary goal kicks or moving back passes.

If the ball does bounce inside a team's area the opponents will receive a point and vice-versa. If a ball fails to reach the zone or goes out of play - the ball will go to the other team.

When a goalkeeper gains control they must distribute the ball within six seconds if it's in their hands. They can gain control by catching the ball directly or controlling it with their body (to replicate a back pass). Try to use one at any time, not both. Keep the game realistic by encouraging the goalkeepers to play quickly.

The example grid can be changed according to the session topic or a diagonal game can be created to work on distribution into wide areas.

Areas Worked

- All kinds of distribution
- Basic handling
- Teamwork
- Communication

Potential Coaching Points

- Judgement of the ball
- Can the goalkeeper biomechanically perform certain distribution methods
- Look out for technical issues with throwing

Chapter 10

Game Starting Positions

- One team starts with the ball
- The coach plays the ball to one of the teams from varying positions
- The coach plays the ball in between the teams' grids – a contest of speed to get the ball is now on

Typical Setup

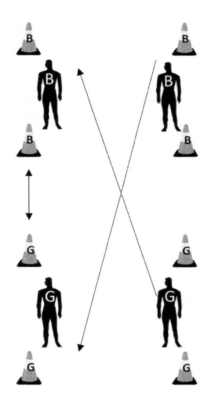

Goalkeeper Bowls

Explanation

The rules are the same as normal bowls with each goalkeeper trying to get their ball nearest the target. It can be played individually (three balls each) or in teams (five balls per team) with the winner the goalkeeper or team getting the ball nearest the target.

The methods of distribution can vary but from experience the best methods are the underarm roll or the simple pass.

The target can be moved at an angle or distance so a variety of situations can be practised such as hitting the ball to wide areas.

Areas Worked

- Accuracy/weight of distribution

Setup

Distribution Gates

Explanation

The aim of the game is to get the ball through the gates by whatever technique is being practised, for example, goal kicks, throwing, or drop kicks. The gates can be moved closer together to increase difficultly, and they can be moved into different positions or distances from the goalkeeper's start position.

Each goalkeeper will have three turns to accumulate as many points as they can. The one who scores the most points is the winner. The number of turns and balls can vary depending on how many goalkeepers there are in the session.

This is a great game for keepers to learn about distribution and, in my experience, all the goalkeepers who have taken part have felt their distribution had improved and they were able to have a fun, competitive game at the same time.

Areas Worked

- Accuracy/weight of distribution
- Different methods (both feet and arms)

Setup

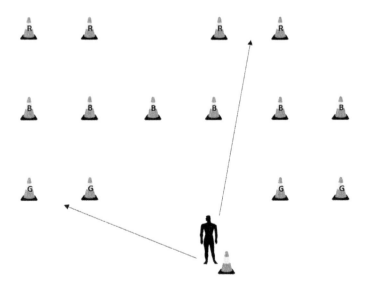

Red = 5 points, Blue = 3 points, Green = 2 points

Accuracy

Explanation

This game uses tennis balls and works on the accuracy of the throw as well as having receiving goalkeepers work on their hand-eye coordination. It's best done indoors, but can also be done on grass and with different types of balls.

All of the distances can vary depending on the age and ability of the goalkeepers. The coach can lay out the game or ask the participants what dimensions they would prefer.

The goalkeepers will throw the ball aiming to bounce it within the red target zone and aiming for an opposition goalkeeper. At first this is done from a stationary position with the receiver of the ball then aiming to return the ball to a different goalkeeper.

The exercise can be progressed with the opposite goalkeepers moving around as targets and the goalkeeper receiving the ball remaining stationary when throwing.

Another progression can achieved be placing goals or targets for the goalkeepers to hit on the floor (see below).

Areas Worked

- Throwing accuracy
- Hand-eye coordination
- Reactions

Setups

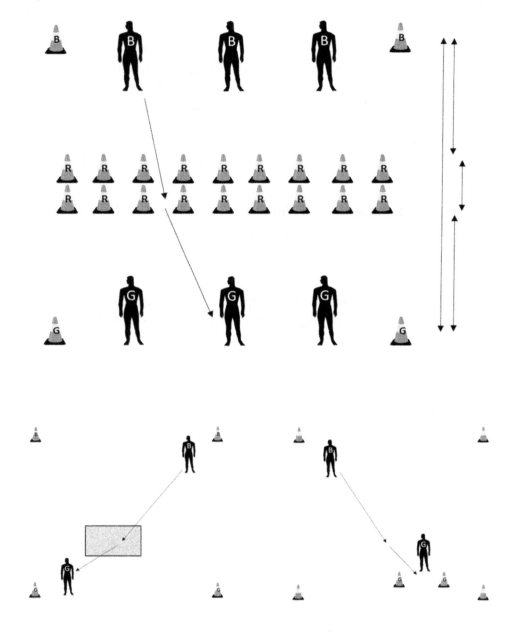

This is a good game to challenge participants and easy to adapt the dimensions and demands according to the group's training needs. Points can be awarded for getting the ball to bounce in the target zone or for scores in a placed goal.

1v1 Situations

Gate Keeper

Explanation

The aim of this game is to get the goalkeeper diving at the feet of the attacker and stopping them getting past. If the attacker gets past the goalkeeper they dribble through the gate then around the side of the grid and return to the back of the line.

This game focuses on 1v1 situations and how a goalkeeper can stop the attacker getting past them and scoring. The attacker will work on their touch and decision making in this game and finish things off when outside the grid by doing a small exercise before returning to the back of the line. For larger groups the grid can be made bigger and more than one goalkeeper and attacker can be worked at the same time.

Areas Worked

- Courage (diving at feet)
- Timing of when to commit
- Positioning from starting ball – front foot

Potential Coaching Points

- Is the goalkeeper in an appropriate starting position in relation to the ball being dribbled in
- Does the goalkeeper move/commit when the ball is under control from the attacker
- Delaying and forcing wide
- Working in unison where there are two goalkeepers trying to save the ball

Game Starting Positions

- From the shown gate on the diagram
- Coach plays the ball into the attacker – the goalkeeper(s) will respond off their first touch

Chapter 10

Typical Setup

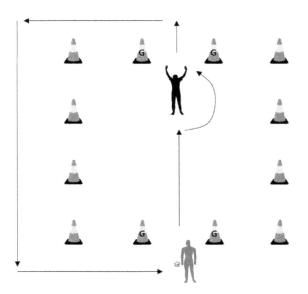

Alternative Setup

The attacker now has a choice and the goalkeeper will have to adjust accordingly, for example there are two goals for the attacker to head for.

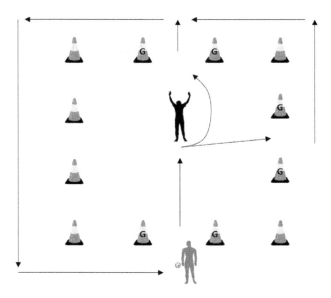

Keeper in the Middle

Explanation

Depending on the number of participants the grid can change size and more than one goalkeeper can be working at a time. The goalkeepers can start by intercepting with their feet but then move on to trying to gain the ball using their hands. This creates a 1v1 situation, and this game would be a good starting point to introduce 1v1 techniques and the skills needed.

A maximum number of touches can be placed on the 'outside goalkeepers' to improve their first touch and composure on the ball.

Areas Worked

- Not committing early
- Timing of interception
- Speed
- Agility

Typical Setup

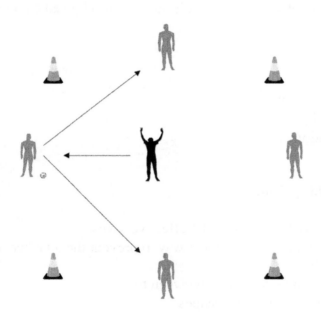

Crocodiles

Explanation

Using two goals in a grid, one team of goalkeepers will be outfield players and one team will play as goalkeepers (with the outfield team overloaded). If a goal is scored the play will switch and the opposite goal will be attacked.

The aim will be for the outfield players to score and for the normal goalkeepers to intercept or save the ball – an interception or a save will count as a goal if they do.

The idea behind "Crocodiles" is that the goalkeepers are protecting something, in this case a goal - the outfield goalkeepers can't allow the Crocodiles to get the ball as they can't get it back off them!

The outfield goalkeepers use their feet to start with - using passing and dribbling. When the drill progresses the goalkeepers playing outfield can use their hands to throw and drop kick if required.

Different conditions can be put on the game such as 'two touches maximum' and players will rotate roles once five goals have been achieved by a team.

Areas Worked

- Footwork
- Communication
- Positional play
- Organisation
- Tactics

Potential Coaching Points

- Does the goalkeeper(s) make effective saves
- Does the goalkeeper(s) find a way to prevent the attackers coming too close to the goal
- Does the goalkeeper(s) know when to set
- Diving angles and hand shapes

Game Starting Positions

- Coach plays the ball anywhere into the grid
- Coach plays to the attackers who go for goal
- The goalkeepers start with the ball – distributing the ball to the attackers

Typical Setup

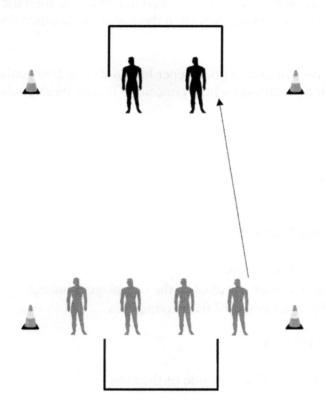

Parallel Goals

Explanation

There are two separate games which the coach will play balls into at random. Either side could be chosen so the goalkeepers must be paying attention and focusing on the ball. When the ball is entered into one side then the attacking player can go for goal or choose to switch the ball into the other side and play from there.

The roles will be rotated once a goalkeeper has conceded five goals. Or you could swap things to winner-stays-on where conceding two or three goals results in a change.

Areas Worked

- Concentration
- Reaction time

Potential Coaching Points

- Front foot starting position
- Does the goalkeeper re-adjust to the ball played through
- Forcing the attacker out of the playing area

Game Starting Positions

- Coach plays the ball either side of the area

Typical Setup

Reaction 1 v 1

Explanation

The ball will start with the server and they will play a pass into the attacker who will take a shot at either goal they wish. The shot must be first time.

The goalkeeper will try to keep the ball out of the goal using quick reactions. The goalkeeper with the least number of goals scored against them in the allotted time will be the winner.

This can be done as a winner-stays-on game or the positions can be rotated.

Areas Worked

- Concentration
- Reaction saves
- Fast and strong hands

Typical Setup

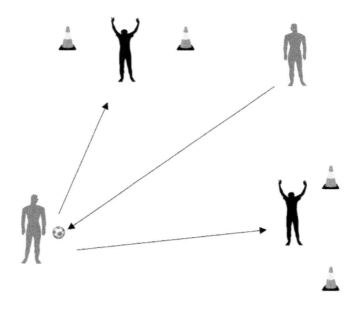

Goals Galore

Explanation

Inside the designated grid (can be smaller when working on 1v1s and reaction saves) there will be a series of mini goals that the goalkeepers will have to defend.

The game can be played with one ball per group and the outfield players passing, or one ball per outfield player.

Each goalkeeper will have his or her own goal and will score a point by making a save and lose a point for a goal conceded. The other non-working goalkeepers will act as outfield players and their objective is to score. They can do this by dribbling through their goal or passing to a team member (if the game is with one ball).

If the goalkeeper gains control of the ball they will distribute the ball to another player. That player cannot directly score back into that goalkeeper's goal.

If a goal is scored or the ball goes outside the grid - the coach will play another ball into the grid, either to a player or space.

When the designated time is up the goalkeeper with the most points will be the winner. If the whole group is made up of goalkeepers, then people will swap positions.

Chapter 10

Areas Worked

- Concentration
- Reacting to changing situations

Potential Coaching Points

- Staying big to block the goal
- Scanning the field for potential attacks
- Is the goalkeeper ready for attack on their goal
- Can the goalkeeper take the ball when it's out of the attackers' feet

Game Starting Positions

- One attacker starts with the ball
- The coach plays the ball into the area from varying angles and distances
- A goalkeeper starts with the ball and distributes to any attacking player

Example Setup

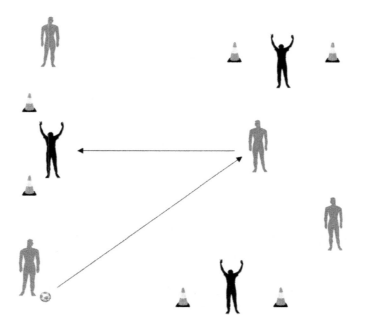

Crossing

Cross Goal

Explanation

There will be a number of servers placed at a variety of different positions around the designated working area - serving crosses. Balls can be thrown or kicked towards the goalkeeper depending on the ability of the group. For the group to get a feel for the exercise - throwing the ball, to start with, might be a good idea.

When a colour is called by the coach the working goalkeeper must touch that coloured cone then move into a position in relation to the ball to be able to claim the cross and stop the ball going into the goal.

The serve order can be determined by working along the line or by issuing numbers - when a colour is called so is a number: the goalkeeper will need to react to the position of that number in relation to the goal area.

To make the exercise more game based the servers will gain a point for a goal and the goalkeepers for a save or an effective dealing with the cross.

This exercise doesn't have to be game based if the technique of dealing with crosses hasn't been done by the group before.

Defenders and attackers can be introduced to make the exercise opposed. The example setup looks more at straight crosses – but the position of the crossers can be any width or depth.

Potential Coaching Points

- Re-adjusting position
- The timing of the jumping movement
- Look for all the standard crossing coaching points – e.g. deal with ball at highest, safest point, etc.

Chapter 10

Game Starting Positions

- Each crossing player has a ball
- The crossing players pass a ball between themselves
- The coach gives the goalkeeper a cross, who then distributes the ball to any of the crossing players who control the ball and look to cross.

Example Setup

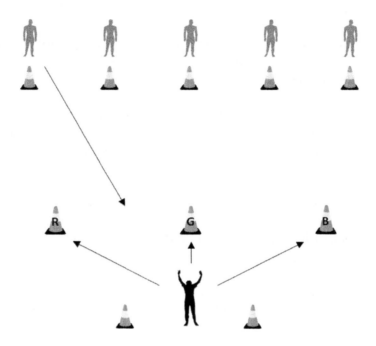

Don't Cross Me!

Explanation

Similar to the original "Cross Goal", the concept here is the same such that the servers will look to produce a delivery that will test the goalkeeper's ability to deal with crossed balls.

The servers will aim to score in the opposite goal, at the far post, making the goalkeeper come and deal with the ball at the far post. The height of the side goals should be the same as the main goal.

The goalkeeper's positioning in relation to the ball and the goal will be important here. Once again attackers and defenders can be added to make the exercise more game realistic.

Typical Setup

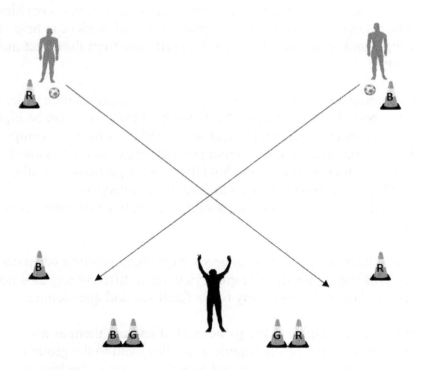

Chapter 10

Summary

As discussed before - games based goalkeeper training is an alternative to the traditional goalkeeping curriculum. The approach also looks to bridge the gap between isolated technical training, and the whole team training environments. This is a potentially neglected area where goalkeepers are proficient in technical practices but then struggle when faced with the reactive and ever changing game environment. The games shown alleviate this transition and are used when the goalkeeping coach takes their sessions.

The games take the goalkeeper out of their comfort zone and the concept accepts errors and mistakes will be made. From the coach's perspective these exercises should increase a goalkeeper's ability to figure out appropriate techniques and movements for themselves.

With the diagnostics being done by the goalkeepers and coaches – through questioning and guided discovery – a motivated and relevant learning environment is created. The goalkeepers will be able to self-regulate their own performance making their own judgements and observations to see what works best for them. The coach, by giving different performance cues (coaching points, buzz words, triggers, encouragement or praise for hard-work) can help stimulate the goalkeeper and ignite their learning. It is different from the direct model or command style.

If you're planning a session with perhaps two or three games then make sure there are rest periods in between as the intensity of the games can be high – a tip to break the games up would be to break away and do something completely different. I've separated games by small possession exercises or some isolated technical work – such as volleys or shots that work a particular handling technique. Or even watching a video to give the goalkeepers a physical break – but still keep them engaged by doing something fun but at the same time bringing in variation.

A key bit of advice would be to change your coaching position when carrying out the games. This way you will get a great view from different angles – not fixed into one place. This will add variety to the feedback and questioning.

Now you've seen examples of the games go out and use them as a starter! Put your own twists and spin on each game and tailor them to the group you're working with. Your goalkeepers should love them. Every coaching environment I've been involved with has benefited in some way from each of the games. They are a great way to bring a new group together, teach new skills to existing goalkeepers or give an experienced group a taste of something different from the norm.

11

Training Methodologies and The Future

"**We would accomplish many more things if we did not think of them as impossible.**"

(**Vince Lombardi**)

This chapter will introduce people whom I consider 'like-minded' from the goalkeeping world. People who see a problem. People who want to change goalkeeping for the better. People who share my passion. There will be input from high level international coaches from different countries as they share how they train their goalkeepers.

In this chapter we will cover:

- Polish Methodology
- Spanish Methodology
- Vision and Awareness for Goalkeepers
- Goalkeeping Innovation
- GK Icon

Let's start by visiting Poland to see how their goalkeepers are developed.

Chapter 11

Goalkeeping in Poland

Daniel Pawlowski is a goalkeeping coach from Poland who has worked with the country's youth international teams, as well as top teams in Poland, and who runs his own Academy. He is a former goalkeeper, and was educated in Sports Sciences in Edinburgh. For him, Messi and Ronaldo would have been the best goalkeeping coaches. In his coaching career he has visited many football academies around Europe and learned various goalkeeping training methods at FC Porto, Tottenham Hotspur, Fulham FC, Valencia CF, PSV Eindhoven and FC Barcelona. He discusses aspects of goalkeeping with great passion and deep knowledge of this peculiar position.

Daniel writes…

A few months ago, I was asked – what is goalkeeping in Poland?

I would have loved to reply and talk about the structures, philosophies and methodologies of something that could commonly be called the Polish Goalkeeping School, but sadly to say we do not have transparent structures, philosophies and methodologies when coaching goalkeepers.

Despite this Polish goalkeepers were (and still are) praised in European football competitions, and as Arsene Wenger put it in one interview: "In Poland they produce some fantastic goalkeepers".

It is difficult to explain this phenomenon. No one has conducted research into Polish goalkeepers yet the country has produced a nice historical line of excellent goalkeepers naturally. Józef Młynarczyk in the 1980's, Wandzik in the 1990's, and Dudek in 2000. Then Boruc, Fabiański, and Kuszczak appeared a few years later, and we now have Szczęsny, and Tytoń.

On the streets you can see young lads wearing T-shirts with goalies names on the back. Goalies are idols. Whilst we still have living memories of Jan Tomaszewski (our hero from Wembley in 1973 when he singlehandedly held back England) the message is clear – Polish goalies can succeed. This is a powerful motivational kick for youngsters. I do not want to be controversial but I worked for nearly 30 months in Scotland, visited many football academies in Europe and I never saw the motivation and eagerness to succeed that I see on the faces of Polish goalkeepers. We do not have excellent facilities, or medical and educational support - the only way for a young goalkeeper to succeed seems to be through hard work, dedication and constant motivation.

The game

Throughout my semi-professional playing career and almost 10 year coaching career I developed different teaching and learning strategies. In simple terms I would coach by using different methods in Scotland compared to England or Poland. Cultural differences must be taken into consideration first. However, I believe that the most successful coaching concept needs to be based around the game itself.

I always thought that I knew a fair deal about the game, but I view the game a little bit differently these days. In fact, I would say that there are underlying problems in understanding the game of football. For years it has been viewed from a deterministic, mechanical point of view, that if A passes the ball to let's say B then something happens. If B passes to C something happens, etc. But we never asked: what happens after the ball is passed? What has happened to B before he received the ball? How has the movement of the A influenced the decision made by B and C?

As a goalkeeping coach I think we have to resolve crucial questions like: how can goalkeepers improve their positioning against *particular* opponents? Or how can a keeper use the space left by opposition midfielders? This is much more than simply – what is the best shape of a keeper's hands or the best footwork.

Neurosciences and Mourinho

The former top English player and TV pundit Jimmy Greaves said that "*Football tactics* are rapidly becoming as complicated as the *chemical* formula for splitting the atom.*"* He was right, with new discoveries in science, especially in neurobiology the actual thinking of the game has changed. Look at the human brain and how our neurons communicate, its analogy is similar to the football field. Look at José Mourinho's latest book *Por qué tantas victorias* where he mentions *Periodización Táctica* (Tactical Periodization) and *Modelo de Juego* (Game Model), which nicely touches upon the complexity of the game and presents a different understanding of soccer training and conditioning too.

If we do not know what the game is, we do not know its proper training methods. Quite frankly, there is no valid algorithm that might help to understand the complexity of the game. Software like ProZone and others do not tell us enough about it. However there are nice approaches from network analysis perspectives in team sports. Using them might be a big shift towards knowing more about its complexity. Great coaches actually feel the game, have this intuition. The best coach in the NBA, Phil Jackson at the Chicago Bulls, developed triangle offence, which was basically a mutual sharing of the ball. Obviously we had seen this sharing before, during Rinus Michels times, for example.

Who do we develop – master of the training or the game?

I always believed in learning the game. As former player I always asked questions like: how will this training help me to improve myself? Traditionally, goalkeeper training is performed away from the dynamics of decision making and lasts between 50 and 80 minutes. It is very isolated. The coach shoots the ball, the goalie makes the saves, and you might think – this is ok, he is making fabulous saves, let's take this type of training and apply it to my athletes. But after such training - when the goalie is back in a game situation - he will struggle. Why you might ask? Because he had just trained in the context of a simple situation and now he is back in a dynamic, complex one he will not function properly. This creates what I have called "Master of the Training". Coaches often say: "He is excellent during training but chokes during games". I am not saying that isolated technique training is wrong but one also has to include: decision making, the impact of emotion and cognition, the positioning of the goalkeeper (in particular dynamic action).

Human movement studies are an emergent phenomenon. We have to understand an athlete's 'intrinsic dynamics' (i.e. those coordination tendencies that are present within an individual). So saying to the goalkeeper – "Keep your elbows bent at some magic angle" is not a proper approach. Elbows will simply bend because of momentum and that's it. There is no biomechanical need to improve it. Football does not belong to some closed skills classification as many apparently believe.

Simply speaking, as the coach, my role is to match *intrinsic dynamics* with *task dynamics* (i.e. those coordination tendencies that are required to successfully perform a task). From a motor learning based perspective, within a dynamical systems perspective, learning is a "search and refinement" process. The coach is there to help structure practice environments and channel movement dynamics by allowing players to explore different configurations in changing settings.

In simple terms, specially designed games for goalkeepers allow them to explore new movements and be faced with the opportunity to use techniques to succeed. When I look back on my development, I started kicking the ball around by

playing and the goalkeeper should be faced with environments such as these.

Załuska creatively succeeding. But for some it is the wrong technique.
(Photo by: Richard Tucker)

Messi and Ronaldo

For many, saying that Messi and Ronaldo would/could have been two of the best
goalkeeping coaches is blasphemy. But, as I have said previously, if I could have
had Messi and Cristiano Ronaldo at my practices, developing goalies would have
taken little time.

Let's imagine two distinct situations: a coach is shooting the ball at the
goalkeeper, low drives, higher ones, etc. He kicks it from the ground, maybe does
some half volleys. In the second scenario, the coach can use the services of Messi
and Ronaldo playing together against two defenders and the goalkeeper. Look at
the shoots, the variety, difficult spins on the ball, not much time to think for the
goalkeeper; anticipation is involved, and communication. What scenario do you

think will make a better goalie? I leave the answer to you.

Coaching senior goalkeepers

It is important to talk openly with players about emotions. I particularly like the quote from Guus Hiddink: "To get to the highest level, the first thing people must do is to have a better understanding of themselves." Would you disagree with that? At a professional level we have to create caring environments where players can develop this mutual, open understanding. Read what great players, Champions League and World Cup winners, are saying about their teams and they often talk about team chemistry. This is not achieved by accident, you have to talk openly about emotions which may sometimes lead to conflicts but a real leader can channel such conflict into positive outcomes.

Ancient wisdom

I do tactical questioning. It's a Mourinho paradigm, but known before him, and involves asking players meaningful questions like: how did the position of this player influence your movement? What happens if your starting position is here or there? Etc.

This is guided discovery learning; players are more attuned to important sources of information; get them to understand the game better. In ancient times it was already applied (*Tell me and I will forget, show me and I will remember, engage me and I will understand* – Confucius) and I think we have to come back to sheer fundamentals in terms of communication so the player feels that the answer *belongs to him*, not directly provided by some other source.

Normal training session for footwork, but this is footwork for this training not for the game. Footwork in a game is totally different.

Coaching young goalkeepers and 10,000 hours of training

I do not see why we should train youths differently to seniors. Of course, there are physiological, psychological and physical differences that we have to take into consideration, but if you look at FC Barcelona's methodology, youth player training sessions are similar to those done by seniors - 80% of the time.

There is one powerful framework in developing talent called 'ten thousand hours' or the 10 year rule. Research into expertise has regularly shown that many athletes who reach international level devoted at least ten thousand hours on their way to becoming great. Putting it into numbers: that's devoting three hours per day for ten years. Obviously, you have to take that message into the perspective of long term athlete development because it does not mean that training more will make you better. Quite surprisingly, English players who sign international contracts at the age of 16 started very early and engaged mostly in football activities. Apart from that, they spent many hours in non-led coaching practices, that is, they just played the game with friends. There is evidence from Brazil telling us that many players, who went international, had not participated in structured activities led by a coach up to the age of 15 or 16; street soccer was their teacher!! Due to these street games intrinsic dynamics match smoothly with task dynamics and we can see great creativity being born. For youth goalies my advice would be: play the game and be passionate about it!

Chapter 11

Structure of the session

I will offer you a simple session now with three 16 year old male goalies. I like informing my players about the content of any session and I put a note on the wall detailing what we will do tomorrow. On the day of training players come better prepared. Concisely, we start as usual with:

- Dynamic warm up: having the ball at the goalkeeper's feet, adding the ball to the feet, some passing, movement, and communication.
- Technical work, i.e. catching balls in the grid, lots of catches and we gradually build the tempo up (12-15 minutes).
- Adding more tactical actions to this, let's say if a rebound is on offer one goalkeeper tries to win the ball. The main part of the session is a designed game for goalies, and lasts for 20-30 minutes. With three keepers and me we set up some 2v1s in one part of the field or various 1v1 attacks from various angles, usually central.

If I notice some recurring pattern, for instance the goalie (in the goal) makes wrong decisions by jumping backwards before the shot is made I will stop the action and correct it either by discussing the matter (because I am unsure whether the keeper is doing it on purpose as he responds to the particular dynamics of the play) or by applying some kind of rule on him (any jump backwards gives one point to the opposition). If I only have 30 minutes to prepare these goalkeepers I focus on technical parts for a short period of time and a specially designed game that matches the content further. We talk a lot about tactics, how a goalkeeper can take advantage of the space, etc.

You can measure intensity by applying technologies that are available but simple. The RPE (Rate of Perceived Exertion) method is reliable.

Conclusions

As we can notice, the position of the goalkeeper is changing; Frans Hoek put their development on one scale with two ends – anticipating and reacting. We have to design special practices to match their changing roles, responsibilities and match actions. That's it. The game is different to the sum of its parts.

Example 1

1. Description:

The goals and players are set up as per the picture. Goalkeepers (C, D), are standing next to the posts as they cover their near post area. Player (B) does a movement; this is a signal for (A) to pass the ball (1) towards him. (C) and (D) change their positions quickly and cover as much of the goal as possible. (B) Has to shoot first touch on whatever goal he wants, and he always goes for any rebound. If the goalkeeper catches the ball he plays it back to (A). No corners. (B) At the beginning must not shoot full power onto goal (60-70% of power). He can go full power after hitting around 20 shots. Change goalkeepers after 6-8 shots.

2. Coaching points:
- (A) has to play a solid pass on the ground.
- Goalkeepers have to react very quickly, move in straight lines, their first step will be crossover.
- Goalkeepers have to be in the set position before the shot is made, however they can read body movements of the striker and react to them.
- (B) can shoot by using any part of his foot.
- The Coach only looks at one keeper at time.

3. Modifications:
- (B) holds two cones (for instance: blue and white), he puts one in the air. Two goalkeepers have to turn their head and shout the visible colour of the cone. After that, (A) continues to pass the ball.
- Coach tells (A) that he can shoot on the goal but goalkeepers must not hear it thus they do not know when it might happen; they have to be constantly alert.
- Coach can go for a rebound as well.
- Coach plays as the defender standing at the back of (B), (B) has to make proper decisions based on how the defender (Coach) moves,
- (B) can change his starting position (going wide or short), and goalkeepers have to make appropriate decisions.

Example 2 – Progression

1. Description:
Goalkeeper (A) passes the ball to (B), he takes two touches and plays wide to (C), who takes two touches and plays a solid pass on the ground, across the goal for (D) who shoots on the goal (100% power); he goes for any rebound. No corners. Change the goalkeepers after 6-8 reps. Change the side after having done all reps. Full concentration.

2. Coaching points:
- (B) and (C) ask for the ball, just like in a back-pass scenario.
- Appropriate, fluid touches of the ball.
- First touch finish.
- Goalkeeper (A) has to move quickly and in straight lines, getting into the set position before the shot is going to be made.
- Goalkeeper reads the body language of the players.
- (A) has to decide in advance where to parry/block the ball if the striker (D) attacks from a particular angle.

3. Modifications:

- Coach tells only (B) to shoot on goal, goalkeeper has to be alert.
- Coach tells (C) that he can shoot on goal too, goalkeeper has to be alert.
- (B) Works as the defender for (D) after passing the ball to (C).
- As the defender (B) moves to cover (D), (C) after passing the ball towards (D) can go up the corner of the penalty area and (D) can pass the ball towards him for a shot.

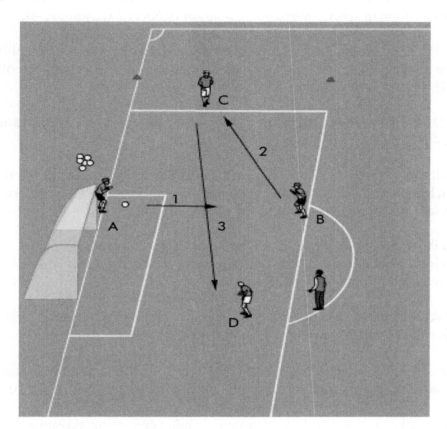

Literature:

Baker J., Côté J., & Abernethy B. (2003) Sport-specific practice and the development of expert decision-making in team ball sports, *Journal of Applied Sport Psychology*, 15, 2–25

Bar-Or O. (1996) *The Child and Adolescent Athlete*, Blackwell Scientific Publications, London

Chapter 11

Czajkowski Z. (2004) *Nauczanie techniki sportowej*, Biblioteka Trenera, Warszawa 2004.

Davids K., Button Ch., & Bennett S. (2008) *Dynamics of Skill Acquisition. A constraints-led approach*. Champaign, IL: Human Kinetics

Fajen B.R., Riley M.A., & Turvey M.T. (2009) Information, affordances, and the control of action in sport, *International Journal of Sport Psychology*, 40, 79–107

Ford P.R., Ward P., Hodges N.J., & Williams A.M. (2009) The role of deliberate practice and play in career progression in sport: the early engagement hypothesis, *High Ability Studies*, 1(20), 65–75

Lee T.D., Swinnen S., & Serrien D. (1994) Cognitive effort and motor learning, *Quest*, 46, 328–344

Mitchell S.A., Griffin L.L., & Oslin J.L. (1995) The effects of two instructional approaches on game performance, *Pedagogy in practice: Teaching and coaching in physical education and sports*, 1, 36–48

Passos P., Araujo D., Davids K., & Shuttleworth R. (2008) Manipulating constraints to train decision making in rugby union, *International Journal of Sport Science & Coaching*, 3, 125–140

Petryński W. (2001) Dwa wzorce opisu czynności ruchowych: strukturalny i funkcjonalny, *Sport Wyczynowy*, 1–2, 433–434

Williams A.M., & Hodges N.J. (2005) Practice, instruction and skill acquisition in soccer: Challenging tradition, *Journal of Sports Sciences*, 223, 637–650

www.arsenal.com/news-archive/wenger-polish-keepers-came-via-same-coach

Spanish Methodology

Spain is at the forefront of modern day football. Not only do they produce fantastically creative outfield players, they have produced some of the best goalkeepers in recent times. For this section I would like to introduce Iñaki Samaniego, a highly experienced Spanish goalkeeping coach who worked for various professional clubs in his native Spain before moving to Holland to coach at the elite youth professional level. He now spends his time running the FUTURE High Performance Goalkeeping Center (*www.future-prokeeper.com*) which looks to give the latest training in technical, tactical, physical and psychological skills as well as performance analysis and nutrition. His insight into the Spanish Methodology is fascinating and having seen it first-hand his training is second to none.

Iñaki writes…

Before I get myself into the intricacies of Spanish goalkeeping training, I would like to thank Andy for the opportunity to collaborate in his book. People like him are helping to finally give goalkeeping training the place it deserves in football.

Now, let's do a bit of goalkeeping history first of all. As you can see, in football there are always cycles, where different countries dominate the competition for a few years, Brazil was the team to beat in the 70's, Argentina was the biggest rival in the 80's, Germany in the 90's, Italy in the 00's, and from 2008 it has been the time of Spain.

Now, if we look at goalkeepers, Spain has always had world class players: Zamora, Iribar, Arconada, Zubizarreta, etc. but for a while now we have been bringing a fairly high number of top class goalkeepers through the system; players such as Iker Casillas, Pepe Reina, Victor Valdes, Diego Lopez, Andres Palop and individuals on the up like David De Gea, Guaita, Joel, Ruben, Roberto, etc.

It is not a coincidence that this flow of top level goalkeepers has happened at the same point in time as the development of goalkeeper coaching in Spain, names like Luis Llopis, Jose Sambade, Jose Manuel Ochotorena, and Roberto Navajas have most definitely helped to make this possible.

These are all professional Spanish coaches who have analyzed goalkeeping from every angle possible: technical, tactical, physical and mental. They have turned our position inside out to make sure nothing remains untouched, and every aspect

355

of this important position gets trained in an effective way.

As you probably know, every time FIFA, UEFA or the local FA makes a change in the rules, the player that gets affected the most is the goalkeeper. As they always try to promote the attacking game this automatically means a change in the level of involvement of our goalkeeper in the game.

I am going to explain some of the basic foundations of the methods and guidelines that are used in Spain with regard to goalkeeping training. First of all we are going to take a look at the three different methods used in goalkeeping training: Analytic, Mixed, and Global. This is how drills and exercises are organized in Spain.

Analytic Method

This method, as the name suggests, is used to work on the technical aspects of goalkeeping, analyzing every technique, dissecting them - in order to pinpoint the segments that need to be worked on.

The Analytic Method is the base of goalkeeping training, and is the one used to learn the basic techniques and to improve and optimize these techniques as well as the more advanced ones.

The main feature of the analytic approach is the repetition of gestures, a repetition that will allow the goalkeeper to automate a certain technique that is being put in practice. Techniques such as a catch, a transition, a goal kick, etc. It can be as specific as a 'part' of a technique. They are exercises performed with or without the ball where there is no opposition of any kind; this simplifies the part of the game that is being worked out. The main objective of this type of drill is to correct deficiencies that show up in simple and basic game situations where they would not really improve by playing real game exercises.

This type of exercise leaves aside more complex mechanisms like perception or decision making.

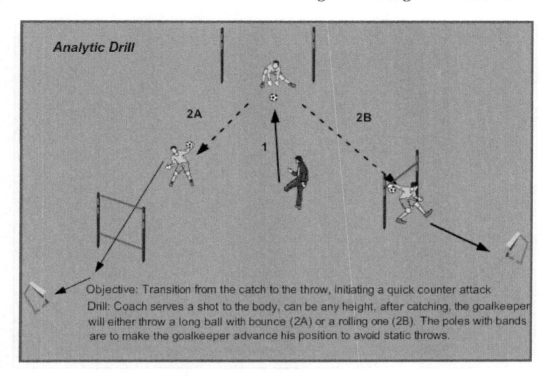

Analytic Drill

2A   2B

1

Objective: Transition from the catch to the throw, initiating a quick counter attack
Drill: Coach serves a shot to the body, can be any height, after catching, the goalkeeper
will either throw a long ball with bounce (2A) or a rolling one (2B). The poles with bands
are to make the goalkeeper advance his position to avoid static throws.

Analytic drills are also used to improve the fitness of the goalkeepers, exercises composed of footwork plus an action, or plyometric jumps finished with a technical action are good examples.

Global Method

This method of training is closest to a real game situation, and is called global because it covers all aspects of the game.

The exercises with this method are drills with playing situations very close to what would happen in a normal competition game, always involving two teams with at least two players, and with the most basic objective of scoring more goals than the opponent.

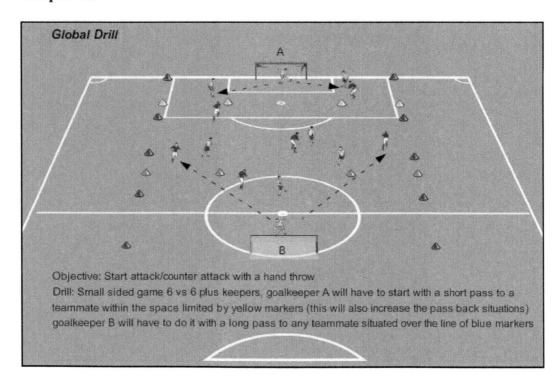

Global Drill

A

B

Objective: Start attack/counter attack with a hand throw
Drill: Small sided game 6 vs 6 plus keepers, goalkeeper A will have to start with a short pass to a teammate within the space limited by yellow markers (this will also increase the pass back situations) goalkeeper B will have to do it with a long pass to any teammate situated over the line of blue markers

These exercises have to be designed with the age and level of the players in mind, whilst also taking into account the objectives that the team has for that moment in the season. Once we have these factors we will design the situations with different levels of difficulty; these levels will be determined by the number of players in situations with, or without, overload.

We can then reduce the space and the number of players so the goalkeeper can increase the number of interventions. This will improve concentration and the greater number of game situations means that the goalkeeper can present different solutions to the same problem. They can evaluate which ones are most successful so they can be used during competition.

The use of standard sized pitches and a full number of players will help our goalkeeper to develop his ability to read situations and boost his interaction with his team mates. This approach progressively improves perception, analysis, and decision making capacities - reducing the time the goalkeeper needs to execute his play.

These situations will put the goalkeeper through a learning process that will then be reflected in competition. The goalkeeper will increase his knowledge about the theory and practice of the game, become able to evaluate his actions during the game, and also able to evaluate the results obtained with each decision taken.

Mixed Method

The Mixed Method, as you can guess from the name, is a step in-between the Analytic and the Global. These are drills where decision making starts making an appearance in exercises, although they are situations that are somewhat simpler than the ones you will find in competition.

These exercises simplify the game situation but we can provide the goalkeeper with repeated situations that will increase the level of work on whatever needs to be developed. The higher the number of situations faced by the goalkeeper - the higher the rate of success in that action; the confidence of the goalkeeper during competition increases accordingly.

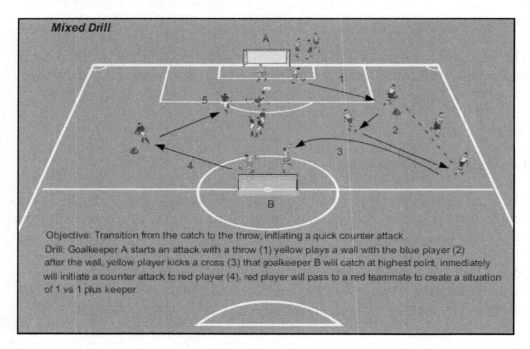

Mixed Drill

Objective: Transition from the catch to the throw, initiating a quick counter attack
Drill: Goalkeeper A starts an attack with a throw (1) yellow plays a wall with the blue player (2) after the wall, yellow player kicks a cross (3) that goalkeeper B will catch at highest point, immediately will initiate a counter attack to red player (4), red player will pass to a red teammate to create a situation of 1 vs 1 plus keeper.

Also the experience of the goalkeeper in these situations will allow him to *identify* the same situations during competition in a faster way.

Now we have witnessed the different types of method used for training in Spain, it is time for us to see how each of these methods can play a part in the evolution of goalkeepers, from early stages to professional competition.

We divide the evolution process into five levels: Initiation, Learning, Development, Command, and Performance.

Initiation (6 and 7 year olds)

In the early years, when a player is beginning to practice the sport, it is crucial that the goalkeeper gets used to handling the ball, and also starts learning the basic technical concepts according to this age group.

This first level is mainly characterized by global drills, where you can work on general objectives. Also, it is important to get the players to play in all positions, to get to understand the game better. Global work is complemented with a small part of analytic and mixed exercises to work more precisely on particular basic techniques.

The game situations that the global method brings, alongside drills with decision making involved, will identify technical aspects to be worked on via the analytic method.

Learning (8 to 11 year olds)

The main objective for this age level is to achieve a reasonable grade of common actions that happen regularly during games. Goalkeepers will also begin to work on certain specific technical actions.

At this level, the majority of the work is done using exercises from the global method, alongside work on specific techniques (mentioned above). The Analytic Method starts taking greater prominence for players in this age bracket.

Real game situations remain the primary scenario of our goalkeeping training but there should also be a higher proportion of analytic drills that work more intensely on the previously mentioned specific techniques.

Development (12 and 13 year olds)

For this age bracket we look for a higher level of performance in usual game situations as well as the perfection of a certain number of technical actions. Once we have reached this level, the amount of work done with Global and Analytic methods are evenly distributed. We start to work more often in closed and analytical tasks that are then combined with situations more related to the real game.

Command (14 to 16 year olds)

The objective at this age is for the goalkeeper to achieve a high level of command of the general aspects of the game as well as mastering the technical actions that we have been working on up to this point.

We see now that analytic work takes a bigger space in the training methodology, as we use the Analytic Method to increase other aspects of the game besides technical ones such as speed, power, reaction time, etc.

We notice that a focus on the technical side of goalkeeping becomes the main theme of our training. By this stage, the goalkeeper has a sound knowledge of the real game, and is being trained in sessions with the team, but specific training will look to improve technique.

Performance (17 onwards)

Once we arrive at this stage the objective is clear, the goalkeeper must be at a high level in all the technical aspects of the position and also should feel comfortable and confident in all game situations.

The methodology at this stage becomes mainly analytic and game situations are limited to competition and group tasks during the training sessions.

It becomes mainly analytic because, since we have a sound control of technique, we have to work on speed, power, strength, etc. and these abilities are mainly worked on via closed drills.

What we should get from this training structure is as follows. During a player's formative years (from the beginning until 14 or 15 years old) we should concentrate on building a strong technical base, a good knowledge of the game, quick tactical thoughts and all the other qualities that come with the position.

The competition is important because a player needs to learn to feel comfortable in the game, to read situations and communicate accordingly with his team mates. We should not sacrifice the development of the player in order to achieve results at these early stages.

Vision and Awareness for Goalkeepers

Kevin McGreskin is a world leader in vision and awareness within football. Having worked at the highest level of the sport he knows that fine margins can be the difference between success and failure.

Kevin holds the highly accredited UEFA A coaching license with three different governing bodies – making him a highly knowledgeable and experienced coach. He runs a consultancy called Soccer eyeQ (*www.soccereyeq.com*) where he uses a variety of different methods to improve vision and awareness for football at all levels – and in any position.

Here's what Kevin has to say:

Vision and awareness truly is the difference maker at the elite level of the game.

It is one of the most important yet under-developed skills that a player can possess.

It is a passion of mine, which I have studied deeply, and I have been privileged enough to share my ideas for developing players as a key speaker on the prestigious UEFA Pro Licence and UEFA A Licence courses, the highest coaching awards in Europe, and be a featured clinician at the NSCAA Convention, the biggest football coaches convention in the world.

I don't know about you but when I first heard people talking about sports vision, the first image that came to mind was Charlie Sheen in his skull and crossbones glasses in the baseball film *Major League*! Sheen plays a pitcher who throws an amazing fast-ball, but lacks any degree of accuracy and sends it all over the place. It's not until he's in the coach's office and about to get cut from the roster, when he squints at a picture, that they realise the problem is with his vision. A simple prescription helps sort out his problems and he becomes a star of the team.

In football, when we talk about vision we are normally on about something much more than just 20/20 vision but that's one of the foundations the whole visual system is built upon - how good the quality of the information coming in is. Have you ever considered that maybe the goalkeeper you are working with, the one that struggles so badly with crosses, maybe does not have a technical problem?

It has been shown that the visual system is the dominant sensory mechanism (Posner et al, 1976) for taking in information yet it is readily apparent that, from a coaching point of view, visual performance during soccer has been largely neglected as an area of importance during player development.

From a sporting perspective, there is an increasing body of research into areas such as visual search, anticipation, advance cue utilization, attention, perceptual expertise and decision making. However, in most of these studies the participants have only been asked to view action scenes that have been displayed directly in front of them. In the real world of sports performance, athletes carry their head and gaze in ways dictated by the inherent constraints of the task. That is both for soccer, and other team sports.

Of particular interest to goalkeepers are the studies, from a variety of other sports (soccer, ice hockey, field hockey), into the visual performance of goalkeepers facing penalty kicks. Whilst these studies have been carried out in rather sterile settings, which are infrequently encountered in real life, they have revealed that expert goalkeepers have a significant advantage over non-experts by more accurately predicting where the resultant shot will go. This is because they rely upon more advanced visual strategies and use subtle cues in order to predict where the ball is going to go.

But when we talk about vision, what is it we are really on about?

For me, when we consider helping a player develop 'vision' there are two fundamental components to consider - Visual Skills Training and On-field Training.

Visual Skills Training is largely based upon training the muscles around the eyes to improve speed, endurance and efficiency of movement. This is mostly done with computer-based training software or technology-based training equipment. The efficacy of such programs is still up for debate with researchers providing evidence both for and against; with those against saying that athletes don't necessarily need any better than average everyday eyesight. But our players don't perform in the 'everyday' environment; they perform in a fast-paced dynamic arena where key information is constantly changing. After all, isn't this one of the reasons we have our players supplement training with work in the gym?

Sherylle Calder and Gail Stephenson are names that are unfamiliar to the majority of you, I am sure. Yet, Sherylle is the proud owner of two rugby World Cup winners' medals and Gail has played her part for a team that has won 9 domestic championships, 2 Champions Leagues and 13 other domestic and international titles whilst she has been involved with them.

In their roles as vision specialists they have proven to be incredibly beneficial for the teams they have worked with. Before helping South Africa to success in 2007, Sherylle was a member of Sir Clive Woodward's backroom staff for the 2003 England Rugby World Cup winning team, for which Clive had famously left no stone unturned in his search for the "critical non-essentials" - those little one percent things that could just make the difference. Sherylle implemented a visual skills training program with both squads, as well as introducing ideas to incorporate aspects of visual performance during training exercises. Meanwhile, Gail has been quietly working her magic under Sir Alex Ferguson at Manchester United, where she screens every member of the playing staff and issues them with a personalized training program. And Manchester United's enduring success over the last two decades is testament to the fact that everything new their manager brings into the club is for the sole purpose of doing one thing - winning!

If we recommend that our players go to the gym to supplement their training in order to be at their physiological optimum, doesn't it make sense for our players to use an 'eye gym' to help their visual performance be at its optimum? I strongly recommend that all coaches consider incorporating a visual skills training package into their players' development program.

However, for me, the most important aspect of visual performance is what happens out on the field of play - after all, it doesn't matter how good your visual skills are if you stand with your back to play! This is why I am a strong advocate of incorporating aspects of visual performance into training exercises at every opportunity.

As coaches, we must start to address the need to include more visual aspects into our training - and this can be done in very simple ways. For example, I see many coaches who start their drills with an audible command such as shouting a command or blowing a whistle but audible triggers are not what we primarily react to in the game - we react to what we see.

I will now look at three exercises that are in common use by goalkeeping coaches around the world, if not exactly - then very similar.

The first is a fast feet exercise, the second a handling and shot stopping exercise, and the third a 'dealing with crosses' exercise.

Fast Feet

Many goalkeeping coaches use fast feet exercises with their players and implemented correctly, they can be very effective. However, I frequently observe goalkeepers performing these exercises with poor form and this largely goes uncorrected by the coach. Look at most goalkeepers whilst they are performing fast feet exercises and they will have their head down and be looking at their feet. I believe that this is a bad habit that we should not allow them to develop. Instead they should be holding their head in a more neutral position with the field of play in front of them being the primary focus of their attention and using their peripheral awareness, or quick eye movements instead of head movements, to view the series of cones or the ladder they are going through.

Handling

The following handling exercise may be familiar to you with the goalkeeper in a box made of four different coloured cones (red/yellow/blue/green).

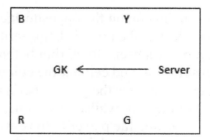

The goalkeeper makes a save from the Server before turning to face the coach who will then call out a colour, which the goalkeeper must go to before returning to the centre of the box - getting into the set position and saving the next serve.

A simple, yet very effective way, to adapt this exercise is to draw four coloured marks (red/yellow/blue/green) on the ball. Now, instead of using an audible command, the coach can use a visual trigger by holding the ball with one colour facing the player and this dictates the cone the player must go to. This simple method has the added benefit of encouraging the player to get his/her eyes straight onto the ball, a good habit to develop in any goalkeeper. One other point of importance in this exercise is that when moving to the specified cone, and back to the centre, the player should keep their body oriented towards the ball - too often I see sloppy technique and the player being let off when turning their back on the ball, even if only slightly.

Crossing

For my last example, I will use the visual component for a slightly different purpose in an exercise for dealing with crosses.

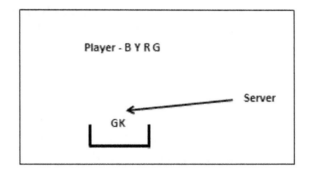

I will have a spare player standing out at the opposite apex of the penalty area with four coloured markers. Just as the cross is being struck the spare player will hold up a cone. After the cross has been struck (but before the goalkeeper has caught the ball) he/she must look at and call out the colour of the cone being held up. What I am trying to develop here is the goalkeeper's ability to quickly and accurately assess the flight of the ball, whilst only seeing the early part of its trajectory. Because I will be asking the player to look away at something else they need to become more accurate at judging trajectory so that when they turn their eyes back to the ball they have a good degree of accuracy of where it is in the air.

Here, I have given a brief insight into why vision is important and how we can incorporate some simple methods into the exercises that we already commonly use with our goalkeepers.

However, I really believe that Game Based Goalkeeper Training should also be incorporated into your regular practice sessions as this methodology regularly exposes your players to the dynamic visual triggers that they will encounter, and have to react to, during competitive performance.

Goalkeeping Innovation

In recent years there has been an influx of goalkeeping training aids - including rebound nets and boards. Due to increasing technology and the ability to create goalkeeper specific products the market has increased a great deal. One man who is at the forefront of this emerging market is Glenn Robertson. His innovation brainchild, the 'RESPONSEBALL', has gone from strength to strength since its launch in 2009, and there are now a number of different unique training balls.

The balls are designed to increase reaction times, improve speed, agility, co-ordination, and motor skills. RESPONSEBALLs are the only balls in the world that will guarantee a combination of regular and irregular bounce, providing a completely unpredictable outcome for the coach and keeper.

Three of the balls in the current range are shown here:

Origin   *Elite*   *Touch*

Each ball is different and offers a different dimension for the goalkeeper. The 'Origin' and 'Elite' have strategically placed bumps on the exterior of the ball which means they could either bounce in any direction or not change direction at all. For the goalkeeper this creates a good learning environment because they cannot commit too early; having to wait for the ball and lead with the hands…or they may be embarrassed!

The latest ball, the 'Touch', is a traditionally shaped football. The innovation here, however, is how the development team have structured the inside of the ball to give it an off centre weight, thus providing irregular flight and movement in the air and on the ground. Again this optimises a keeper's concentration and attention as the player has to watch the ball closely and be in an appropriate position when the ball reaches them.

Having used each of these balls in my own coaching, the benefits from a technical point of view are almost immediately evident – my goalkeepers now watch the ball more closely and can respond to small deflections off players or diversions off the pitch very well.

The balls are suitable for use at absolutely any level from grassroots up to international. They have been embraced by a number of different football clubs, including Liverpool, West Ham and Barcelona. They have entered the International arena being used in training by the England Futsal team, beach soccer team and even the Israeli 2012 Olympic squad!

They are absolutely a must have in every goalkeeping coach's equipment bag and will add a different dimension to your training sessions.

Glenn is very much a visionary within the goalkeeping world, a pioneer of innovation in specific product development and has produced other items too, such as the 1kg MAX Ball for use in handling and core strength/speed work, GloveGlu, and the new IMPACT pad. GloveGlu for example, enhances the grip of any goalkeeping glove with its unique formula. It can be applied before and during training and games and is effective in both wet and dry conditions.

The IMPACT pad has been specifically designed for goalkeeper contact, pressure and reaction work. Taking high balls, quick feet, movement, evasion and recovery saves are all examples of when the pad can be used.

The RESPONSEBLL brand is ever growing and with first mover advantage is paving the way for future goalkeeping innovation. From a goalkeeping development point of view these innovations allow goalkeepers to be involved in new training environments, and coaches can add a new element to training sessions.

Glenn is not only a product innovator but also an excellent coach and all round nice guy! Nothing is ever too much trouble and you can always catch him online on the socials: *facebook.com/responseball* or *twitter.com/academygk*

Finally Glenn has also recently created the GCA – Goalkeeper Coaches Association. This organisation is designed to share ideas/resources, put on goalkeeping days for any coach and bring like-minded people together in an open environment. For more information on the above and to purchase any of the training aids go to: *www.responseball.com* or *www.thegca.com*

GK Icon

GK Icon (*www.gkicon.com*), in a nutshell, offers goalkeepers and coaches of all ages and standards everything they could possibly need:

- A platform for top goalkeeping coaches to run a successful goalkeeping centre and all the aid they could possibly require (If you are a coach and interested please email RichardLee@gkicon.com and he will personally send further information on what they can offer you).
- The chance for goalkeepers to find a venue nearby where they can learn new skills and help improve their game from some of the best coaches in the game.
- A hub of education via their innovative 'keepers corner' on the website.
- A large selection of products via the GK Icon superstore
- And much more…

Check out the website for further details….

Summary

The main ethos within this chapter is to offer some different perspectives on the position and how people go about assisting goalkeeping development.

The contributors offer their development ideas at different ages and levels of football. This helps shape their philosophies but the over-riding theme is they train in realistic game environments, they train a lot with the ball at an early age, and keepers are placed within the team training to develop tactical understanding.

At the latter part of the chapter, you can see how other contributors have found ways in which to target niche areas of goalkeeping; from vision and awareness training to innovative training aids. All the people in this chapter are at the top of their fields and the calibre of their ideas and work is first class. For more information on any of the people involved, please use the suggested links.

12
Conclusion

"The first guy through the wall.......he always gets bloody."

(John Henry, *Moneyball*)

I wouldn't say I'm trying to revolutionise goalkeeping, I would come to the conclusion that I'm trying to help evolve it… and give the position its rightful standing in football.

Like all the previous chapters I have put in a quote (above) which I think is relevant and quite poignant. Trying to change the way people do things, breaking traditions, invoking new thinking, or offering new perspectives can be hard, very hard. I hope this book does this. There has to be the resolve to prepare young goalkeepers for the demands of the match – to equip them with all the tools to succeed. To make what they do autonomous.

Psychologically, physically, and tactically - the goalkeeper should enter the field of play positive and confident in their own ability no matter what the circumstances. From a training perspective: "Until you've seen something you can't act upon it."

This book is fundamentally a resource to improve your understanding of the goalkeeper; whether that is as a coach, analyst, parent… or maybe a goalkeeper yourself.

Chapter 12

The book is an evidence-based and interdisciplinary approach to goalkeeping that provides practical answers to questions. All of these sub-sections can't work without the other. To be a top goalkeeper you need all these chapters to succeed and to perform at your best: week in, week out. Each chapter gives you an insight into that part of goalkeeping – I'm sure every chapter could be a whole book on its own with the detail you could go into! Every area has hopefully been given the necessary coverage it deserves to enable the development of young goalkeepers.

There are many theories within this book. Whatever your role in goalkeeping - develop your own philosophy and stick by it at all costs. Every coach will always work differently. I've had many knockbacks in the past but I truly believe that the position of the goalkeeper is special and unrivalled in sport. It takes a different type of person to be a goalkeeper, crazy... maybe(!) but committed and passionate definitely. One key thing I've learned is that there's always more than one way to do things.

The philosophy of this book comes from lots of different viewpoints. From playing at various different levels, from coaching at various different levels, working goalkeepers' physical development at various different levels, and of course being a performance analyst at various clubs has given me a huge advantage in being able to dissect the position.

Goalkeeping isn't an exact science – but it's not rocket science either! I hope the aims of this book have been fulfilled and the position of the goalkeeper given the importance it deserves. The goalkeeper is part of the team not apart from the team – they are a major cog in the team dynamic.

References

Origins and Experiences

1. Baker, J., Cobley, B. & Fraser-Thomas, J. (2009). What do we know about early sport specialization? Not much! *High Ability Studies,* 1 (20), p77-89.

2. Barynina, I.I., & Vaitsekhovskii, S.M. (1992). The aftermath of early sports specialization for highly qualified swimmers. *Fitness and Sport Review International, 27* (4), p132–133.

3. Clemence, R. (1997). Goalkeeping - Dealing with the Back Pass. *FA Insight.* 1 (2), p23-24.

4. Gulbin, J. (2008). Identifying and developing sporting experts. In D. Farrow, J. Baker, & C.MacMahon (Eds.), *Developing sport expertise: Researchers and coaches put theory into practice,* New York: Routledge, p60-69.

5. McBrewester, J. (2009). *History of English Football*. London: Alphascript.

6. Mulqueen, T. (2010). The Complete Soccer Goalkeeper. Champaign, IL: Human Kinetics.

References

7. Ruiz, L. (2002). *The Spanish Goalkeeping Bible*. USA: Reedswain.

8. Smith, S. (2004). *The Specialist: Goalkeeping for soccer*. Leeds: Coachwise Business Solutions.

9. Wade, A. (1997). The Goalkeeper's Role. In: *Positional Play - Goalkeeping*. Spring City, PA: Reedswain, p2-3.

Chapters 1, 2 & 3 – Psychology, Physiology & Athletic Development and Biomechanics

1. Abernethy, B. (2001). Attention. In R. N. Singer, H. A. Hausenblas, & C. Janelle (Eds.), *Handbook of research on sport psychology* (2nd ed, p53–85). New York: Wiley.

2. Aruajo, C.G.S. (2004). *Flexitest; An Innovative Flexibility Assessment Method*. Leeds; Human Kinetics.

3. Arts, M. (2002). *The Soccer Goalkeeper Coach*. Spring City, PA: Reedswain.

4. Bachi, N., Baron, R., Calderon, M.F.J., Di Salvo, V. & Pigozzi, F. (2007). Performance Characteristics According to Playing Position in Elite Soccer. *International Journal of Sports Medicine,* 28, (3), p222-227.

5. Bandura, A. (1977). Self-efficacy: Toward a unifying theory of behaviour change. *Psychological Review*, 84, p191–215.

6. Bangsbo, J, Franks, A & Reilly, T. (2000). Anthropometric and physiological predispositions for elite soccer, *Journal of Sports Sciences*, 18, (9), p669-683.

7. Bartlett, R. (2007). Introduction to Sports Biomechanics: Analysing Human Movement Patterns, *Identifying Critical Features of a Movement*, New York: Routledge.

8. Beswick, B. (2001). *Focused for Soccer*. Champaign, IL: Human Kinetics.

9. Buchheit, M., Mendez-Villanueva, A., Brughelli, M & Ahmaidi, S. (2010). Improving repeated sprint ability in young elite soccer players: repeated shuttle sprints vs. explosive strength training, *Journal of Strength & Conditioning Research*, 24, (10), p271.

10. Butler, R.J. & Hardy, L. (1992). The performance profile: Theory & Application. *The Sport Psychologist*, (6), p253-264.

11. Carlock, J.M., Smith, S.L., Hartman, M.J., Morris, R.T., Ciroslan, D.A., Pierce, K.C., et al. (2004). The relationship between vertical jump power estimates and weightlifting ability: a field-test approach. *Journal of Strength and Conditioning Research*, (18), p534–539.

12. Cashmore, E. (2002). Sport Psychology: The Key Concepts, London: Routledge.

13. Cashmore, E. (2008). Sport Psychology: The Key Concepts (2nd Ed), London: Routledge.

14. Cassidy, T., Stanley, S., & Bartlett, R. (2006). Reflecting on Video Feedback as a Tool for Learning Skilled Movement, *International Journal of Sports Science & Coaching*, (3), p279-288.

15. Chu, D. (1998). *Jumping into plyometrics* (2nd Ed.). Champaign, Illinois: Human Kinetics.

16. Clemence, R. (1997). Goalkeeping - Dealing with the Back Pass. *FA Insight*, 1, (2), p23-24.

17. Clemence, R. (2003). An interview with Ray Clemence. *FA Insight*, 6, (2), p3-4.

18. Coles, D. (2004). Goalkeeping – The Specialists View. *FA Insight*, (7), p4-32.

19. Cox, R.H. (2007). *Sport Psychology: Concepts and Applications* (6th Ed).

References

London: WCB/McGraw-Hill.

20. Cumming, J., & Hall, C. (2002). Deliberate imagery practice: The development of imagery skills in competitive athletes. *Journal of Sports Sciences,* (20), p137-145.

21. Davis, S, D., Bosley, E. E., Gronell, C. L., Keeney, A. S., Rossetti, M. A., Mancinelli, A. C., Petronis, J. J. (2006). The relationship of body segment length and vertical jump displacement in recreational athletes. *Journal of Strength & Conditioning Research*, 20, (1), p136.

22. Deci, E.L. (1975). *Intrinsic motivation.* New York: Plenum Press.

23. England, N. (2007). Running and Fitness, *Journal of Sports Medicine*, 357, (2), p198-199.

24. Evans, L., Jones, L. & Mullen, R. (2004). An Imagery Intervention during the Competitive Season with an Elite Rugby Union Player, *The Sport Psychologist*, (18), p252-271.

25. Farrow, D. Young, W. & Bruce, L. (2005). The development of a test of reactive agility for netball: a new methodology. *Journal of Science, Medicine and Sport*, (8), p52–60.

26. Feltz, D. L. (2007). Self-confidence and sports performance. In D. Smith & M. Bar-Eli (Eds.), *Essential readings in sport and exercise psychology*, Champaign, IL: Human Kinetics, p278–294.

27. Fleck, S.J. & Kraemer, W.J. (1996). *Periodization breakthrough!* Ronkonkoma, New York: Advanced Research Press.

28. Getchell B. (1979). *Physical Fitness: A Way of Life*, (2nd Ed.) New York: John Wiley and Son.

29. Goss, S., Hall, C., Buckolz, E., & Fishbume, G. (1986). Imagery ability and the acquisition and retention of movements. *Memory and Cognition*, (14), p469-477.

30. Graham-Smith, P. and Lees, A. (1999). Analysis of technique of

goalkeepers during the penalty kicks. *Journal of Sports Sciences*, (19), p916.

31. Gregg, M. & Hall, C. (2006). The Relationship of Skill Level and Age to the Use of Imagery by Golfers, *Journal of Applied Sport Psychology*, (18), p363–375.

32. Groom R., Cushion, C., & Nelson, L. (2011). The Delivery of Video-Based Performance Analysis by England Youth Soccer Coaches: Towards a Grounded Theory, *Journal of Applied Sports Psychology*, (23), p16-32.

33. Hall, C., Mack, D., Paivio, A., & Hausenblas, H. (1998). Imagery use by athletes: Development of the Sport Imagery Questionnaire. *International Journal of Sport Psychology*, (29), p73–89.

34. Hardy, L., Jones, G. and Gould, D. (2007). *Understanding Psychological Preparation for Sport: Theory and practice of elite performers*. Chichester: John Wiley & Sons.

35. Hedrick, A. (2002). Manipulating Strength and Conditioning Programs to Improve Athleticism, *Strength & Conditioning Journal*, 24, (4), p71-74.

36. Hoff, J. & Helgerud, J. (2004). Endurance and Strength Training for Soccer Players, *Sports Medicine*, 34 (3), p165-180.

37. Honeybourne, J. (2004). *Acquiring Skill in Sport: An Introduction*. Abingdon: England: Taylor & Francis.

38. Horn, T. (2008). *Advances in Sport Psychology (3rd Ed)*. Champaign, Illinois: Human Kinetics.

39. Hughes, M.D. & Franks, I.M. (2004). *Notational Analysis of Sport*, London: Routledge.

40. Hughes, M.D. & Franks, I.M. (2008). *The Essentials of Performance Analysis*, New York: Routledge.

41. Jennings, C.L., Viljoen, W., Durandt, J. & Lambert, M.I. (2005). The reliability of the FitroDyne as a measure of muscle power. *Journal of*

References

Strength and Conditioning Research, (19), p859–863.

42. Jones, R. L. (2006). S*ports Coach as Educator, The: Re-conceptualising Sports Coaching.* London & New York: Taylor & Francis.

43. Karageorghis, C. (2007). Competition anxiety needn't get you down. *Peak Performance,* 243, p4-7.

44. Kreighbaum, E. & Barthels, K. (1996). *Biomechanics: a qualitative approach for studying human movement.* Boston: Allyn and Bacon.

45. Kurz, T. (1994). *Stretching Scientifically: A Guide to Flexibility Training*, Stadion Publishing Co. Inc.,U.S

46. Lambert, I.M., Viljoen, V., Bosch, A., Pearce, A.J. & Sayers M. (2008). General Principles of Training, *The Olympic Textbook of Medicine in Sport*, 1st edition. Edited by M. Schwellnus. Blackwell Publishing.

47. Lees, A. & Nolan, L. (1997). The biomechanics of soccer: A review. *Journal of Sports Sciences*, (16), p211-234.

48. Lees, A. (2003). Biomechanics applied to soccer skills. In: *Science and Soccer 2nd Edition.* New York: Routledge.

49. Leitert, H. (2009). *The Art of Goalkeeping.* (2nd Ed). Anton Lindemann: Onli Verlag.

50. Lyle, J. (2002). *Sports Coaching Concepts: A Framework for Coaches' Behaviour*, London: Routledge.

51. Mancini, R. (2011). Italian chief questions England stopper's concentration levels, Burke, M, *www.goal.com/en-gb/news/2900/fa-cup/2011/01/18/2311542/manchester-city-boss-roberto-mancini-urges-joe-hart-to*, 18/01/2011.

52. Mangan, J.A. (2000). *Athleticism in the Victorian and Edwardian public school: the emergence and consolidation of an educational ideology. (3rd Ed).* London: Frank Cass.

53. Manzo, L. (2002). Enhancing sport performance: the role of confidence

and concentration, p247–71 in Silva, J.M. and Stevens, D.E. (Eds) *Psychological Foundations of Sport,* Boston MA: Allyn & Bacon.

54. Manolopoulos, E., Papadopoulos, C. & Kellis, E. (2006). Effects of combined strength and kick coordination training on soccer kick biomechanics in amateur players. *Scandinavian Journal of Medicine and Science in Sports*, (16), p102-110.

55. Martens, R., Vealey, R.S., & Burton, D. (1990). *Competitive anxiety in sport,* Champaign, IL: Human Kinetics.

56. Medvedev, A.S., Marchenko, V.V. & Fomichenko, S.V. (1983). *Speed-Strength Structure of Vertical Jumps by Qualified Weightlifters in Different Take-off Conditions (Condensed)*. 19. pp. 164–167.

57. Meylan, C., Cronin, J., Oliver, J. & Hughes, M. (2010). Talent identification in soccer: the role of maturity status on physical, physiological and technical characteristics. *Journal of Sport Science and Coaching*. 5, (4), p571-592.

58. Miller, J.M., Hilbert, S.C. & Brown, L.E. (2001). Speed, quickness and agility training for senior tennis players. *Strength and Conditioning*, 23, (5), p62-66.

59. Mulqueen, T. (2010). *The Complete Soccer Goalkeeper.* Champaign, IL: Human Kinetics.

60. Murphy, S. M. (1994). Imagery interventions in sport. *Medicine and Science in Sports and Exercise*, (26), p486–494.

61. Nideffer, R. (1976). *The Inner Athlete: Mind plus muscle for winning,* p115-117. New York: Crowell.

62. Paish, W. (1999). *The Complete Manual of Sports Science.* London: A & C Black.

63. Pelletier, L. G., Fortier, M. S., Vallerand, R. J., Tuson, K. M., Brière, N. M., & Blais, M. R. (1995). Toward a new measure of intrinsic

References

motivation, extrinsic motivation, and motivation in sports: The Sport Motivation Scale (SMS). *Journal of Sport & Exercise Psychology, (17),* p35-53.

64. Perrotta, F. (2010). The beneficial effects of sport on anxiety and depression, *Journal of Physical Education and Sport*, 28, (3), p94-99.

65. Reber, A.S. (1985). *Dictionary of Psychology*. London: Penguin Books, p64.

66. Reilly, T. & Williams, A.M., (2003). *Science and Soccer*. London: Routledge.

67. Reilly, T. (2003). Motion analysis and physiological demands. In: *Science and Soccer 2nd Edition.* USA: Routledge, p62.

68. Richardson, D., Gilbourne, D. & Littlewood, M. (2004). Developing support mechanisms for elite young players in a professional soccer academy: Creative reflections in action research. *European Sport Management Quarterly*, 12 (9), p1250-1264.

69. Rimmer, E. & Sleivert, G. (2000). Effects of a Plyometrics Intervention Program on Sprint Performance, *Journal of Strength and Conditioning Research,* 14, (3), p295-301.

70. Ruiz, L (2002). *The Spanish Goalkeeping Bible*. USA: Reedswain.

71. Savelsbergh G, Williams M, Van Der Kamp, J. & Ward, P. (2002). Visual search, anticipation and expertise in soccer goalkeepers, *Journal of Sports Sciences,* (20), p279-287.

72. Schmidt, R.A. & Wrisberg, C.A. (2000). *Motor Learning and performance: A problem-based learning approach, (2nd Ed.)* Champaign, IL: Human Kinetics.

73. Shellock, F.G. & Prentice, W.E. (1985). Warming-up and stretching for improved physical performance and prevention of sports-related injuries. *Sports Medicine* (2), p267–278.

74. Sheppard J.M., Young, W.B., Doyle, T.L., Sheppard, T.A., & Newton, R.U. (2006). An evaluation of a new test of reactive agility and its relationship to sprint speed and change of direction speed. *Journal of Science, Medicine and Sport*, (9), p342–349.

75. Simpson, K.J, Ciapponi, T. & Wang, H. (2000). Biomechanics of Landing. In *Exercise and Sport Science*. Philadelphia, USA: Lippincott, Williams & Wilkins.

76. Smith, S. (2004). The Specialist. In: *Goalkeeping for soccer*. Leeds: Coachwise Business Solutions, p5.

77. Sorensen, H., Thomassen, M. & Zacho, M. (2008). Biomechanical Profile of Danish Elite and Sub-Elite Soccer Goalkeepers, *Football Science*, (5), p37-44.

78. Spennewyn, K. (2008). *Journal of Strength and Conditioning Research*, January, (22), 1.

79. Stevanja, J. (2008). *The G Code: Unlocking the Scientific Secrets to Goalkeeping Success*. Self published ebook

80. Stevens, H. (2002). The goalkeeper as a full-fledged member of the staff. In: *The Soccer Goalkeeper Coach*. Spring City, PA: Reedswain. p58.

81. Stone, M.H., Collins, D., Plisk, S., Haff, G. & Stone, M.E. (2000) Training principles: evaluation of modes and methods of resistance training. *Strength and Conditioning Journal* (22), p65–76.

82. Stratton, G., Reilly, T., Williams, A. and Richardson, D. (2004). *Youth Soccer: From Science to Performance*. USA, Routledge.

83. Suzuki, S., Togari, H., Isokawa, M., Ohashi, J. & Ohgushi T. (1988). Analysis of the goalkeeper's diving motion, in *Science and Football* (Eds T. Reilly, A. Lees, K. Davids and W.J. Murphy), E & FN Spon, London.

84. The Football Association. (2010). *UEFA B Goalkeeping Module*.

85. The NBA. (2010). *Fitness Tests for the NBA Draft*, www.nba.com

References

86. The Sports Psychologist. Performance Profiling, *www.sportspsychologist.co.uk*

87. Thomas, M. (2005). FA Goalkeeping - Coaching Education. *FA Insight*. 8 (2), p34-37.

88. Thomas, O., Hanton, S. & Jones, G. (2002). An alternative approach to short-form self-report assessment of competitive anxiety: A research note. *International Journal of Sport Psychology*, (33), p325-336.

89. Trininic, V., Papic, V. & Trininic, M. (2009). Role of expert coaches in development of top-level athlete's careers in individual and team sports. *Acta Kinesiological*, 3, (1), p99-106.

90. Vealey, R. S. (2001). Understanding and enhancing self-confidence in athletes. In R. N. Singer, H. A. Hausenblas, & C.M. Janelle (Eds.), *Handbook of sport psychology*, p550–565. New York: Wiley.

91. Vealey, R.S. (2005). *Coaching for the Inner Edge*, p392-395. Champaign IL: Human Kinetics.

92. Weinberg R. S. (2009). Motivation, In *Sport Psychology – Handbook of Sports Medicine and Science.* Ur. Brewer B.W. Str, p7-17. International Olympic Committee. Wiley-Blackwell.

93. Welsh, A. (1998). The Ten Cs to Goalkeeping Success. In: *The Soccer Goalkeeping Handbook*. London: A & C Black, p111-114.

94. Williams, A.M., Lee, D. & Reilly, T. (1999). *A Quantitative Analysis of Matches Played in the 1991–92 and 1997–98 Seasons*. The Football Association, London.

95. Williams, A. M., Davids, K., & Williams, J. G. (1999). *Visual perception and action in sport.* London: E. & F. N.

96. Williams, A. M., & Reilly, T. (2000). Talent identification and development in soccer. *Journal of Sports Sciences*, (18), p 657–667.

97. Williams, J.M. (2006). *Applied Sport Psychology: Personal Growth to*

Peak Performance (5th Edition). London: McGraw Hill.

98. Wilmore, H.J., Costill, L.D., & Kenny, L.W. (2008). *Physiology of sport and exercise*, Champaign IL: Human Kinetics.

99. Yerkes, R. M & Dodson, J.D. (1908). The relation of strength of stimulus to rapidity of habit-formation. *Journal of Comparative Neurology and Psychology* (18), p459-482.

100. Young, W.B., James, R., & Montgomery, I. (2002). Is muscle power related to running speed with changes of direction? *Journal of Sports Medicine and Physical Fitness*, (42), p282–288.

101. Zinsser, N., Bunker, L., & Williams, J.M. (2006). Cognitive Techniques for Building Confidence and Enhancing Performance. In J.M. Williams (Ed.), *Applied sport psychology: Personal growth to peak performance (5th Ed)*, p284–311. Boston, MA: McGraw-Hill.

102. *http://sportsmedicine.about.com/od/abdominalcorestrength1/a/NewCore.htm*

Chapters 4 & 5 – Performance and Video Analysis

1. Arts, M. (2002). *The Soccer Goalkeeper Coach.* Spring City, PA: Reedswain.

2. Coles, D. (2004) Goalkeeping – The Specialists View, *FA Insight*, 11, (7), p15-17.

3. Clemence, R., Thomas, M., Grant, A. & Williams, A. (2000) Goalkeeper Distribution Patterns in the Premier League. *FA Insight*. 3, (2), p23-25.

4. Clemence, R. (2008). An interview with Ray Clemence. *FA Insight*. 6, (2), p3-4.

5. Coyle, D. (2009). *The Talent Code*, New York: Arrow Books.

6. Cross, N & Lyle, J. (1999). *The Coaching Process.* Oxford: Butterworth

References

& Heinemann.

7. Cushion, C.J., & Smith, M. (2006). An investigation of the in-game behaviours of professional, top level youth soccer coaches. *Journal of Sports Sciences*, 24, (4), p355-366.

8. Franks, I.M., Goodman, D., & Miller, G. (1983). Analysis of performance: Qualitative or Quantitative. *SPORTS*, March.

9. Glazier, P.S. (2010). Game, Set and Match? Substantive Issues and Future Directions in Performance Analysis. *Sports Medicine*, 40, (8), p625-634.

10. Groom, R. & Cushion, C. (2004). Coaches Perception of the use of Video Analysis. *FA Insight*, 7, (3), p. 56-58.

11. Groom, R. & Cushion, C. (2005). Using of Video Based Coaching With Players: A Case Study, *International Journal of Performance Analysis in Sport,* 5, (3), p40-46.

12. Groom R., Cushion, C., & Nelson, L. (2011). The Delivery of Video-Based Performance Analysis by England Youth Soccer Coaches: Towards a Grounded Theory, *Journal of Applied Sports Psychology*, (23), p16-32.

13. Hughes, M. & Bartlett, R. (2008*).* The Use of Performance Indicators in Performance Analysis*, Journal of Sport Sciences*, (20), p739-754.

14. Hughes, M. & Franks, I.M. (2008). *The Essentials of Performance Analysis*, New York: Routledge.

15. Jones, R.L., Armour, K.A. & Potrac, P.A. (2004). *Sports Coaching Cultures: From Practice to Theory.* London; Routledge

16. Kolb, D.A. (1984). *Experiential Learning: Experience as the source of learning and development.* Englewood Cliffs, N.J.: Prentice Hall

17. Liebermann, D.G & Franks, I.M. (2004). The Use of Feedback –Based Technologies, in: Hughes, M.D & Franks, I.M., eds., *Notional Analysis of Sport*, E & F.N. Spon, p40-58.

18. Leitert, H (2009). *The Art of Goalkeeping. (2nd ed)*. Anton Lindemann:

Onli Verlag.

19. Lyle, J. (2002). *Sports Coaching Concepts: A framework for coaches' behaviour*. London: Routledge.

20. Magill, R. A. (2001). Augmented feedback in motor skill acquisition. In R. N. Singer, H. A. Hausenblas, & C. M. Janelle, *Handbook of sport psychology, (2nd edition)*, p86-114. New York: John Wiley & Sons.

21. Medina, J. (2008). *Brain Rules: 12 Principles for Surviving and Thriving at Work, Home, and School.* Seattle: Pear Press.

22. Mulqueen, T. (2010). *The Complete Soccer Goalkeeper*. Champaign, IL: Human Kinetics.

23. Murtough, J. & Williams, M. (1999). Using video in coaching, *FA Insight,* 4, (2), p38-39.

24. O'Donoghue, P. (2006). The use of feedback videos in sport, *International Journal of Performance Analysis in Sport*, 6, (2), p1-14.

25. Opta Statistics. (2011) & Sky Sports. (2011). 2010/2011 Football Statistics, *www.opta.com* & *www.skysports.com*

26. Rink, J. E. (2002). *Teaching physical education for learning, (4th edition).* New York: McGraw-Hill.

27. Smith, S. (2004). *The Specialist: Goalkeeping for soccer*. Leeds: Coachwise Business Solutions.

28. Suzuki, S., Togari, H., Isokawa, M., Ohashi, J. & Ohgushi T. (1998). Analysis of the goalkeeper's diving motion, In *Science and Football* (eds T. Reilly, A. Lees, K. Davids &W.J. Murphy), E & FN Spon, London, p468–75

29. Stratton, G., Reilly, T., Williams, A. & Richardson, D. (2004). *Youth Soccer: From science to performance.* London: Routledge.

30. The One Glove. (2006). The Science of Goalkeeping, *www.theoneglovestore.co.uk/article_science_of_keeping.html*

References

31. Thomas, M., Lawlor, J., Riley, P., Carron, J. & Isaacson, M. (2002). Goalkeeper Distribution. *FA Insight*. 5, (4), p78-80.

32. Thomas, M. (2005). FA Goalkeeping - Coaching Education. *FA Insight*. 8, (2), p34-37.

33. Wade, A. (1997). *Positional Play - Goalkeeping*. Spring City, PA: Reedswain.

Chapters 8, 9 & 10 – Games Based Goalkeeper Training

1. Bunker, D., and Thorpe, R. (1982). A model for the teaching of games in secondary schools. *Bulletin of Physical Education,* 18, (1), p5-8.

2. Kidman, L. (2005). *Athlete-centred Coaching: Developing inspired and inspiring people*, Christchurch, NZ: Innovative Print Communications.

Graduation: Life Lessons of a Professional Footballer by Richard Lee

The 2010/11 season will go down as a memorable one for Goalkeeper Richard Lee. Cup wins, penalty saves, hypnotherapy and injury would follow, but these things only tell a small part of the tale. Filled with anecdotes, insights, humour and honesty - Graduation uncovers Richard's campaign to take back the number one spot, save a lot of penalties, and overcome new challenges. What we see is a transformation - beautifully encapsulated in this extraordinary season.

"Whatever level you have played the beautiful game and whether a goalkeeper or outfield player, you will connect with this book. Richard's honesty exposes the fragility in us all, he gives an honest insight into dimensions of a footballer's life that are often kept a secret and in doing so offers worthy advice on how to overcome any hurdle. A great read." **Ben Foster, Goalkeeper, West Bromwich Albion.**

Soccer Tough by Dan Abrahams

"Take a minute to slip into the mind of one of the world's greatest soccer players and imagine a stadium around you. Picture a performance under the lights and mentally play the perfect game."

Technique, speed and tactical execution are crucial components of winning soccer, but it is mental toughness that marks out the very best players – the ability to play when pressure is highest, the opposition is strongest, and fear is greatest. Top players and coaches understand the importance of sport psychology in soccer but how do you actually train your mind to become the best player you can be?

Soccer Tough demystifies this crucial side of the game and offers practical techniques that will enable soccer players of all abilities to actively develop focus, energy, and confidence. Soccer Tough will help banish the fear, mistakes, and mental limits that holds players back.

Around the World in 80 Scams: an Essential Travel Guide by Peter John

Every year, thousands of people fall victim to various travel scams, crimes and confidence tricks while they travel. Most people escape having simply lost a little money, but many lose much more, and some encounter real personal danger

This essential book is a practical, focused, and detailed guide to eighty of the most common scams and crimes travellers might encounter. It is packed with real-world examples drawn from resources across the globe and the author's own travels. Being aware of scammers' tricks is the best way of avoiding them altogether.

Chapters cover all sorts of scams including: Hotels and other accommodation scams, Transport scams, Eating, drinking and gambling scams, Begging and street hustling scams, Extortion, blackmail and fraud scams, and more.

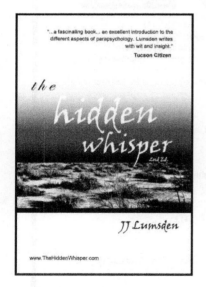

The Hidden Whisper by Dr JJ Lumsden

Want to learn about the science of parapsychology and paranormal phenomena? Follow the exploits of fictional parapsychologist Dr Luke Jackson as he seeks to uncover a poltergeist outbreak in Southern Arizona. Along the way, learn all about paranormal phenomena such as Extra Sensory Perception, Psychokinesis, Ghosts, Poltergeists, Out of Body Experiences and more.

This book works on many levels, an excellent introduction to the concepts current in the field of parapsychology... at best you may learn something new, and at worst you'll have read a witty and well-written paranormal detective story. **Parascience**

...a ghost investigation novel that has all the elements of a good detective mystery and spooky thriller...an engrossing haunting tale... an informative overview of the current theories on the phenomena. **paranormal.about.com**

Lightning Source UK Ltd.
Milton Keynes UK
UKOW05f1806040915

258106UK00004B/280/P